The Activist Classroom: Performance and Pedagogy

Edited by Kim Solga

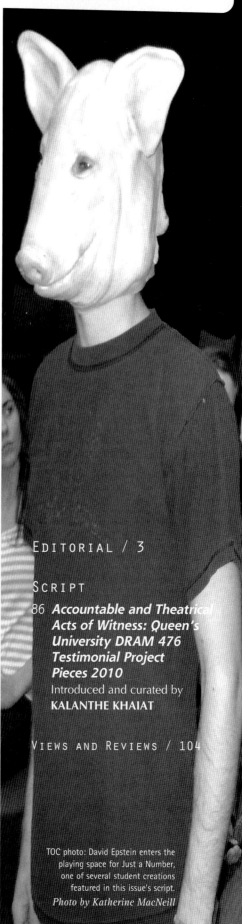

FEATURE ARTICLES

5   **Building the Activist Classroom: Learning to Collaborate, Learning through Performance in English 2470: Canadian Drama**
KIM SOLGA talks with former undergraduate students PAIGE BECK and LAUREN MOORE about the ways in which regular group performance work both helped and hindered their and their peers' experience of "the activist classroom" in Canadian Drama: Performing An Intercultural Nation in winter 2010.

12   **Activist Awareness in the Theatre of the Oppressed Classroom**
Using a case study built around her own Dalhousie University classroom, SUSANNE SHAWYER explores how Theatre of the Oppressed techniques can be used to train theatre students to be activists.

18   **Applied Theatre and/as Activism**
MONICA PRENDERGAST speaks with eight current and former faculty members and graduate students from the University of Victoria's new Applied Theatre program, and discovers that, sometimes, activist pedagogy needs to be moved out of the classroom studio and into the community.

24   **When the Audience is Ourselves: From Intellectual Argument to Visceral Experience**
Sometimes an experience in the classroom can creep up and wallop both teacher and student alike. What then? JAN SELMAN remembers one such instance, and reflects on the value of creating disturbance as part of educational processes in all theatre classrooms.

31   **Minstrels in the Classroom: Teaching, Race, and Blackface**
For instructors of theatre and performance history, the traditions of blackface minstrelsy present a pedagogical challenge. How to foster sensitive and critically productive discussions about race and representation in the undergraduate classroom? NATALIE ALVAREZ and STEPHEN JOHNSON start the conversation.

38   **A Pedagogy of Justice**
In university classrooms where art is both subject and praxis, canon and methodology frequently converge to reproduce asymmetrical systems of power. The disruption of these systems is arduous and rewarding work, work that requires a committed consortium of students, teachers, and extended community. NAILA KELETA-MAE explores the risky business of building a pedagogy of justice in which both teacher and student agree to let go of the moorings that tether their worldviews.

43   **Making it Up as We Go Along: Improvisation and Environmental Education**
Improvisation and environmental education have a lot to learn from each other, argues JULIA LANE. Although improv is often associated with sketch comedy shows like *Whose Line is it Anyway?*, what might happen if we take literally Gary Paul Nabhan's understanding of life on earth as "the Great Improvisation"?

49   **"A Precise Instrument for Seeing": Remembrance in *Burning Vision* and the Activist Classroom**
Marie Clements' 2002 play, *Burning Vision*, challenges teachers and students to remember our shared histories with a difference. But it also poses a problem: how model critical memory practices to a group of students eager to make sense of complex problems and move on? ALLISON HARGREAVES examines the risks and rewards of Clements' work in the activist classroom.

Cover photo: Animating in role, engaging the audience: Shannon Larson in *Are We There Yet?* by Jane Heather (Concrete Theatre, 2002).   *Photo courtesy of Epic Photography Inc.*

EDITORIAL / 3

SCRIPT

86 *Accountable and Theatrical Acts of Witness: Queen's University DRAM 476 Testimonial Project Pieces 2010*
Introduced and curated by KALANTHE KHAIAT

VIEWS AND REVIEWS / 104

TOC photo: David Epstein enters the playing space for *Just a Number*, one of several student creations featured in this issue's script.
Photo by Katherine MacNeill.

Canadian Theatre Review
Volume 147, Summer 2011

Editor Laura Levin

Associate Editors Catherine Graham and Reid Gilbert

Editor, Volume 147 Kim Solga

Editorial Advisory Board Jenny Munday, Margaret-Gail Osachoff

Review Editors Natalie Alvarez and Jenn Stephenson

Managing Editor Anne Marie Corrigan

Editorial Assistant Ofer Ravid

Editorial Coordinator Sheree Pell

Advertising Coordinator Audrey Greenwood

Production/Layout Artist Amy Desrochers

Founding Editors Don Rubin, Ross Stuart, Stephen Mezei

Publisher University of Toronto Press Incorporated

Founding Publisher Joseph Green

CTR gratefully acknowledges the financial assistance of the Canada Council for the Arts and the Ontario Arts Council.

CTR is available through subscription from the Journals Department, University of Toronto Press Inc., 5201 Dufferin Street, Toronto, Ontario M3H 5T8. Phone: (416) 667-7810; Fax: (416) 667-7881; Fax toll free: 1-800-221-9985; journals@utpress.utoronto.ca, www.utpjournals.com.

Subscriptions inside Canada: institutions $105 per year; individuals $45; students $35; Theatre Ontario Members $35. Single copies $15.00. Orders from USA and abroad submit payment in US funds. Overseas postage add $20. *CTR* is also available on microfilm through Micro Media Ltd, Toronto. Indexed in the Canadian Periodical Index.

Editorial enquiries and manuscripts should be sent by email to info@canadiantheatrereview.com, or by mail to *CTR* Editorial Office, 317 Centre for Film and Theatre, York University, Toronto, Ontario M3J 1P3. Opinions expressed are those of the authors and not necessarily those of *Canadian Theatre Review*.

Copyright © 2011, University of Toronto Press Inc.

ISSN 0315-0836 E-ISSN 1920-941X ISBN 978-1-4426-1055-2
PRINTED IN CANADA at Thistle Printing.

Publications Mail Agreement number 40600510, Toronto, ON.
Published quarterly.
Periodicals postage paid at Buffalo, NY.

US Postmaster: Send address changes to U of T Press Inc., 2250 Military Road, Tonawanda, NY 14150-6000

US Periodicals Registration Number 006628

Canada Post: Send address changes to University of Toronto Press Inc., 5201 Dufferin Street, Toronto, ON M3H 5T8.

55 Creative Copying?: The Pedagogy of Adaptation
While it may seem counterintuitive to promote creativity through "copying," **JAMES MCKINNON** argues that teaching drama and theatre through adaptation-based methods fosters creative and critical thinking. Learning how many of the great masterpieces of the dramatic canon are actually adaptations themselves pierces the mystique surrounding the creative process, making it less intimidating for students.

61 The ICE Approach: Saving the World One Broken Toaster at a Time
GRAHAME RENYK and **JENN STEPHENSON** of the drama department at Queen's University discuss their use of the ICE method in a first-year theatre studies classroom. Although Renyk and Stephenson use ICE for assessment, here they explore how the technique can be employed in assignment design, challenging learners to take both initiative and pleasure in their own learning.

68 "Elder up!": A Mentor/Mentee Memoir
Teaching isn't always for teachers, and learning isn't exclusive to students; sometimes, the activist classroom is carried in bodies, hearts, and minds across cultural, generational, and national divides. **TARA BEAGAN**, the newly appointed Artistic Director of Native Earth Performing Arts in Toronto, remembers her mentors and considers her own process of coming-to-elderhood.

74 "Elephants in the Classroom": A Forum on Performance Pedagogy
Organized and edited by **MARLIS SCHWEITZER** and **LAURA LEVIN**
Transcription by **CASSANDRA DEE BALL** and **MEGAN MACDONALD**
Workshop participants: Natalie Alvarez, Allan Boss, Barry Freeman, Catherine Graham, Nelson Gray, Nicholas Hanson, Andy Houston, Erin Hurley, Stephen Johnson, Aida Jordão, Laura Levin, Megan Macdonald, James McKinnon, Mia Perry, Monica Prendergast, Marlis Schweitzer, Annie Smith, Kim Solga, Jenn Stephenson, Richie Wilcox, Lydia Wilkinson

Views and Reviews / 104

105 Unclassified and Controvertible: *The Edward Curtis Project* and *Beyond Eden* in Vancouver, 2010 by **BEVERLY YHAP**

110 Many Stories, Many Voices: Alberta Aboriginal Arts by **SCOTT SHARPLIN**

113 Humanizing Strangers Near and Far: Ethics and Irony in *The Middle Place* and *A Taste of Empire* by **BARRY FREEMAN**

117 The Politics of Distraction: Spectatorial Freedom and (dis)Enfranchisement in Toneelgroep's *Roman Tragedies* by **NATALIE CORBETT** and **KEREN ZAIONTZ**

121 Dancing in the dark: *Tu vois ce que je veux dire?* by **NATALIE REWA**

Toward the Activist Classroom

by Kim Solga

In the spring of 2005 I spent several months in the Department of Theatre and Dance at the University of Texas at Austin. I was there to be a part of an innovative PhD stream called "Performance as a Public Practice." My colleagues and I worked closely with extraordinary, socially engaged practitioners. We made work of our own and we talked again and again about how, when, and where theatre becomes a force for political and cultural change and when, where, and how it does not.

When I returned to Canada to take up my first full time teaching job in September that year, I was full of the theories and practices I had absorbed at UT and determined to implement the ethos of Performance as a Public Practice in my own teaching. My new job was in an English department, in which students were accustomed to calling plays "novels." I knew immediately that by demanding the students learn by *doing*—by performing, embodying, making personal the very political work we would read together—I could help them to see theatre's potent public strengths. We began (in the wake of Hurricane Katrina) with a simple exercise: what if you were a theatre artist in Houston, in Baton Rouge, or in Nashville, I asked them; how would you muster your resources to help the people of New Orleans? I was amazed at the eager, smart responses—something that continued each week thereafter as students, divided into teams for the term, made outstanding poor theatre and spoke with sensitivity about what they and their peers were accomplishing, for whom, and whether or not it mattered. We were on our way.

Six years on, I am now a decorated teacher at my school, something that makes me proud but also makes me laugh. After all, I'm not doing anything that my peers in theatre and drama departments across North America aren't doing; I'm just a queer presence on a campus where "Theatre" no longer formally exists. I've always known that my students and I do good work, but I've also always known that we're not special. I've been wanting to tap into the teaching and learning knowledge of my fellow theatre and performance teachers for a long time; this issue has grown from my hunger to know not just how my work fits in, but how it could be better, stronger, for the help, advice, and encouraging war stories of my peers. What makes us good teachers? What makes our classrooms collaborative learning spaces? What makes our classrooms safe spaces to try out unsafe ideas? What makes our classrooms places where large-scale change can, in tiny steps, appear to begin? What makes our teaching activist, anyway? How do we—teachers and students—define that term for ourselves?

My activist classroom is constantly evolving, and it will be so much richer for my experience of putting this issue of *CTR* together.

For those looking for concrete suggestions to improve their teaching, Julia Lane, James McKinnon, Grahame Renyk, and Jenn Stephenson offer exercises that can be transported straight from these pages into the classroom. Lane considers the natural weave between improv performance and environmental education, and provides simple, excellent exercises from a recent workshop. McKinnon asks us to consider the creativity required to produce a good adaptation, and to use that creativity to help students rethink their capacity to be producers of "real" art. Renyk and Stephenson introduce us to the ICE technique and its capacity to enliven both assessment and assignment design.

Learning to teach better isn't just about absorbing new techniques, of course; it's also about listening to the stories that mark us as teachers, for better or worse. Some classroom struggles can seem intractable, and those of us who fight for sexual, racial, and gendered social justice each day know all too well how hard bridging the divide between activist life choices and activist teaching choices can be. Natalie Alvarez and Stephen Johnson both teach the history of blackface performance. They stage here a conversation about the challenges of that work and share strategies that they have developed to help their students recognize the "real"ness of race. Allison Hargreaves struggles with similar challenges in her classes on Indigenous performance: in her contribution she considers Marie Clements' *Burning Vision* as a vehicle through which to help students recognize what damage neoliberal discourses of remembrance and redress can do. Alvarez, Johnson, and Hargreaves are, in their ways, all striving toward what Naila Keleta-Mae, in her memoir-manifesto, calls a "pedagogy of justice": a space "co-constituted" by teachers and students and able to "unmoor" us all in productive ways.

Over the years since Austin I have learned that my own best teachers are my students—they don't have my resources or my experience, to be sure, but they know when it's not working. Two of my former students, Paige Beck and Lauren Moore, reflect on their work in my classroom in our lead article, and teach me about exactly *what* I'm teaching when I stand in front of my classes. Monica Prendergast talks to colleagues and students, both former and current, and asks each of them to consider how activism impacts their work in community and applied theatre. Jan Selman remembers one of those unforgettable "teachable moments" and uses it to reflect on the role discomfort and discombobulation should play in any activist learning space. Susanne Shawyer reflects on her students' struggle with the very *idea* of activism in a class on political theatre, and recounts an exuberant term's end performance that changed some minds but not others. Finally, Tara Beagan takes up her new role as Artistic Director of Native Earth Performing Arts by thinking through her formative relationship with her friend, mentor, and colleague Yvette Nolan. In this "mentor/mentee memoir," Beagan asks what it means to be mentored, what it means to *become* a mentor, and imagines how a strong mentoring relationship may function as perhaps the ultimate "activist classroom."

Our script for this issue is a shared endeavour, split evenly between teachers and students, the work of teaching and the work of learning. In May 2010 I was fortunate to take part in a workshop called "Elephants in the Classroom," coordinated by Laura Levin and Marlis Schweitzer. Levin and Schweitzer publish the transcript of our discussions here; it offers some excellent classroom exercises (large scale and small scale) as well as candid, topical reflections on life in each of our institutions right now. Then, we honour the labours of our best students with five devised pieces produced by Julie Salverson's senior drama seminar at Queen's University. Curated and introduced by Kalanthe Khaiat, these pieces remind me of the very best student performances I have witnessed over the last few years in my own activist classroom. They deliver not didactic messages and not simplified acts of empathy, but challenging engagements with otherness that ask all of us to consider the potential and the limits of our activisms, both in the classroom and beyond.

I hope you enjoy the issue!

Building the Activist Classroom: Learning to Collaborate, Learning through Performance in English 2470: Canadian Drama

Paige-Tiffany Beck and Lauren Moore
in conversation with Kim Solga

INTRODUCTION

Since September 2005 I have been teaching contemporary theatre and performance in the English department at the University of Western Ontario. From the moment I began working at Western I was determined not to teach drama "as literature"; I wanted my students to understand how performance works as an embodied art form in which audiences, actors, and others come together simultaneously to create meaning and, I believe, political impact. The idea of drama as performance, and of performance as activism, motivated my decision to turn one-third of all class time in my undergraduate courses over to student scene studies and student-driven talkbacks. I divide students into five groups at the beginning of the term and we do a number of initial exercises to build community. I then send them off to create "poor" performances of pre-assigned plays.

Each performance earns a group grade, as well as a page of comments from me. Those comments stress the value of the group's performance choices, the overall quality of their execution, and the strengths and weaknesses of group members' contributions during the post-performance talkback. I stress early and often that lines need not be memorized and acting will not be graded; this is performance as "thought work"—performance for social engagement among an audience of peers.

I recently invited two outstanding former students, Paige Beck and Lauren Moore, to talk with me about their experiences in my classroom during the Winter of 2010. The theme of English 2470: Canadian Drama that term was "Performing an Intercultural Nation." Paige and Lauren speak candidly about the good, the bad, and the productively difficult below.

Kim Solga: What did you think when you first learned how much performing we were going to do in this class? I'm always afraid students are going to freak out and drop before they get a chance to figure out what the class is really all about.

Paige-Tiffany Beck: I was very interested in taking Canadian Drama and had been trying to make the course fit into my schedule for two years before I finally enrolled. I was excited when I found out about the amount of performing we'd be doing because I have always been active in theatre, whether it be through school or in community theatre. My excitement aside, I definitely felt that the general reaction to the performance-based nature of this class was sheer panic. There was a tangible dis-ease in the classroom when it became apparent that this class was not like other literature classes. Because the class also entailed a large amount of group work, and therefore mutual commitment, I was more worried about my peers recoiling from participating and performing than I was about my own nerves.

Each performance earns a group grade, as well as a page of comments from me. Those comments stress the value of the group's performance choices, the overall quality of their execution, and the strengths and weaknesses of group members' contributions during the post-performance talkback. I stress early and often that lines need not be memorized and acting will not be graded; this is performance as "thought work"—performance for social engagement among an audience of peers.

Lauren Moore: I sensed an initially mixed response from the class to the course format. Some (like me) were beyond enthusiastic because they had taken a similar drama course in the past and knew what to expect. Those who hadn't been exposed to drama at UWO, on the other hand, were noticeably petrified. The idea of performance (whether it's "poor" or not) is scary, despite Kim's constant assurance that acting skills would not be evaluated. It seemed contradictory that one would be graded on a performance, and yet zero aspects of the performance are talent-based. Regardless, I feel that this mixture of enthusiasm from some and hesitation from others allowed for a greater exercise of peer leadership and support both within my group and in the class at large.

Solga: What was the group work like? Tell me about the good and the bad.

Moore: Candidly, I generally dislike group work. The idea of relying on others in academic situations makes me uneasy, but that's the beauty of this format: I was forced to confront my issues of depending on my peers, and I (inevitably) learned more about collaboration and delegation than I would in any other circumstance. By encouraging each other to adopt responsibilities that were truly wanted, my group consistently delivered a great final product that was fun to create.

This might sound cliché, but I honestly cannot think of a negative experience of the group work. My group was earnest, hardworking, and eager to deliver a quality performance that pushed our creative limits. I grew to recognize and admire the hidden talents of my group members, and it was fascinating to discuss individual interpretations of a text in-depth.

Beck: I, like Lauren, am very wary about group work. In this situation, group work was for me at times very productive and stimulating, and at others very frustrating. There was a large disparity between the contributions of the students who really wanted our performances to succeed and those who were along for the ride. In my group in particular there were three students out of eight who regularly did not show up for group rehearsals. This made scripting and blocking performances especially difficult. Our group strongly encouraged participation from every member; in practice, however, I found that I or another committed group member would take on a disproportionate amount of work.

For our second performance, in frustration and desperation, the committed members of the group decided to place a large amount of the control in the hands of the group members who had not participated very much in the first performance. We had a disastrous performance as a result, but still I forced myself to commit to everything that was happening, the good and the bad. It was not easy for me; I felt like the performance would have been better if I had stepped in, but I had made a conscious resolution not to do that. As a student committed to the success of the group's performance, I found it especially difficult to give up my control over the situation: that was my biggest challenge in our classroom. By stepping back, though, I feel that I learned a lot from my group members, especially the shy members whose ideas would not have been heard otherwise. In turn, I think that this effort inspired some confidence in those group members and impelled them to speak up more and to trust their contributions.

Solga: You both clearly learned a lot about yourselves thanks to the group work. How else did it affect your learning? Did it improve your grasp of course content?

> Our group strongly encouraged participation from every member; in practice, however, I found that I or another committed group member would take on a disproportionate amount of work.

Beck: At its best, the group work allowed us to interrogate our reactions to a play and to share them with our peers. I found this, in the context of the [multicultural/intercultural] material we were learning, to be particularly stimulating because we could not discuss our reactions to a play without considering the challenges of performing it. I found that, within our group, there were varying reactions to the plays that we studied—specifically from those students who had lived experiences of immigrating to Canada—and that these reactions complicated our whole group's understanding of the play and informed our performance choices. As this was a learning environment and the performances were geared toward putting theories about theatre and representation into action, the failings and successes of group performances were opportunities to learn about what theories might "work" and which do not work in praxis.

> We had a disastrous performance [...] but still I forced myself to commit to everything that was happening, the good and the bad. It was not easy for me; I felt like the performance would have been better if I had stepped in, but I had made a conscious resolution not to do that. As a student committed to the success of the group's performance, I found it especially difficult to give up my control over the situation: that was my biggest challenge in our classroom.

One of the best moments for my group was when the "thesis" of our performance was recognized by our peers in one of our talkbacks. Our group came up with a performance of James Reaney's *The Donnellys: Sticks and Stones* that we were particularly proud of. Our staging pointed to the exploitation of the Donnellys' personal history and to their "blackness" by playing up the minstrelsy of Reaney's play. This performance in particular felt like an accomplishment because we were all so invested in our version of the play and, during talkback, our peers were excited about what we had done and saw its social value.

Moore: As interesting and valuable as it was to put on a performance, I benefitted most from viewing other groups' interpretations of a play. On Thursdays, I found myself predicting what themes and circumstances from each play would be highlighted in the performance, and I was almost always wrong. It fascinated me to watch my own interpretation unravel ... It forced me to consider the purpose of *each* artistic decision, and analyzing small-scale performances allowed me to comprehend the value in each liberty taken.

Lauren Moore graduated from the University of Western Ontario in June 2010 and now works as a writer in New York City.
Photo by Michelle Moore

Further, breaking down each performance during group talkbacks was equally valuable. Since I developed a closer bond with my group members than with other classmates, I felt safe vocalizing my intellectual explorations of each performance. I found that participating in class was a beautiful, rare thing; I wanted to discuss and analyze for the sake of sheer knowledge, whereas for most courses, I participated only for the academic pay-off.

Solga: I stress that our classroom is a "collaborative" space. Did it feel that way to you?

Moore: I absolutely feel that the classroom was a collaborative space, and it's a rarity in a university setting. In Canadian Drama, there were no taboos; any question, no matter the subject, could be raised and not judged. Discretions were cast aside, and issues that are normally uncomfortable (like racism and sexual identity) were discussed in a mature, intellectual manner. Class discussions forced me to realize that my perspective isn't always the right one. I developed a comprehension of the texts and their greater meanings that I could not have discovered on my own.

Beck: Lauren is absolutely right to point to the rarity of this collaborative experience and the freedom to discuss uncomfortable issues allowed by the course format. Engaging in collaborative discussions during our talkbacks made the classroom feel like a learning community. At the same time, though, talkbacks were also sometimes provocative due to the fact that many of the plays we discussed hinged around racial or cultural issues.

Students Heather Monteith and Stephanie St John enjoy a laugh while working on discussion questions to share during the talkback for *Goodness*.
Photo by Keely Kwok

Solga: This was intentional, of course: I theme Canadian Drama around the notion of "performing an intercultural nation" in part to get students thinking and talking critically about how racial and cultural difference works (both positively and negatively) in Canada. In this context, I use group performance to make our learning "active," but also politically charged, "activist." What, if anything, did you learn about "activism" in our classroom?

Beck: Canadian Drama made theatre real for me. My experiences of working in my group and working closely with a text in order to stage it gave me a sense of theatre as a living thing. Furthermore, I now understand how theatre *is* a potential tool for activism because I have intimately felt how political the act of dramatizing a text can be.

When my group performed Nina Aquino and Nadine Villasin's *Miss Orient(ed)*, I was most conscious about the potential dangers of our creative choices. We attempted to perform a hyperbolized racial "drag," assuming over-the-top, stereotypical "Asian" accents in order to address the fact that we were a predominately Caucasian company performing a play about the lived experiences of Filipina immigrants, experiences to which we had no claim. Our thought-work behind this performance was comprehensive and well intentioned, and we imagined that by dressing our single male group member as a woman [the Beauty Icon] we were clearly pointing out that we were following Aquino and Villasin's satirical tone and commenting on the impossibility of our fully embodying the experiences of the play's characters.

Solga: What happened?

Beck: The talkback was very tense. Because our performance ran long, we had to pick up our discussion during the next class. In the interim, there were some very intense debates regarding our performance on the course website between a member of our group and another member of the class who felt that our performance was insensitive. On the day of the talkback, only half of our group came to class. It was clear to the present members of the group that those absent were consciously avoiding answering for the perceived pseudo-racist nature of our performance. To make matters worse, the students who were absent were those responsible for the majority of the creative choices we would discuss in the talkback. Many members of the class were clearly viewing our performance through the lens of the heated online debate and it was plain that much of what the class wanted to say was deliberately left unsaid. There was a very long period of silence during which I felt ashamed for our performance, though I did not give up on trying to defend our creative choices.

> Breaking down each performance during group talkbacks was equally valuable. Since I developed a closer bond with my group members than with other classmates, I felt safe vocalizing my intellectual explorations of each performance. I found that participating in class was a beautiful, rare thing; I wanted to discuss and analyze for the sake of sheer knowledge, whereas for most courses, I participated only for the academic pay-off.

In retrospect, this experience led our group (and probably many members of the rest of the class) to understand that acting, and theatre itself, can be a tool for opening up theoretical discussion, but that these things can also be very dangerous. Through this experience of trying but failing to perform our take on the text—to perform the intricacies of race—in an activist way I learned the most about the power of theatre. I saw the power of theatre to polarize. I saw how theatre could become more than one-sided: the audience and the actors were engaged in a web discussion about the performance for weeks after. The experience became truly

Students Sandy Martin, Rebecca Watson, and Inna Yasinska prepare their presentation of Michael Redhill's *Goodness* for English 2470: Canadian Drama, March 2011.
Photo by Caroline Plancke

Moore: There was a moment in one performance that I will never forget. It made me extremely uncomfortable, and I feel like the entire class felt so, as well. We staged Guillermo Verdecchia's *Fronteras Americanas,* and, without realizing it, cast our group's only non-white member to play an overt Latino stereotype [Wideload]. When this was called to our attention in talkback, a billion thoughts flew through my mind. At first, I worried that we had accidentally made a racist move by subconsciously associating this student with the least white-acting character in the play. Then, I felt uncomfortable *for* the girl, who must have thought the same thing. And, since this all happened at the end of class, I felt that this issue wasn't particularly resolved, nor should it have been. I realized that the fact we cast this student without considering the racial implications is actually a *great* thing, because clearly my group ceased to see her as any different from our other members.

participatory ... In the end our performance was not a failure because it generated passionate response and allowed us to come at the seemingly untouchable topics of race and the politics of cross-racial casting. In Canadian Drama I learned how to be an activist performer, but also how to be an activist audience member.

Solga: That's an ideal outcome.

Beck: It was ideal, at least in my experience, though it was a difficult process to arrive at the point where it all clicked.

On the subject of difficult performances, I have a question for Lauren: did you feel that there were some things that your group could not perform? Did you ever question whether your group should do something? My group ended up regretting our racial "drag" performance of *Miss Orient(ed)*—did you ever feel like you made the wrong choice in a performance?

Small-group discussions centred on student performance work encourage active participation by all class members, especially those nervous to speak up in larger discussion settings.
Photo by Keely Kwok

> Through this experience of trying but failing to perform our take on the text—to perform the intricacies of race—in an activist way I learned the most about the power of theatre. I saw the power of theatre to polarize. I saw how theatre could become more than one-sided: the audience and the actors were engaged in a web discussion about the performance for weeks after.

Solga: I think about this moment a lot as well; for me as a teacher it was genuinely traumatic. I was terrified that the student felt "called out," her skin on display for all to see. I agonized over the way we handled this moment—the question; the student's rather bewildered reply. Is there anything we, as a class, or I, as a teacher, could have done better in this moment, to respond to the taboos we were raising or to take care of your group?

Moore: As much as I would love to say that, retrospectively, there was an easy solution to ease the situation, I think that it was handled very well. Everyone was undoubtedly uncomfortable, but, again, it proved the importance of this class's

Rebecca Watson lifts Inna Yasinska as they experiment with dance as part of their preparations for *Goodness*, March 2011.
Photo by Caroline Plancke

Moore: I feel that the greatest but least obvious challenge is learning to open your mind to the perspectives shown by your classmates. We all have our opinions and judgments, and learning to combat personal beliefs is a difficult but rewarding process. For example, acknowledging the differences between us without feeling racist is a hard experience that has been tabooed for our generation, but it's important to recognize these cultural disparities.

This class forced me to vocalize questions that I wouldn't normally ask for fear of offending or disturbing others.

As well, this class forced me to vocalize questions that I wouldn't normally ask for fear of offending or disturbing others. If anyone enrolls in an activist-formatted classroom, I highly encourage him or her to leave judgments at the door, and to soak in the different values of class members. There are valuable, life-long lessons to be learned if we let down our guard, and it was refreshing to be in a classroom where I aimed to succeed not for academic reasons, but in order to acquire skills, a mindset, that can accompany me for the rest of my life.

structure. It was obvious that the student's skin colour wasn't called out in any whim of racism; rather, her difference was acknowledged via mature, intellectual, and academic inquiry. Sure, it was terribly awkward, but ultimately, the goal of the class was achieved: students felt comfortable to speak of what's normally not spoken, and the artistic risks of multiculturalism were explored using a day-to-day example.

In Canadian Drama I learned how to be an activist performer, but also how to be an activist audience member.

Solga: What was the hardest thing about English 2470? In other words, what cautionary tales can you, as students, tell about teaching and learning in this way?

Beck: The most challenging aspect of the course was also its greatest strength: the large emphasis on group work. If I were to tell a cautionary tale to incoming students it would definitely be: do not expect that every person in your group will be as vested in and as excited about the work you are doing as you might be. I feel that students' experiences of this course are greatly impacted by the quality of the group work and the group atmosphere. That being said, learning this way was a great opportunity to interrogate my personal reactions to texts and to test them against others' often opposing opinions, and the process of collaborating on the performance work amidst differences of approach was valuable and ultimately a welcome challenge. This course had staying power with me: I often left the classroom still thinking about what we had done in class that day.

Students in English 2450: Modern Drama at the University of Western Ontario engage in a talkback discussion of their performance of Griselda Gambaro's *Information for Foreigners*. (l-r): Rebecca Myers, Jordan Stanton, Kate McRae, Maria Halabi, Stewart Orr, Ynina Kapustin, Stephen Matlovich, Alexandra Berney, and Brittany Kosir.
Photo by André Cormier

Paige-Tiffany Beck is currently pursuing an MA in English at the University of Western Ontario. Her research interests centre on women's experiences of literary creation and poetic voice, specifically in Victorian women's poetry.

Lauren Moore graduated from the University of Western Ontario in 2010 with a BA in English Literature. Moore, now in New York City, reports on entertainment and fashion for various publications.

Kim Solga is Associate Professor in the Department of English at the University of Western Ontario, where for the past six years she has taught Canadian Drama: Performing An Intercultural Nation, among other courses on contemporary theatre and performance. In 2009 she was awarded Western's Marilyn Robinson Award for Excellence in Teaching.

Activist Awareness in the Theatre of the Oppressed Classroom

By Susanne Shawyer

What is activism? Doing.[1]

Students stride through Dalhousie University's Killam Library with urgent purpose. It is the last week of classes, and the library's atrium bristles with energy. A few students lounge by the coffee shop and snack bar, but most walk briskly, focused on study. Papers, textbooks, and laptops cover scattered tables. Cellphone chatter and casual conversation fills the airy space. Without warning, the amplified sound of a booting laptop throbs through the air. Conversation falters. Students look up from their books and papers as pencils tap on table tops and hands slap course calendars. A heavy textbook falls to the floor. The sounds repeat, again. Throughout the atrium, people stop to listen as the noise crescendos then gently dissipates. Just as the spectators begin to wonder what is happening, a strong voice shouts, "Oppression!" Ten students immediately run to the centre of the atrium and freeze in place. Their pose is strong, their stance is firm. "Stress!" the strong voice shouts, and the performers create another frozen image. A passerby halts to watch, and welcoming smiles greet her. "Want to sign the banner?" friendly voices ask, offering coloured markers and a chance to discuss the impact of student stress. She hesitates, unsure why the library atrium is suddenly a performance space. Tentatively she asks, "Is this for a class?"

I am oppressed. Everyone has faced oppression at some point.

Theatre of the Oppressed is a popular applied theatre form that uses improvisation and audience participation to explore social issues. When Brazilian theatre director and activist Augusto Boal created Theatre of the Oppressed in Brazil and Peru in the 1960s,

Students performing Image Theatre in Dalhousie's library as part of the Theatre of the Oppressed class project.
Photo by Susanne Shawyer

he worked with the economically and culturally oppressed: illiterate farm workers and exploited native peoples. Compared to much of the world, Canadian university students are not oppressed. While many do struggle with debt or juggle employment and child care with full-time studies, they nevertheless enjoy an enviable literacy, lifestyle, and freedom of expression. Yet Boal's Theatre of the Oppressed techniques offer much to Canadian theatre students. His exercises promote physical and emotional expression and develop improvisation skills—useful for actors and directors. His Joker System encourages potential teachers to hone their facilitation skills. A theatre student trained in Theatre of the Oppressed techniques has skills applicable to the fields of development, social work, education, politics, and the fine arts. A Theatre of the Oppressed class therefore has obvious practical value for theatre students. But because Theatre of the Oppressed is rooted in social and economic activism, perhaps it should also have political value for students. Can a Theatre of the Oppressed class train students not only to be performers and facilitators, but also to be activists?

By participating in a system that privileges me over others, that leads to their oppression, I oppress others.

The question of whether a Theatre of the Oppressed class can have political value guided my development of a half-year course at Dalhousie University in the Fall term of 2010. On a basic level, the course served as an introduction to the theory and practice of Theatre of the Oppressed. While some students had encountered Boal's writings in a previous theatre theory course, most entered the course with no knowledge of Theatre of the Oppressed. Students read Boal's seminal book, *Theatre of the Oppressed,* as well as case studies of Theatre of the Oppressed performances. They researched Canadian artists and theatre companies using Boal's techniques. Students debated Boal's argument about the coercive nature of theatre that strives for emotional catharsis. They tested his notion of social alienation by playing improvisation games about social status. Each class we practiced exercises from Boal's *Games for Actors and Non-Actors*, activities meant to develop self-expression or explore social stereotypes. By the end of the course, the class had a broad understanding of how Theatre of the Oppressed methods could be applied in a variety of Canadian contexts.

I am of an unbelievably privileged class, race, generation, population, country, hemisphere.

> A theatre student trained in Theatre of the Oppressed techniques has skills applicable to the fields of development, social work, education, politics, and the fine arts. A Theatre of the Oppressed class therefore has obvious practical value for theatre students. But because Theatre of the Oppressed is rooted in social and economic activism, perhaps it should also have political value for students.

Yet I was also curious to see if the course had an impact on the students' attitudes towards activism. Some were already politically or socially active, volunteering with the campus Women's Centre and local youth organizations, or working with socially-conscious theatre in Halifax. Others were interested in exploring issues, but felt that their busy schedules prevented activist engagement. A few took the class simply because it fit their schedule. While the students saw themselves as theatre actors, technicians, directors, audience members, and scholars, few firmly identified themselves as theatrical activists. Would weekly discussions about Boal's socially-conscious theatre inspire them to create their own activist theatre? Would the chance to devise their own Theatre of the Oppressed performance at the end of term encourage them to see themselves not just as theatre artists, but also as political activists? Could a Theatre of the Oppressed course bolster their awareness of activism, or increase their activist commitment? To help answer these questions, students tracked their course progress with short self-reflection papers, and twice filled out a questionnaire. This survey logged whether they self-identified as activists and recorded their definitions of words like "oppression" and "activism."

I live under a system that devalues and limits my person and my agency. I have the extraordinary privilege of both education and awareness, and am much less limited than many, but having the tools to withstand my oppression doesn't make it any less a cage.

"Oppression" can be a tricky word in the Canadian university classroom. On a global scale, Canadian theatre students enjoy a privileged literacy and access to education. Yet one cannot assume the absence of oppression: in the first questionnaire some students identified as economically oppressed due to large loans, lack of available credit, and long hours worked in minimum wage service jobs in order to afford tuition. Many had experienced gender discrimination and bullying, either at school or in the workplace. Some connected to the notion of self-oppression. Boal refers to this internalizing of oppressive social norms as submission to the "Cop in the Head" (*Rainbow* 42). While the class was strongly aware of economic systems and cultural norms that can lead to oppressive situations, some felt that oppression was a term reserved for the least privileged of the world, and not applicable to their own situation. A portion of the class considered "oppression" too weighty a word, or too negative in its connotations. They worried that labeling a community or population as "oppressed" could itself be an oppressive act. Ambivalent about the word "oppression," the class hesitated to embrace the term "Theatre of the Oppressed."

At times I feel momentarily oppressed, but on the whole, no, I do not allow myself to feel inferior to people.

Class members felt that the negative connotations of "oppression" contradicted the inclusive nature of Theatre of the Oppressed, which encourages both oppressed and oppressor to work together to end inequalities. Early in the course the class responded enthusiastically to an exercise titled "Vote with Your Feet." This simple activity asks participants to imagine the playing space as a continuum, with one side of the room representing "strongly agree" and the other side symbolizing "strongly disagree." As the facilitator calls out statements of issue, participants vote with their feet by taking a position in the space to signify their stance on the issue. In discussion after the exercise, students appreciated how physical embodiment not only allowed for nuance and uncertainty, but also allowed everyone's opinion to be represented at once. The question of inclusivity popped up again at the end of October when we adapted a warm-up game of "Duck, Duck, Goose" for a classmate with a leg injury. In lieu of competitive running, we substituted zombie walks. Instead of competition, there was cooperation: participants chose their own rate of speed and worked as a group to ensure no one was left outside of the circle for more than two turns. In subsequent self-reflections, several students commented on how easily traditional playground games and theatre warm-ups can be adapted to curtail competition and instead encourage teamwork. Thus while students understood Boal's intellectual debt to fellow Brazilian Paulo Freire's *The Pedagogy of the Oppressed*, they nevertheless brainstormed alternate names for Theatre of the Oppressed. Inspired by its inclusive nature, they suggested: Theatre of Unity, Theatre of Audience, Theatre for All, Theatre of Coexistence, and Theatre of Conversation. Although the class never agreed about the word "oppression," or indeed how to define it, their lively discussions revealed a growing awareness of the nuances of political debate and the need to look beyond perceived binaries and simplified oppositions.

I don't carry signs or march but I guess I'm somewhat of a "quiet" activist in that I choose not to accept stereotypes or limits others place on me.

> "Oppression" can be a tricky word in the Canadian university classroom. On a global scale, Canadian theatre students enjoy a privileged literacy and access to education. Yet one cannot assume the absence of oppression.

The students were also ambivalent about the term "activism." Like "oppression," the word "activism" for them carried some negative connotations. Students discussed a stereotype of activists as strident and aggressive, perhaps related to media images of summer 2010's G20 demonstrations in Toronto that resulted in violence and vandalism. Even when self-identifying as activist, students defined themselves against the stereotype of aggressive public action. One wrote, "While I am not out on the streets with a loudspeaker, I do regularly try to raise the voices of those less empowered through community engagement" (Anonymous). This stereotype firmly places activism in the public sphere, and ignores the possibility that small scale, personal actions can be activist. Because of this stereotype, it is not surprising that some students hesitated to identify as activist. They wrote that they could not call themselves activists because they did not "organize or engage with the community enough," or they "only try to spread information," or they are "a far too lazy, passive, self-centred person" to be an activist (Anonymous). At the start of the class they acknowledged their interest in and desire to do activist work, but harshly critiqued their own lack of direct public action.

I am an activist. The choice to recognize inequalities and gain knowledge ... makes me an activist.

Early in the course the class responded enthusiastically to an exercise titled "Vote with Your Feet." This simple activity asks participants to imagine the playing space as a continuum, with one side of the room representing "strongly agree" and the other side symbolizing "strongly disagree." As the facilitator calls out statements of issue, participants vote with their feet by taking a position in the space to signify their stance on the issue.

The students wanted to engage, but seemed unsure how. Frustration appeared when the class experimented with Forum Theatre, in which audience members are invited to intervene in a short theatrical piece by proposing alternate behaviours or improvising new actions for the characters. Student volunteers played a scene about sexism in the local bar and restaurant industry. By stopping to add characters' inner monologues, the actors revealed the complex oppressive systems behind character motivations: the bar manager yielded to corporate financial pressure, the female server needed to pay the rent but hated her low-cut uniform, the sexist patron was self-oppressing. The class eagerly suggested options meant to change the inequalities in the scene. While some proposals were briefly successful, the class was unable to solve the overall systematic class and gender oppression at work. In their desire to solve the problem at hand, they forgot that Boal writes that the job of Theatre of the Oppressed is not to "show the correct path, but only to offer the means by which all possible paths may be examined" (Boal, *Theatre* 141). They realized the activist potential of Theatre of the Oppressed, but perhaps felt frustrated by the pervasive economic and gender inequalities they experience daily.

I'm trying to be an activist—I believe in things strongly and speak about them, keep getting ideas. I'm a bit of a lame duck, trying to get off the ground.

An interactive banner targets stress-relief strategies, part of the class performance project.
Photo by Susanne Shawyer

Boal famously wrote that Theatre of the Oppressed is a "rehearsal of revolution," a chance to explore actions and options (*Theatre* 141). I wondered if participating in a performance of their own devising would inspire students' activist awareness, as it might focus their attention on a community for which they felt a particular affinity and perhaps allow them to see how even rehearsing a revolution can be an activist act. The students chose other students from both Dalhousie University and University of King's College as their community, and devised a performance that addressed

---

The students were also ambivalent about the term "activism." Like "oppression," the word "activism" for them carried some negative connotations.

---

issues of stress within the institutional setting of the university. The performance included a flash mob-style soundscape (in which students used the sounds of studying to draw attention to stress levels at the library); a short Image Theatre demonstration (in which frozen tableaux commented on the structures that create stress in student lives); and an interactive banner that encouraged audience members to respond to the performance by articulating their own desires about how they would like to combat stress. A live Twitter feed reported participant responses. Although the activist goals for the performance were modest, most of the class felt strongly about the need to raise awareness about stress during the pressure of final exams.

A close up of the interactive banner.
Photo by Susanne Shawyer

Boal famously wrote that Theatre of the Oppressed is a "rehearsal of revolution," a chance to explore actions and options (*Theatre* 141). I wondered if participating in a performance of their own devising would inspire students' activist awareness, as it might focus their attention on a community for which they felt a particular affinity and perhaps allow them to see how even rehearsing a revolution can be an activist act. The students chose other students from both Dalhousie University and University of King's College as their community, and devised a performance that addressed issues of stress within the institutional setting of the university.

Activism is actively hindering or eliminating oppression by taking effective, intentional, and organized action against it—it's following through on a promise and being completely invested in your purpose.

At the post-mortem discussion, some in the class declared the performance a success. They argued that their performance transformed the library space into a space of community: many passersby stopped to watch, library staff hopefully asked if there would be a repeat performance, and crowds gathered around the banner to talk about stress. They pointed out that they themselves coped with their own stress by performing, focusing attention outward away from self-involvement. Others felt that the performance only worked because student facilitators discussed issues of stress with audience members after the performance, arguing that the message of the performance itself was not clear enough. A few felt that the premise of the performance was flawed, arguing that the chosen community was not oppressed: most students freely choose higher education, and many create stress by procrastinating. A passionate group countered that the performance succeeded in rehearsing the revolution because it made people stop, watch, talk, and think. In the end, the students never reached a consensus on whether the class performance constituted activism. Nevertheless, the debate was lively and individual reflections were thoughtful.

I am an activist because I define myself that way after taking this class. But no, I'm not—because I haven't found a balance between being active and being happy and healthy.

"Is this for a class?" asked the audience member at the library performance. The answer is both yes and no. During the post-performance discussion, class members expressed their desire for the performance project to expand beyond the thirteen-week university term. They suggested repeating the performance to reach more students. They proposed adding to the soundscape and expanding the frozen tableaux to clarify their meaning. They entered the banner into the university's annual student/faculty/staff art exhibition. Thus the techniques and ideas explored in the Theatre of the Oppressed class did have an impact beyond the classroom. But did this Theatre of the Oppressed class have political value? Did the class have any impact on students' activist commitment? Results were mixed. On the second questionnaire, one student firmly embraced the term "activist," stating that

A Dalhousie teaching assistant stops to sign the banner while watched by a curious crowd.
Photo by Susanne Shawyer

she supported her political beliefs through direct action and daily life. But another argued that his attempts to change minds about important issues rarely worked. The class did not seem more eager to self-identify as activist, and many participants remained suspicious of the word. Critically engaged class debates over definitions of "activism" and "activist," however, left me hopeful for the future. Although the class did not embrace activism, they embraced an activist awareness:

I am an activist more or less. I've the ideals of one, if not the time ... I also have the tools and the knowledge, so when I have some time to actually do something, I'm totally prepared.

Note

1   All words in italics are anonymous student responses to two class questionnaires meant to record changing attitudes to and awareness of political activism.

Works Cited

Anonymous. Questionnaire responses. THEA4921: Special Topics II: Theatre of the Oppressed. Halifax: Dalhousie University. 14 Sept. 2010 and 7 Dec. 2010. TS.

Boal, Augusto. *Theatre of the Oppressed*. Trans. Charles A. and Maria-Odilia Leal McBride. New York: TCG, 1985. Print.

———. *Games for Actors and Non-Actors*. Trans. Adrian Jackson. New York: Routledge, 1992. Print.

———. *The Rainbow of Desire: The Boal Method of Theatre and Therapy*. Trans. Adrian Jackson. New York: Routledge, 1995. Print.

Freire, Paulo. *Pedagogy of the Oppressed*. Trans. Myra Bergman Ramos. New York: Continuum, 2000. Print.

Susanne Shawyer is Assistant Professor in the Department of Theatre at Dalhousie University where she teaches theatre history, performance analysis, and Theatre of the Oppressed. Her research interests include the history of applied theatre, dramaturgies of protest, and virtual performance.

Applied Theatre and/as Activism

By Monica Prendergast

INTRODUCTION

Applied theatre is becoming recognized worldwide as a field of theatre that encompasses a range of practices, all of which are carried out in non-theatrical or extra-theatrical settings. While Augusto Boal's Theatre of the Oppressed may seem quite dissimilar to Pam Schweitzer's Reminiscence Theatre, or to Museum Theatre, Popular Theatre, or Theatre in Education, all of these applied theatre forms require trained facilitators with a broad set of skills in theatre performance, direction, and design as well as in facilitation, collective creation, and pedagogy. The Applied Theatre program in the University of Victoria's (UVic's) Department of Theatre offers a BFA specialization as well as special arrangement graduate degree programs (MA and PhD). Before the Applied Theatre program began at UVic in 2004, the Department of Theatre had long delivered a BFA/MA program in Theatre/Drama in Education (TIE/DIE).

While the new Applied Theatre program has a broader focus than extra-theatrical work in schools, the foundation of educational theatre remains visible. So, if UVic's program is most interested in educational applications of applied theatre, it becomes a question whether or not its teaching philosophy carries any overt or subtle activist agendas. It is this topic—the relationship, the tension between applied theatre practice and social activism—that I discussed with eight present and former faculty members and graduate students. The questions I offered to the interviewees were intentionally generalized and open-ended to provide an opportunity for each person to talk from their own particular background and philosophy of praxis:

1. What is social activism in your view?
2. How do you see the relationship between your training and practice in applied theatre and social activism?
3. What are the responsibilities and ethics of taking a group of participants in a more activist-oriented direction?
4. Why is it important/not important for us to consider our work in applied theatre as a form of activism?

I have chosen to render these interview transcripts in monologue form, as I believe it is useful to see each speaker as an individual. In addition, this process closely mirrors Applied Theatre practice, which involves the translation of interviews into dramatic texts of various kinds (including scenes and monologues). My own work in arts-based and practice-based research presses me to consider not only the *what,* but also the *how* of representation.

It is this topic—the relationship, the tension between applied theatre practice and social activism—that I discussed with eight present and former faculty members and graduate students. The questions I offered to the interviewees were intentionally generalized and open-ended to provide an opportunity for each person to talk from their own particular background and philosophy of praxis.

Anne Cirillo as Joanne, Reid Sparling as MJ, and John Krich as Grandpa have an intergenerational debate in *No Particular Place to Go*, written by Warwick Dobson. The play is based on devising rehearsals as part of a SSHRC-funded collaborative research project on older drivers carried out between the Centre on Aging and the Applied Theatre program, University of Victoria (2008–2011).
Photo by Don Chaput/Angel Communications, www.donchaput.com

INTERVIEW MONOLOGUES

I. Faculty

Warwick Dobson: (Warwick is a drama educator, director, and playwright and is the University Scholar in Applied Theatre at the University of Victoria.) I don't know what activism is. Edward Bond tells us it's not the business of theatre to change the world—politics does that. What I'm trying to do is probe the roots of inequality by understanding where social injustice comes from. My work at The Dukes Theatre in Education Company in the 1980s was concept-based rather than issue-based. These two different positions were hotly and politically debated at the time through the Standing Council of Young Peoples' Theatres (SCYPT) in England. I felt that issue-based work was ineffective. Kids know the "right" answers and will say what adults want to hear. I doubt this changes people. When adults are around, [kids] amend their racism. At Dukes our work was concept-based, in which we subjected a social problem to analysis. For example, where do the roots of racism lie? It's about a change in understanding more than cosmetic amelioration. Activism, however, lives on the border of propagandizing. In order for real change to take root, it requires understanding. For me, it all goes back to Brecht—the whole idea of epic theatre and acting are cornerstones of Applied Theatre practice. The use of narration, slightly distanced acting, political content, and an episodic quality with the audience forging links between episodes. That said, there is the perennial problem of propagandizing and didacticism—the problem of preaching to the choir and how to reach the right audience. So it's about keeping political content and didacticism in balance. I certainly come from a political upbringing—my father was a card-carrying communist and Labor party activist—and I saw how politics can polarize people. Politics gets sanitized in North America. I would want an Applied Theatre student interested in activism to be realistic—theatre does some things well and other things not terribly well. There are always pitfalls.

Barb Hill: (Barb is a retired elementary school teacher and drama specialist from Ontario with a Master's degree in education. Her interests are in effective drama pedagogy and arts-based education. She teaches the third year Applied Theatre course in Drama/Theatre Education at UVic.) For me, when I was in a classroom, it was about Dorothy Heathcote's idea of a prism, which changes what you see and how you see; it's about seeing things in their all-sidedness. It's less about telling and more about showing and doing as students become empowered decision-makers and thinkers. The arts provide the possibility of seeing the world afresh. I signed up for a summer course in computers, but it was full, so I did drama education instead! I had never really understood the purposeful learning of children until then. I went on to conduct pro-

Reid Sparling as MJ and John Krich as Grandpa play air guitars to Chuck Berry in *No Particular Place to Go*.
Photo by Don Chaput/Angel Communications, www.donchaput.com

fessional development workshops in my board and to develop a number of arts-based curriculum projects. I used drama as a vehicle for curriculum delivery using social studies as a focus. As a result, my students were happier, more enthusiastic, open, willing, and had a better grasp of material. It was more interesting for us, as this was a way of transformational teaching: teacher as fellow artist. My Applied Theatre students take away principles of planning and facilitating and conduct an assessed workshop in schools. Internal coherence [in the planning] and felt understanding [as an outcome] are vital.

> I don't know what activism is. Edward Bond tells us it's not the business of theatre to change the world—politics does that. What I'm trying to do is probe the roots of inequality by understanding where social injustice comes from.

Juliana Saxton: (Juliana is Professor Emeritus in the Department of Theatre at UVic and ran the TIE/DIE program there for twenty years. Her co-authored books have been centred on best practices in pedagogy, drama pedagogy, and story drama.) Social activism is about change ... surely a classroom is about change? Taking students from where they're at and moving them somewhere else. Theatre in education has always been about change. Education is an institution that presumably has change at its heart, although there are always political issues to deal with. University is a place with young people who are beginning to see the world more clearly; theatre becomes a way to help people see the need for change. My devised projects were always tied to curriculum, most often based on interviews in schools. Many were on health issues (bulimia/anorexia was one we did), but also tackled gossip, bullying, and friendship. How we treat each other was at the core, with curricular dimensions, how we work and play together. Good social health. I felt I was already doing Boal's work in terms of Image Theatre—tableaux work is a significant arrow in our quiver as drama educators. I saw Boal as spreading our work into the non-English-speaking world, and this broke open my eyes to the power of the work with marginalized people, other than children. But I was equally influenced by Pam Schweitzer's work with the elderly; it was mind-blowing to have our awareness raised about the capacity of seniors as seen in

> Social activism is about change ... surely a classroom is about change? Taking students from where they're at and moving them somewhere else. Theatre in education has always been about change.

Reminiscence Theatre. I was also influenced by the work of other UK drama practitioners such as Jonothan Neelands, David Davis, and Geoff Gilham when they came to Canada. The work seemed heavily political, [and] in my view Canadians are apolitical; so this work was wonderful but needed to be adapted. What I love about Applied Theatre is it gives voice and form to people's issues ... finding the language. All good stories, the kind of stories we look for, have a kind of Shakespearean frisson that reaches beyond: "and then, and then, and then ..."

II. Graduate Students (Present and Former)

Robert Birch: (Robert is a long-time activist. His use of theatre within the HIV/AIDS community in North America generates research into how theatre can support health and well-being. He completed his MA in Applied Theatre in 2008 and is currently an assistant professor in the Department of Theatre at UVic.) I'm interested in how communities struggling with HIV/AIDS have been drawn to the arts. I focus on the notion of "frozen stories" and make use of Playback Theatre to explore how painful stories ... get frozen, stuck, immobilizing the lessons our experiences offer. How can activism and other creative initiatives work together to safely support people to "thaw their stories out" in service of themselves and others? Activism, like theatre, requires action. Why do people become activists? Because we are compelled to move out of pain, move beyond fear. Where activism and performance connect is that both enliven, both have an erotic nature. Systemic oppression deadens people's ability to respond to conflict, numbing us to what we feel. Creative action awakens and eroticizes our experiences. For the duration of the action participants see and are seen as more than their circumstances. We are endowed with more agency, that of the cause … And yet we can be myopic in our

Anne Cirillo as Joanne and John Krich as Grandpa discuss Grandpa's driving record in *No Particular Place to Go*.
Photo by Don Chaput/Angel Communications, www.donchaput.com

work as artists if we don't consider and welcome the dangers inherent to activism … We live in a time when activists are branded as terrorists. When I work with students, they know much of the social justice rhetoric. What they don't recognize is how they have internalized it. I often lecture and assign performance art projects that support classes to move beyond their known identities as students and children, challenging them to consider how they might experience their world as artists, to actively explore how to bust through consensus reality. Inevitably tears of upset emerge. Their emotional push back often helps them have self-empathy, to recognize their surprising reaction to their own chosen material is the anger (or grief) of awakening. [My work] is about bringing activism to our classrooms as an arts-based, interpersonally aware pedagogy.

Anne Cirillo: (Anne completed her BFA in Applied Theatre at UVic and is now in the second year of an MA program. Her interests are in prison theatre, effective facilitation, and education. She has worked for the past four years on various projects at William Head Institution [a minimum security federal correctional institution] outside of Victoria.) When I think of activism in applied theatre, I think of voice, a voice that needs to be heard, desperately. Through activism those voices are heard, at least by those who have spoken out loud, regardless if they fall on deaf ears. There is urgency in the world today, on the streets of Victoria, in Canada, around the world. Disparity between rich and poor is growing due to corruption in the systems that run the world. I love the concept of theatre as a weapon against [those systems] because they are destroying our world. I'm here as an Applied Theatre practitioner because of them, because I want to change the world. In the prison the men say we appreciate that you're not here to fix us, that we have the freedom to just "be." Lots of times the guys would say, "I've waited all week for this, having the choices within the work to express myself." My drama workshops at William Head engage the participants in an experience that provides a reprieve from the everyday life of prison and that encourages and invites participants to access the "freedom" of self and collective expression by way of the drama. This work is not easy for many, especially those who are incarcerated. The physical and emotional demands of drama contradict or cut against the grain of prison decorum, if you will. These men live in an environment where letting your guard down, physically or emotionally, can be very dangerous. It takes courage to participate in drama in prison. Time and time again, I bear witness to individuals struggling through the work, yet they stay with it and continue to come to the workshops.

Activism, like theatre, requires action. Why do people become activists? Because we are compelled to move out of pain, move beyond fear.

Lauren Jerke: (Lauren is a second year MA student who is interested in Theatre in Health Education and Theatre for Young Audiences. Her research project involves adapting the documentary theatre form "Living Newspaper" into an applied theatre context.) Applied Theatre and activism is about public action, making the issue at hand seen, heard, and known. When I was an undergrad acting student I felt disenchanted with theatre. I thought, "There's got to be more to theatre than this!" The mainstream ideas that go along with traditional theatremaking weren't enough. That's where I started my own work. I guess it started in a physical theatre class with Boal Image Theatre. I drew on my own experiences in Mexico and El Salvador and made theatre pieces on that. I also began to work on some projects with new immigrants in Lethbridge. I remember in grade two seeing a TYA play in our school about the safety of the wetlands … I remember the songs … one moment and I was hooked. I find hope in the personal connections I make in my work. In the past year, I've been working with outpatients at a Psychiatric Day Hospital. Even though the play we created began with a rocky start, the cast performed the best I'd ever seen them do, and maintained a positive attitude about the project afterwards. That's where I find the hope for me.

Yasmine Kandil: (An Egyptian practitioner with an MFA in Directing from UVic, Yasmine is now working on a PhD in Applied Theatre. Yasmine's practice has been centred on Theatre for Development both in Cairo and in Victoria. Her doctoral research is on her work as theatre facilitator with the Victoria Immigrants and Refugees Centre Society.) Theatre

---

> When I worked with child garbage collectors in Cairo, I didn't know what I was doing. It was a struggle [...] I walked into this community and wanted to be human to them. I was foreign because of the way I dressed and the car I drove, I was foreign to them. But something happened [...] after the performance (of comic scenes and other scenes from these children's lives). It was enough for once. People didn't want to leave after the show ... they stayed to hang out with the kids.

---

for Development doesn't just happen in developing countries ... there are developing communities right here in Victoria in this wealthy country of Canada. There is a different understanding of activism in different cultures. In simple terms, it's being passionate about something and the words "social change" come to mind when I think of activism. Is this an idealist vision? A lot of Applied Theatre imposes agendas. Observing the Applied Theatre process unravel itself and seep into the community's hearts and minds is as natural a process as when animals give birth and innately know how to feed their young and look after them. I know why I'm alive while it's happening and I see it when it happens. When I worked with child garbage collectors in Cairo, I didn't know what I was doing. It was a struggle [...] I walked into this community and wanted to be human to them. I was foreign because of the way I dressed and the car I drove, I was foreign to them. But something happened [...] after the performance (of comic scenes and other scenes from these children's lives). It was enough for once. People didn't want to leave after the show ... they stayed to hang out with the kids after that. It changed the kids, they were changed, and they wanted more. It happened, change happened. Finding a jewel in the midst of a mound of garbage. And it happens in every single workshop and I think it's the earthiness of the process for me.

Will Weigler: (Will is the author of *Strategies for Playbuilding: Helping Groups Translate Issues into Theatre* [Heinemann, 2001]. His doctoral dissertation theorizes innovative ways for artists to co-create aesthetically engaging plays with community members.) I think it's useful to differentiate between the work of Applied Theatre and political theatre. In my view, activism in political theatre is about storming the citadels, marshalling theatre to promote a political agenda. Applied Theatre is about something else. I'll give you an example. After Bethlehem Steel closed its plant in Pennsylvania, Applied Theatre artists [Cornerstone Theater and Touchstone Theater] worked with that town's residents to produce an adaptation of *Prometheus Bound* addressing the resulting devastation experienced by the community. Afterwards, one of the professional non-resident actors involved in the show criticized the artistic team for failing to use this opportunity to attack Bethlehem Steel for the damage they had done. Sonja Kuftinec responded by explaining that the critique missed the point of the work. This was not about using theatre as a weapon; it was about a healing ritual that allowed people to redefine the story of what happened to them on their own terms. For me, this is activism in Applied Theatre. Activist community development in this context means leveraging the imaginative framework of theatre to enable a community to counter externally imposed, hegemonic narratives that

---

> Activist community development in this context means leveraging the imaginative framework of theatre to enable a community to counter externally imposed, hegemonic narratives that define their stories according to outsiders.

---

define their stories according to outsiders. In addition to the valuable experience of participating in a creative project that allows one's voice to be heard, activism in Applied Theatre also involves the ethics of the relationship between artists and community participants during the creative process. A defining feature of Applied Theatre work is the conscious decision by artists to engage in a relationship with community members that is based on equity and mutuality.

CONCLUDING COMMENTS

As an Applied Theatre practitioner myself, what strikes me most after transcribing and rereading these interview monologues is the sense of a lack of separation between classroom and community as experienced and expressed by interviewees. All subjects spoke about the topic of activism (however defined) as completely interwoven with their community-based practice, and inseparable from the processes and pedagogies involved in training. In UVic's Applied Theatre program, students take their work out into the community in every course from second through fourth year. Much of the focus in the classroom/studio is on preparing for the task of working with community members and/or groups. In these ways, activism becomes an integral part of the teaching of Applied

---

What strikes me most after transcribing and rereading these interview monologues is the sense of a lack of separation between classroom and community as experienced and expressed by interviewees.

Theatre as an interventionist theatre practice, albeit ever-mindful of the ethical and social responsibilities necessary to work in wholly reciprocal, non-didactic, and non-propagandistic ways with community collaborators. Whether the focus is educational, interventionist, or revolutionary, in Applied Theatre as practiced at UVic, theatre is an efficacious means for many kinds of participant-initiated activism, both in the classroom and beyond.

Monica Prendergast, Ph.D. is Assistant Professor of Drama Education and Adjunct Assistant Professor of Applied Theatre at the University of Victoria. She has published widely on spectatorship, audience education, drama education, and applied theatre.

When the Audience is Ourselves: From Intellectual Argument to Visceral Experience

By Jan Selman

Location: A graduate seminar in theories and methods of popular theatre, Department of Drama, University of Alberta.

Topic: The dramaturgy of scenes for participatory theatre.

Assignment: In small groups, create a scene that launches character-driven participatory theatre. Engage with the principles provided.

Principles for structuring participatory theatre for change:

1. Know your intended audience.
2. Put a character that is like your audience in a situation that leads to a crisis or dilemma that they (and you) want to/need to explore.
3. Catapult the character (who is like the audience) out of the scene at the point of crisis to ask the audience for help/advice/solutions.
4. Seek and try out as many suggestions as possible.
5. Live in a state of curiosity—respect and learn from your audience.

Outcome: oh! ... this is about us!

This is the story of how a group of graduate students and their professor shifted our understandings of what theatre can do. We experienced the nature of theatre's capacity to radicalize from the inside out.

There are two giant barriers to radicalizing the theatre/acting classroom. One: so much foundational theatre training is necessarily about self. Emerging artists need to

Participatory actor in the midst of an audience: Guillermo Urra in *Are We There Yet?* by Jane Heather (Concrete Theatre, 2005).
Photo by Chris Bullough

invest in developing their own expressiveness by developing their bodies, voices, imaginations, and emotive powers, as well as their interpretive capacity, communication skills, and critical tools. Two: university and college walls are high. While community-based experiences are possible, and while there are many examples of successful engagement between theatre students and specific communities, barriers to consistent interaction with a wider community's multiple viewpoints and issues include the huge amounts of time theatre artist/students must spend in cloistered rehearsal halls and studios, as well as ethical matters related to the varying needs and expectations of such an exchange.

We like to think that courses and programs in community-based theatre (also called applied or popular theatre, among other labels [see Jackson 1–2]) can overcome these barriers. In many cases they do. However, as they seek to stretch beyond the cushioning of the studio environment, several ethical questions must be addressed: when and how, and can and should, students interact with "community"? How can community needs be responded to ethically within the standard time span of a university course? And, when is a student sufficiently prepared to work purposefully, ethically, and usefully with and in communities at risk? While I regularly witness spectacular outcomes when members of underrepresented communities and students meet in the context of coursework, I have also witnessed highly problematic outcomes: communities left hanging, with high expectations which are not realized, as the end of a course intervenes; student theatre facilitators working without sufficient safeguards and supports in place for either community members; or students not knowing what to do after newly embraced theatre techniques open up difficult issues.

As an artist who wants theatre to reach out and make a difference in the world, and as an educator who seeks to enable theatre students to grow as artists while also confronting and taking responsibility for theatre's potential power to make change in communities, I struggle with these pedagogical and ethical matters. Meanwhile, I share educational philosopher Maxine Greene's belief in "the need for students to develop a sense of agency and participation and to do so in collaboration with one another" (104).

In cloistered studio settings we can all fall in love with ourselves: our sense of the importance of self-expression, our engagement with personal growth, and our commitment to theatre work and theatre learning. Our experience can seem like the most important thing on earth. We read each other's codes and celebrate each other's breakthroughs. We revel in great moments when experiential exercises are fully embraced. A natural counterpoint to this luscious and sometimes incestuous teaching and learning environment can be to put on our shoes and walk out the door, past university walls, and into our communities.

Rather ironically, then, one of the moments of greatest impact on my teaching world emerged some years ago from a decision to "stay inside." Teaching a graduate course on theory and methods of popular theatre, I was looking for ways to deepen students' engagement with the activist theories which underpin this branch of interventionist theatre.[1] The course combined classroom and studio work, marrying critical and case study readings and discussions on transformative, community-based theatre with simulations, and other experiential opportunities to explore creating and leading participant-based theatre for change. This kind of theatre work is based in Freirian educational philosophy[2] and involves uncovering and expressing the stories, experiences, and conditions of a

---

This is the story of how a group of graduate students and their professor shifted our understandings of what theatre can do. We experienced the nature of theatre's capacity to radicalize from the inside out.

Animating in role, engaging the audience: Shannon Larson in *Are We There Yet?* by Jane Heather (Concrete Theatre, 2002).
Photo courtesy of Epic Photography Inc.

community, so that these can be examined, "decoded," and ultimately altered. Fascinating and sometimes controversial international case studies (e.g., Bappa and Etherton, Etherton, Kidd, van Erven) were taking us to a certain point, as were some of the more theoretic readings (e.g., Freire, Kershaw, Matarasso, Salverson). This field does not neatly separate itself into theory and practice, nor theory and project narratives. Students entered into intensive dialogue about the roles of theatre in society, exploring the relative merits of theatre for, theatre with, and theatre by the people (Kidd). They generously engaged with various techniques, plunging into weekly lab sessions that investigated a variety of exercises common to the group development and issue identification stages of popular theatre: image, sculpture, metaphor games, story creation, and story-for-analysis, among others. They were presented with creative problems to solve, problems which involved adapting core exercises to suit particular communities, contexts, and themes. The students were outstanding: involved, intellectually curious, risk taking, willing to challenge, prepared, focused. Yet nevertheless, the need for greater engagement was on my mind. How could these ideas and experiences be deepened? How could they be more deeply

---

When and how, and can and should, students interact with "community"? How can community needs be responded to ethically within the standard time span of a university course? And, when is a student sufficiently prepared to work purposefully, ethically, and usefully with and in communities at risk?

---

grounded for North American students? How could this course challenge students to ask: why make theatre?

Oddly, an answer came on a day that was apparently about "learning a new theatre technique," rather than about confronting theatre's capacity to transform. We were studying the dramaturgy of creating scenes that lead to participation with an audience. These were the steps used for this experiential learning-based investigation:

1. *Know the community that will form your audience.* Student teams designed mini-workshops to learn "what matters to our audience." Because the audience was to be themselves, fellow graduate students, the task appeared to be an exercise in self-reflection. However, students were asked to both learn something new and identify things that made them a community before starting to create participatory scenes. The challenges of listening and hearing took on new meaning for them.

Connecting with the audience: Jared Matsunaga-Turnbull in *Are We There Yet?* by Jane Heather (Concrete Theatre, 2002).
Photo courtesy of Epic Photography Inc.

2. *Structure a scene for improvisation that will leave a character that is like the audience in a dilemma or crisis.* The class's scene issues included money, competition for a position, several relationship upheavals, an intractable problem with a supervisor, a rejected request for help from a peer, a housing dispute. Fictions that could be true. (Of course, this simple list does not communicate the layered, counter-pointed scenes that were ultimately devised.) Scenes were then improvised, built from who-what-where and objective-obstacles-stakes scenario planning.

3. *Catapult the character in crisis out of the scene and into the audience for help, advice, strategies.* As characters struggled with apparently intractable problems, students practiced techniques and experienced some of the challenges and payoffs of this interactive theatrical style. Meanwhile, everyone worked collaboratively on recognizable issues, issues that connected with their lives.

One of the scenes, which wove together characters' ideological differences, intellectual badgering, being broke, and a request for a loan, hit its crisis and the character exploded into the audience with: "I won't deal with him, I refuse!"

Pause.

"What the hell can I do with him?"

Pause.

"What can I say?"

An audience member, a member of our class, ran out of the room. Jolt. Silence. Racing hearts. Two went to check he was okay. The rest of the class, creators and audience members alike, were left to face themselves. To unpack what had happened—and what was happening.

> In cloistered studio settings we can all fall in love with ourselves: our sense of the importance of self-expression, our engagement with personal growth, and our commitment to theatre work and theatre learning. Our experience can seem like the most important thing on earth.

Suddenly our object of study—theatre for transformation—became known to us in a new way. Intellect, emotion, and physical experience were fused. Implications of and responsibility for our scene work were in our faces. "Relevant" took on new meaning...

I should clarify: this is not a story of a group of students having a first experiential moment in the studio and revelling in the newness of the connection of body-mind-heart that theatre can provide. Previously, their work had been connected—sometimes impassioned—and the group had already explored themselves and their social circumstances in some depth. They were well into what Maxine Greene terms "social imagination: the capacity to invent visions of what should be and what might be in our deficient society" (5). As grad students, so often in their heads, they had enjoyed the self-expression and physical/personal experiences of drama and popular theatre exercises, and they vigorously linked their studio experiences with the course readings and debates about social transformation and students' roles in movements for justice. But this was different—this was new. A shock, a disturbance, beyond the expected. We were out on an edge, naming the previously unsayable. Jolted into meaning.

Class reflections about this experience were not easy, but ultimately rich. Beyond addressing their own community's previously unstated but pressing matters, the group's discussions re-examined theatre's power and artists' culpability. Direct responsibility for the theatre we make was felt and understood by them in a new way … in two new ways. On one hand, we had felt how much, how intimately, theatre can matter. When created with full attention to who is our audience, what makes them a community, and with what issues and injustices they experience and struggle—both within their own community and because of other interests—theatre actually does what artists always hope it will do in some way—it meets people where they live and touches them deeply. It can acknowledge their lives, clarify struggles, and offer new ways to see. Why ever aim for less? But further than that, students also learned that if we can tap this power, which surely we hope to do every time we create, we also take on a new level of responsibility for our work. Audiences need places to unpack and direct these responses and insights. We need to ensure that we are working in conditions where new-found passion, emotion, understanding, and insight can be supported, and even put to use. The community that is our audience needs to have ways to act as a community.

Could this rich moment of learning have occurred using a different theatre technique? Likely. However, the power of participatory theatre, the form under exploration on that day, should not be overlooked. If certain principles are adhered to (which I believe they must be during creation, rehearsal, and performance if social change and further action are the goals), this theatrical form is particularly powerful. Why? In this kind of participatory theatre, fictional characters that are recognizable to the audience go through a fictional experience that audience members also recognize and believe is important and could be true. Characters face a crisis or impasse that is urgent and palpable, and then they face the audience. There is no mediating joker or facilitator. The character stands before spectators, in a sense representing them. He or she looks to audience members as confidantes and endows

---

> One of the scenes, which wove together characters' ideological differences, intellectual badgering, being broke, and a request for a loan, hit its crisis and the character exploded into the audience with: "I won't deal with him, I refuse!"
> Pause.
> "What the hell can I do with him?"
> Pause.
> "What can I say?"
> An audience member, a member of our class, ran out of the room.
> Jolt. Silence.

A graduate seminar in the Department of Drama, University of Alberta.
Photo by Curtis Comeau

terms, "participatory communal relationships between spectator and performer" (76). Many artists are working on a return to and explorations of theatrical forms that connect more directly with theatre's audiences: forms that combine the power of story and character with a recognition of the need for audience engagement, insight, and power. This kind of work suggests one way back to a theatre that is essential, and central to our social transformation.

In that classroom of some years ago, the scene's moment of crisis led on to a classroom crisis. The course was never the same. The power of theatre *in* community had been felt—experienced. And with that knowledge and power came responsibility. Though we had dissected, critiqued, and championed topicality and the importance of telling the stories of the "voiceless" collaboratively and ethically, the understanding that we were all deeply implicated, always, as we create, perform, and present theatre was now visceral

them with the status of expert and ally. If built well, the play or scene enthrals its audience, and that audience works with the character to move beyond impasse to strategize for success. As the audience experiences empathy with the character and recognition of his or her situation, the character's stakes become the audience's stakes. Everyone feels the need to find a way forward. When the actor/character needs spectators, when he or she earns their respect, hears them, and tries their ideas, they further invest in the character's successful passage through the crisis to another level. When a scene creates the contradictions and dilemmas that are at

> The rest of the class, creators and audience members alike, were left to face themselves. To unpack what had happened—and what was happening.

Promotional image for Jane Heather's *Are We There Yet?* The performer pictured on the right is Jana O'Connor.
Photos and image design courtesy of Epic Photography Inc.

the heart of a community's conditions, the interactive performance can act as a lightning rod: it can surprise an audience, moving the group from a polite, proper, cool set of theatregoers to an engaged group of citizens. The invitation to participate is the catch. When a piece of theatre is constructed so that a character who is stuck (or confused, or giving up, or furious but impotent) may discover and test ways beyond an impasse *because of audience intervention*, the piece supports a community in exploring actions that it could take in real life.[3]

Lancaster, referencing critics from Aristotle to Turner and Brecht to Bennett, proposes that at this mediatized and consumerist period in our history, there is a hunger for opportunities to *do*—to get to play, to interact. People seek opportunities that enable them to rediscover, in today's

for us. Bappa and Etherton's statement, "'Theatre' in this context becomes nothing less than the *actual social process* whereby the people come to make their own political and economic analysis for future action" (56) had shifted from a good theory to something for us to acknowledge and grapple with continuously. The event shook us up. Using theatre-making and performing meta-critically, in order to interrogate theatre's potential power, function, and roles, crept up and walloped us, making "education" highly personal, politicized, and urgent. Perhaps in that moment some of us experienced, in Greene's terms, a decision to "break from anchorage and insert [ourselves] into the world with a particular kind of identity and responsibility, a particular mode of valuing what lies around and of straining toward what ought to be" (70–71).

Actor Natasha MacLellan engages with Nova Scotia audiences in Mulgrave Road Theatre's production of Jane Heather's participatory play *Are We There Yet?*
Photo by Emmy Alcorn

Of course viscerally linking theatremaking, theatre theory, and theatre's potential for potency when strategically tied to a community and its issues is more feasible in a course that focuses on popular theatre, a kind of theatre which overtly sets out to provoke and pursue social justice. When I teach courses that focus more on foundational techniques such as acting and directing, I wonder if we can meet the goals of those courses and also embed, viscerally as well as intellectually, this level of knowledge of social responsibility

> We need to ensure that we are working in conditions where new-found passion, emotion, understanding, and insight can be supported, and even put to use. The community that is our audience needs to have ways to act as a community.

and ethical commitment to an audience that can accompany theatre practice. While risky, using our art form to investigate its own power and creating experiential conditions in theatre classrooms where students are jolted into realizations about that power may be one method of keeping our classrooms entwined with our communities, while also provoking students to link their artistic expression with their views of social justice.

Some glimmers of a way forward emerged for me when I purposely linked script choices in an acting class with character and dialect research assignments in local and culturally appropriate communities, then invited those providing re-

search to attend the performances. For example, Romanian-Canadians assisted with preparations for a production of Caryl Churchill's *Mad Forest*. Intensive and overt responses from these audience members to the material which was directly reflective of their experience led to a need for actors to unpack the meanings of those audience reactions. Engagement with audience is key: careful choice of texts that may lead to opportunities for such engagement during rehearsals and for provocative audience responses is a challenge, but is also vital. In directing classes I ask students to make cases for their choices of material in light of their anticipated audiences, which will often be their age-mates; this strategy typically starts a debate about the relative merits of aiming for universality versus aiming for cultural specificity. While audience and student safety and autonomy must be supported, creating "disturbance" as part of students' (and teachers') educational experiences may challenge and jolt while also creating demanding and memorable opportunities for learning.

Notes

1. Popular Theatre normally refers to theatrical processes and performances that deeply engage a community of geography or interest in making and performing theatre for change. Discussions of this definition can be found in Bappa and Etherton and Prentki and Selman.

2. Freire espouses conscientization, or the development of a critical consciousness that engages learners in questioning their social situation. Codification (stories, photos of community) and decodification (analysis of these) are key in this process, which is also called "reading the world."

3. For discussion of a research project that tested these theories about impacts of participatory theatre via interdisciplinary, quantitative, qualitative, and theatrical research strategies, see www.ualberta.ca/awty.

Works Cited

Bappa, Salihu and Michael Etherton. "Popular theatre voice of the oppressed." *Commonwealth* 25.4 (1983): 55–57. Print.

Etherton, Michael. "Third world popular theatre: Reaching and helping unorganized and disadvantaged people." *Courier* 33 (1981): 30–33. Print.

Freire, Paolo. *Pedagogy of the Oppressed*. New York: Continuum, 1983. Print.

Greene, Maxine. *Releasing the Imagination: Essays on Education, the Arts, and Social Change*. San Francisco: John Wiley & Sons, 1995. Print.

Jackson, Anthony. *Theatre, Education and the Making of Meanings: Art or Instrument?* Manchester: Manchester UP, 2007. Print.

Kershaw, Baz. *The Politics of Performance: Radical Theatre as Cultural Intervention*. New York: Routledge, 1992. Print.

Kidd, Ross. "Popular Theatre, Conscientization and Popular Organisation." *Courier* 33 (1981): 21. Print.

Lancaster, Kurt. "When Spectators Become Performers: Contemporary Performance-Entertainments Meet the Needs of an 'Unsettled' Audience." *Journal of Popular Culture* 30.4 (1997): 75–88. Print.

Matarasso, Francois. *Use or Ornament? The Social Impact of Participation in the Arts*. Stroud, Gloucester: Comedia, 1997. Print.

Prentki, Tim and Jan Selman (with contributions from other popular theatre artists). *Popular Theatre in Political Culture: Britain and Canada in Focus*. Bristol: Intellect Books, 2000. Print.

Salverson, Julie. "Performing Emergency: Witnessing, Popular Theatre, and the Lie of the Literal." *Theatre Topics* 6.2 (1996): 181–191. Print.

Van Erven, Eugene. *Community Theatre: Global Perspectives*. New York: Routledge, 2001. Print.

Jan Selman is Professor of Drama at the University of Alberta where she teaches acting, directing, and popular theatre. A specialist in participatory theatre forms, her recent work includes co-facilitating *Transforming Dangerous Spaces*, which uses theatre to explore coalition in women's activist communities, and leading the *Are We There Yet?* interdisciplinary research program, which links social science and theatre researchers, health agencies, and theatre companies to create and assess theatre for change.

Minstrels in the Classroom: Teaching, Race, and Blackface

By Natalie Alvarez and Stephen Johnson

INTRODUCTION

What follows is a conversation about how we engage with issues of "race" in the undergraduate theatre and performance classroom. Our interest arises from a shared belief in the importance of examining the traditions of blackface minstrelsy as a conduit for discussions about race and representation—discussions that are undeniably awkward and difficult, and for this reason, perhaps, often avoided in undergraduate contexts. We come to this conversation with research interests in the subject but also with an interest in articulating the pedagogical challenges that minstrelsy presents. Our intention is not to propose solutions to these challenges—indeed, whether or not solutions are possible is questionable—but to approach the topic interrogatively in order to initiate a discussion that, we hope, will make us less apprehensive about addressing the subject of "race" in the classroom.

Two opening statements: First, we use "race" in quotation marks in order to acknowledge the ways in which this category has been complicated by historians and scholars of race theory and dismantled by biologists and geneticists. As Nell Irvin Painter states in her introduction to *The History of White People*, "Today […] biologists and geneticists (not to mention literary critics) no longer believe in the physical existence of races—though they recognize the continuing power of racism (the belief that races exist, and that some are better than others)" (xii). Second, it is our experience that we are, as a society, ill equipped to talk about constructions of race at all, let alone in the classroom. This is perhaps in part a result of the so-called "post-racial" landscape left in the wake of Canada's idyllic project of multiculturalism. Multiculturalism has, as Alicia Arrizón reminds us (following Vera M. Kutzinski), "created the façade of cultural diversity, which diverted attention from the inequalities that continued to divide people of colour from whites" under the banner of cultural pluralism (7). Even under Pierre Trudeau's policy of multiculturalism, "ethnic groups" beyond those defined by the 1967 Royal Commission on Bilingualism and Biculturalism as English or French maintained a merely "symbolic function," with no clear articulation of how they would impact "the practice of Canadian society" (Gómez 28–29). The lack of such an articulation at the federal level is, perhaps, symptomatic of our ineptitude in articulating questions of cultural difference and race at an interpersonal level.

CONTEXT

STEPHEN: It is nothing new that the subject of race finds its way into the classroom, and I would say I am no more than representative of the challenge all instructors face—to discuss race fairly and openly, but to ensure that there is sufficient critical distance, so that the emotions that are so abundantly (and justifiably) associated with the subject are set aside, creating a safe space. Because, however, I am a historian of performance, and one of the things I research is the history of blackface minstrelsy, I bring to "the table" a very specific kind of racial profiling. It makes sense that, since I know about it, I should explore ways to use it in the classroom.

NATALIE: I incorporate the study of minstrelsy in undergraduate courses that undertake the cultural history of theatre because I feel it's important to address in light of its continued, and unsettling, resurgence: as minstrelsy scholar W.T. Lhamon writes, "The twentieth-century tendrils of the story of minstrelsy are still spreading, both in life and in cultural reckonings" (152). I want to give my students—and myself, as an educator—an opportunity to develop the critical skills to address the fraught and difficult questions of race this tradition invites, in order to better navigate its recursions in twenty-first century popular culture. But to do so in a predominantly "white" classroom—as Theatre Studies classrooms tend to be for reasons that warrant a sustained examination elsewhere—as a white/Hispanic instructor is admittedly awkward, anxiety inducing, and challenging. In the hours before this particular class each year, I invariably feel my anxiousness about the impending discussion intensify—a discussion that will no doubt confuse a generation weaned on the comfortable, neo-liberal denial of racial difference in a so-called "post-racial" society and uncomfortably betray the mechanics of white privilege that essentially affords us the luxury (and power) to address these issues at our convenience.

CASE STUDIES: THE INSTRUCTOR'S DILEMMA

STEPHEN: I want to give you an idea of the challenges as I have experienced them, and I'm choosing two incidents for very particular reasons.

When I first started teaching undergraduates, I showed the 1915 film *The Birth of a Nation* in a large introductory film studies course. This is a very important film to the study of cinema; it is also an aggressively racist film, in which the Ku Klux Klan is portrayed as heroic, and all black characters are portrayed as by turns docile simpletons and sexually violent predators, normally by white actors in blackface. It can be a tough film to watch, but I thought that if I could just give it sufficient context, set the students up to watch it "in

---

> In the hours before this particular class each year, I invariably feel my anxiousness about the impending discussion intensify—a discussion that will no doubt confuse a generation weaned on the comfortable, neo-liberal denial of racial difference in a so-called "post-racial" society.

---

a certain light," we would be all right. I gave my lecture, I showed the film, and as I remember there was no protest, no outrage. There was, however, one letter, from an older student, explaining to me in persuasive terms that I had made an error in judgment. As much as she understood why I would want to show this film, as important as it was to the history of cinema, and as capable as I may have been in providing the socio-cultural and the aesthetic context—the tools with which we might understand the racism in this work and then move past it to other matters—the fact was, she argued, that no amount of context would be sufficient to "get past" the racism in this film. Certainly I couldn't do the job in the short time I had with this class. It could never be historicized or contextualized sufficiently to a class of this size, and this demographic. That being the case, it can do damage to members of that class, reinforce prejudices and self-images already inherent in the classroom, and possibly incite further hatred. Her conclusion was that it simply should not be shown.

Twenty years later, in another setting entirely, I was involved in a workshop-demonstration on melodramatic acting style, to which I brought some brief examples of the precision of gesture and the extremes of emotion that are the hallmarks of that style. There isn't a film in existence that better demonstrates this style—its uses and abuses—than *Birth of a Nation*. Time was short, as it often is in workshops, and I did not have or take the time to give the kind of contextual introduction I had prepared. Given the circumstances, I had to rely on the possibility that we might *only* talk about acting style *and not race*. This was, of course, impossible. The acting style existed exactly to serve the racial message of the film, a service it still provides even after ninety-five years. There was discomfort on all sides (and, thankfully, an honest debriefing afterwards). The fact was that the discussion could never not be about race.

> There is no means to acknowledge the racialized treatment of character in art and then, somehow, tell everyone to ignore it in order to look at something else (acting style, film technique); and no amount of context will be sufficient to distance every student from this aspect of the work, so that it does not cause hurt. This leaves us with two straightforward alternatives: never show such works or talk only about race. These do not seem like useful answers.

I take two lessons from these episodes in the life of an instructor: there is no means to acknowledge the racialized treatment of character in art and then, somehow, tell everyone to ignore it in order to look at something else (acting style, film technique); and no amount of context will be sufficient to distance every student from this aspect of the work, so that it does not cause hurt.

This leaves us with two straightforward alternatives: never show such works or talk only about race. These do not seem like useful answers. It should be beneficial to confront and not suppress these works, and clearly we need to talk about race. How do we strike the balance we need in the classroom, between an admission of complexity and a need for clear thinking?

NATALIE: Yes, and the problem becomes how to preface a discussion with "an admission of complexity and a need for clear thinking" without exacerbating apprehensions students might already have talking about these issues. Students are, understandably, reticent about tackling the difficult questions of "race" particular texts elicit. For example, I often centre a class discussion around the infamous case of Ben Jonson's *Masque of Blackness,* the seventeenth-century masque that ostensibly marked the first instance on record of performers "blacking up" (Queen Anne among them), rather than donning the traditional "vizards" or masks. Our discussion is framed by an effective reading of this performance by Kim Hall, who persuasively demonstrates the interlocking logic of gender, class, and race at work in the masque as "Britannia" embarks on a project of national identity formation in the face of colonial encounters with cultural "others." Even though Hall's argument serves as a companion piece to tease out the imbedded discourses of race, gender, and class in Jonson's masque, the students are often more confident in criticizing what they perceive as Hall's "agenda" than the implications of the masque's representations of difference, absolving the masque's participants with arguments such as, "they didn't know any better back then." Other students simply don't participate in the discussion, steering clear of the minefield that questions of race and representation present. In one memorable case, a group of students conducted a "Research in Performance" project on the masque and, through the entire course of their presentation, made not one single mention of the issues of race the performance raises, settling much more comfortably into discussions of gender and class. I was faced with the delicate task of bringing the discussion around to the colonial narrative and the dichotomized language of "blackness" and "whiteness" that the masque deploys. The students seemed mortified by the fact that I was "pushing" the problem of race when, from their point of view, it was not a problem.

> In one memorable case, a group of students conducted a "Research in Performance" project on the [*Masque of Blackness*] and, through the entire course of their presentation, made not one single mention of the issues of race the performance raises.

STEPHEN: I am also struck by just how passive students can be in the face of the obvious delineation of race that is "blackface." On the other hand, we can never know what they have experienced outside the classroom door. I think it is important to understand just how much "race" infuses every pore of our cultural body. On the face of it, blackface performance seems archaic, obsolete, expunged from all performing arts culture with the Civil Rights movement in the early 1960s. And yet we have all seen something like an "eruption" of this form in various media—used self-consciously in film, television, and the web, but also more locally. The last two years running, Halloween parties in

"Daughter of Niger": design by Inigo Jones for Ben Jonson's *The Masque of Blackness* (1605). Students are asked to contend with this early instance of "blacking up" in the context of England's colonial encounters with cultural "others." Devonshire Collection, Chatsworth.
Reproduced by permission of Chatsworth Settlement Trustees

Ontario (on a university campus and in a Canadian Legion hall) have given prizes to costumes using blackface. There was protest and apology afterwards, but the significant word is "afterwards"—first they won the competition, voted for by people who did not see the problem.

There has been some question recently as to why this archaic idiom has returned. I believe this is the wrong question. I want to know where it went when everyone thought it had passed away. At the same time I was *not* giving sufficient context to *Birth of a Nation* in a film course, I taught a senior seminar in contemporary theatre. I asked students to bring in evidence of the kinds of performance happening then—circa 1990—in their hometowns and cultures. One student brought in a videotape of a recent performance by his hometown's local service club, of their annual fundraiser. It was a minstrel show.

> The students seemed mortified by the fact that I was "pushing" the problem of race when, from their point of view, it was not a problem.

What I didn't know when I taught *Birth of a Nation* was that there might be someone sitting in the classroom who had experienced the theatrical forms of racism exhibited in the film. I thought that I had the advantage inherent in obsolescence—the distance provided by the dead metaphor. But, as Faulkner tells us, "the past isn't dead—it isn't even past."

> I think it is important to understand just how much "race" infuses every pore of our cultural body. On the face of it, blackface performance seems archaic, obsolete, expunged from all performing arts culture with the Civil Rights movement in the early 1960s. And yet we have all seen something like an "eruption" of this form in various media—used self-consciously in film, television, and the web, but also more locally.

CASE STUDIES: STRATEGIES

NATALIE: In an attempt to bridge that distance and demonstrate how the past "isn't even past," I usually introduce recent manifestations of blackface in classes that otherwise focus on historical case studies. In part, I introduce these recent examples as "teachable moments" and as a way of throwing us headlong into the messy, awkward struggle of developing a critical vocabulary that allows us to identify or "see the problem." But I also introduce them in order to underscore the fact that *not* seeing the problem is itself a racialized experience, that is, part of what it means to be inscribed by "whiteness" and its privileges as a racial category.

In a recent class, I began with the infamous October 2009 *Vogue* layout that features model Lara Stone posing seductively in haute couture fashions in blackface. A student

Images from *Connecting Contemporary Dance and Juba: How Does Art Affect Art?*, an exercise in which senior acting students in the University of Toronto–Mississauga/Sheridan College theatre and drama studies program were asked to examine the life of the dancer Juba, and in particular his role as a performer of colour in a blackface minstrel troupe, and to explore his life and art through movement. The results of the project are posted at http://www.utm.utoronto.ca/~w3minstr/artistrespond/index.html. Clockwise from upper left: Oren Williamson, Leslie McBay, Oren Williamson, and Marissa Ship.
Images courtesy of Stephen Johnson

at the back of the hall evoked a familiar argument to justify the image's innocence: "It's just a look," he said confidently, "it doesn't mean anything. It's not meant to mean anything." Looking back, I question the pedagogical efficacy of my choice to use this static fashion image as a means of catalyzing discussion. As a generation reared in a globalized image economy, perhaps these students have a particular set of interpretive skills by which they process an endless circulation of signifiers hollowed out and detached from their referents.

I followed this with a You Tube clip from an episode of the Australian television show *Hey Hey It's Saturday* in 2009, which featured a Caucasian group performing as the Jackson Five in blackface to a bewildered Harry Connick, Jr. as guest judge. I winced as I screened this, conscious of the few black students in the class who chose not to participate in the discussion that was largely taken up by students attempting to diffuse the "cultural work" these representations were doing. I wondered whether the few visible minorities in the classroom were feeling silenced by this dominant opinion or attempting to comply with it, not wanting to make themselves part of the "issue" of race under scrutiny in the classroom.

Invariably, I find these classroom discussions dominated by the white student majority and expressions of skepticism about racial politics or the existence of racism generally. I wonder if, at the root of this, lies students' fear of making themselves complicit with racism by demonstrating a capacity to identify how it operates in particular performance texts or events; instead students defer to what they perhaps feel is a more politically correct colour blindness and obliviousness to racial politics. But the denial of the historical fact of race relations, or the willful desire to obviate the mechanisms at work in its representations, is a by-product of white privilege. Assertions of "sameness"—as in, we're all the same—and claims of colour-blindness—as in, I don't see race, race doesn't matter—are the luxurious assets of white privilege. But these questions remain: how do I disabuse students of their implicit claims to a "post-racial" society and address the mechanics of white privilege without making them feel targeted as "part of the problem"? and: how do I navigate this delicate topic to ensure that visible minorities in the classroom are part of the critical discussion rather than the objects of it?

Image of William Henry Lane dancing with a minstrel troupe under the stage name "Juba," at Vauxhall Gardens, London. From the *Illustrated London News*, 5 August 1848.
Photo in public domain

know? I think introducing nuanced discussions around empathy in the classroom is crucial. While empathy is often evoked as an imaginative exercise that allows one to understand difference, it also risks erasing difference as an I-centred exercise that colonizes the experience of the "other," reducing the "other" to "the same." I think productive conversations can be had about how *not* understanding need not necessarily mean failure in the undergraduate classroom.

In a recent class, I began with the infamous October 2009 *Vogue* layout that features model Lara Stone posing seductively in haute couture fashions in blackface. A student at the back of the hall evoked a familiar argument to justify the image's innocence: "It's just a look," he said confidently, "it doesn't mean anything."

STEPHEN: So what is a teacher to do? And what is a historian to do when teaching? I have explored a number of strategies over the years—perhaps the appropriate term is "coping skills"—and I'd like to relate two of them here: the use of the extreme historical example, and the performed artist's response.

In the interests of bringing these issues gradually closer and closer to "home," I showed a slide show, also from YouTube (so rife with "teachable moments"), of the infamous incident that took place as part of a Nations of the World event at Wilfrid Laurier in 2007. There, blacked-up white students with buckets of KFC on their heads carrying marijuana joints and legs of chicken "represented" Jamaica. As I showed these clips, I read from a newspaper report of the incident, which outlined the participating students' assertions that they were just having fun. My attempt here was to short circuit claims of innocence and naivety: we were forced to reconcile the words of the Wilfred Laurier students, their assertions that no harm was intended, with the images in front of us that were producing a surfeit of discomfiting meanings that were difficult to metabolize.

I opt for a discussion and analysis of emblematic representations because I am wary of praxis-oriented exercises that invite students to embody, stand in the place of, or speak on behalf of "the other." My concern is with how such exercises often rely on the language of empathy as a gateway to understand the experience of the other. But can one presume to know? Isn't the more ethical choice to assume that one cannot

---

How do I disabuse students of their implicit claims to a "post-racial" society and address the mechanics of white privilege without making them feel targeted as "part of the problem"?

It really doesn't work simply to say "it's complicated" to a classroom full of undergraduate students. We need to show just how complicated it is. Because I research and write in this area, I have run across some examples that, I think, foreground the complexity with which audiences view race on stage, and so in the world. As an example, I talk about the nineteenth-century dancer Juba (William Lane), the alleged progenitor of tap, and a great star during the 1840s. Students appreciate the excellent descriptions of his dancing, which emphasize his skill and innovation. But he performed most famously in a minstrel show, the only performer of colour on a stage filled with white performers in blackface, billed as "authentic," "illustrating the simple dances of his native people." More troubling is this brief quotation: "It has been said that in 1852 [Juba's] skeleton ... was on exhibition at the Surrey Music Hall, Sheffield, England." What does this mean? Can this be true? If it is true, why would it happen? At this point we as a group can begin to discuss—as applied to one great artist in one extreme example—what it means to "see" someone as a part of another race. The historical context I can give them then has some more immediate purpose—yes, skeletons were on display, of the infamous, the peculiar, and the representative, including race. Perhaps, in the case of this artist, all three applied. The individual example is not important; it is part of a larger strategy to find the extreme historical example that has something so unusual about it, to the contemporary undergraduate, that it short-circuits the normal way of seeing (or not seeing) "race."

After the discussion of Juba noted above, students take the descriptions of Juba's dancing and ask each other what they would make of them, given their understanding of his circumstances, a black performer surrounded by the racist environment of blackface minstrelsy. For my undergraduate students, many of whom intend to become professional performers, this is not an arcane question. I then ask what they would do to interpret both description and context through movement—not to re-create, which would be its own kind of minstrelsy, but to find the objective correlative that communicates how they, as students, interpret how this historical figure met this racial challenge. The performance of race is filled with danger. I too am wary of this kind of engagement, and I have only attempted it with senior acting students. What I have found, however, is that given the clear instruction to find the contemporary analogy to the relationship Juba had with the world around him, the performances were strongly stated expressions of pain and outrage on the one hand—images ranging from grotesque physical distortion to ventriloquism and puppetry—and on the other hand defiance and the exuberant passion that comes with skilled artistic expression. These are opinions about and reactions toward racism that we can all use to begin a discussion.

CONCLUSION

While we have, through the course of this conversation, raised more questions—and anxieties—than we have strategies, we hope at the very least to have conveyed the extent to which blackface minstrelsy continues to pervade contemporary culture, providing potentially "teachable moments" that make present the often eluded past. No strategy works all the time, or with every student. Finally, our goal should be to begin a discussion—by any means at our disposal—that does not end at the door of the classroom.

Works Cited

Arrizón, Alicia. *Queering Mestizaje: Transculturation and Performance.* Ann Arbor: U of Michigan P, 2006. Print.

Gómez, Mayte. "Healing the Border Wound: *Fronteras Americanas* and the Future of Canadian Multiculturalism." *Theatre Research in Canada* 16.1–2 (1995): 26–39. Print.

Lhamon, W.T., Jr. *Raising Cain: Blackface Performance from Jim Crow to Hip Hop.* Cambridge: Harvard UP, 1998. Print.

Painter, Nell Irvin. *The History of White People.* New York: W.W. Norton & Co., 2010. Print.

Natalie Alvarez is an Assistant Professor in the Department of Dramatic Arts at Brock University. She received a SSHRC grant for her research on performativity and cultural difference in military training scenarios and immersive dark tourism. She is the editor of two forthcoming books on Latina/o-Canadian theatre for Playwrights Canada Press and serves as co-editor of *CTR*'s Views and Reviews.

Stephen Johnson is Director of the Graduate Centre for Study of Drama at the University of Toronto. His recently completed research project on blackface minstrelsy resulted in a database and website available at http://link.library.utoronto.ca/minstrels/. He is currently developing a web-based project focusing on performance in Southern Ontario during the nineteenth and early twentieth centuries, available as it develops at http://link.library.utoronto.ca/ontheroad/canadawest/index.cfm.

A Pedagogy of Justice

By Naila Keleta-Mae

Justice is like fire; even if you cover it with a veil, it still burns. (Madagascar)
—Hodari and Sobers 156

I painted a large, circular shape for the face with long, vertical brush strokes on both sides of it for two ponytails. Mrs. Cowan, my junior kindergarten teacher, asked our class to paint pictures of ourselves, but as I looked at the array of brushstrokes fashioning face and hair, the task suddenly seemed impossible. I had used black paint. If I used more black paint to paint my eyes, nose, and mouth, my features would be invisible, my face incomplete. I remember standing in front of the easel, perplexed. I surveyed my palette and settled on green paint for my eyes, red paint for my nose, and blue paint for my mouth.

Mrs. Cowan always hung a large picture frame in the hallway outside of our classroom and in it she would display a student's artwork for a few days. She chose my painting. I was proud. When she showed it to my parents she noted that I knew who I was. I had used black paint. I knew I was a black girl. But what nudged up against me, as I stood before the easel in contemplation of a black image that could not hold features to make it human, was that race and colour were not synonymous. I was a little black girl whose face, hair, nose, eyes, and lips were shades of brown. I was and was not black. In those few moments I deepened my understanding of the nuances of blackness and as I fashioned features from green, red, and blue paint, I rehearsed an invaluable skill: the use of art to cleave open space that dominant discourses attempt to foreclose.

In *Arts Under Pressure: Promoting Cultural Diversity in the Age of Globalization,* Joost Smiers argues that, "[t]he arts are pre-eminently a field where emotional incompatibilities, social conflicts and questions of status collide in a more concentrated way than happens in daily communication" (1). I have often acutely felt the reverberations of these collisions as a teacher and student in post-secondary classrooms where art is both subject and praxis. Within these deeply subjective spaces, canon and methodology frequently converge to reproduce asymmetrical systems of power. The disruption of these systems, through the identification and examination of their epistemes and ontologies, is arduous and rewarding work—work that requires a committed consortium of students,

---

> After class during the Winter 2011 semester, a student asked me if black people can create theatre that is not required to be black—"Can't they just make theatre that's about anything or nothing like so many of the shows put on in Toronto?" Through the example of Samuel Beckett's play *Waiting for Godot*, the student and I talked about racial politics imbedded in work that is allegedly about anything or nothing.

---

teachers, and extended community. The Oxford English Dictionary defines "activist" in the following terms: "That advocates or engages in action, *spec.* that undertakes vigorous political or social campaigning" ("Activist"). I teach Black Theatre and Performance, a third year undergraduate course offered by the theatre department at York University. While the work we do there falls shy of "campaigning," it is heavily invested in the overt consideration of what is "political" and what is "social."

My teaching practice is a pedagogy of justice that uses divergent source material to challenge participants to interrogate the historical, political, and cultural components of their frameworks of analysis and those at play in the material at hand. Within the intellectually rigorous learning environment that my pedagogy of justice requires, I aim to teach students to enrich their thinking and communicative skills through critical self-reflexivity. It is this approach that I have found most productive in the wide range of courses, workshops, lectures, and keynote addresses I have created for more than a decade for graduate, undergraduate, high school, and elementary students as well as non-governmental organizations, community organizations, and labour unions. In *Looking White People in the Eye: Gender, Race and Culture in Courtrooms and Classrooms,* Sherene H. Razack argues that "[E]ducation for social change is not so much about new information as it is about disrupting the hegemonic ways of seeing through which subjects make themselves dominant" (10). This is risky business; it asks students and teachers to look closely at their moorings and, at times, to untie systems of meaning-making that have held together their world-views for a long time.

After class during the Winter 2011 semester, a student asked me if black people can create theatre that is not required to be black—"Can't they just make theatre that's about anything or nothing like so many of the shows put on in Toronto?" Through the example of Samuel Beckett's play *Waiting for Godot,* the student and I talked about racial politics imbedded in work that is allegedly about anything or nothing. I suggested to him that the framing of his query was directly tied to his being educated in a Canadian educational system that upholds various modes of white supremacy. I suggested to him that the framing of his question positioned work void of a racial identifier as a marker of creative freedom, something that black theatre practitioners should aspire to. "Oh, white is the standard," he said. "It's what's normal." "Yes," I replied, "and the expectation that everyone aspire to and meet whiteness on its terms is deeply problematic." What might it mean, I asked him, if race was considered in the critique and analysis of all theatre in the city? How might that destabilize the powerful invisibility of whiteness, a key component of its ethnicity? Razack asserts that, "If we can name the organizing frames, the conceptual formulas, the rhetorical devices that disguise and sustain elites, we can begin to develop responses that bring us closer to social justice. That is, we can each begin to stop performing ourselves as dominant" (16).

I call my teaching practice a pedagogy of justice because it emerged from my reflections on what I, and others in the

---

> Razack asserts that, "If we can name the organizing frames, the conceptual formulas, the rhetorical devices that disguise and sustain elites, we can begin to develop responses that bring us closer to social justice. That is, we can each begin to stop performing ourselves as dominant" (16).

---

communities I am connected to, have identified as our most rewarding and discombobulating experiences as teachers and students in academic institutions and other learning environments. Curiosity and self-reflexivity have flourished in learning environments where teachers and students listened carefully and engaged thoughtfully with course materials and one another. On the other hand, there has been a deficit of learning when teachers and students foreclosed areas of inquiry, touted intellectual blind spots, and suspended complex material realities of everyday life. As such, my pedagogy of justice hinges on a co-constituted learning relationship between teacher and student—one that often results in students and teachers who are more autonomous in their exhibition of intellectual agency.

A co-constituted learning relationship requires constant experimentation with ways to rethink, reshape, and redistribute power. It also poses its own set of risks, particularly when negotiated within the encoded space of a western post-secondary classroom where divisions of power are so deeply entrenched that students and teacher perform their roles with the ease of a repertory company playing stock characters. Even when we noisily drag chairs into a misshapen circle in an effort to abandon the lectern and rowed seating, students eventually raise their hands and direct comments to the teacher. The teacher almost always decides who gets to speak, and s/he usually speaks the most.

In the Black Theatre and Performance course that I teach, the lectern and blackboard are shared spaces; students use the lectern, front of the class, and/or classroom as they wish during their oral presentations and I routinely incorporate exercises that require students to write on the blackboard. When I assign group work during class time, I ask students to form groups with as many or as few students as they like, and when they introduce themselves to the group on the first day of class I take notes about their interests and skills. During a class in January 2011 I asked a couple of students who are also dance instructors to lead the class through warm-up exercises, and I asked students who were photographers to record our activities for this article. We started class with a series of pliés and by the end my camera was filled with pictures (some of which are included here).

On the first day of class in January 2011 I was presented with a logistical dilemma. Students had to choose an oral presentation from an existing list of topics assigned to specific days. Just prior to beginning the sign up process several students asked me how it would take place, expressing their anxiety about not getting the topic and day that they wanted. I told them I planned to circulate a sheet and they would choose what they wanted. They diplomatically told me that my plan was colossally unfair. The first student who got to sign up would have an array of choices while the last would have none. We decided that I would call out the topic and day of each presentation and we would see if there was interest from multiple students. When multiple students wanted the same topic, a few gracefully bowed out and when two students still remained, another student suggested they play rock-paper-scissors to decide the winner. We assigned all of the topics in short order. It was fun, it was fair, and I never would have come up with this solution on my own. That day, I left the classroom buoyed by what we had accomplished as a group when I relinquished control over what I thought I should know and decide. I was reminded that in a co-constituted learning relationship, triumphs are often tiny and change is incremental. I was also reminded to measure my effectiveness as a teacher against the extent to which I have guided and been guided by students in our creation of a rigorous, imaginative, and intellectual exchange.

On a cold February evening in Toronto in 2006, I witnessed the performance poetry of Mutabaruka, a highly acclaimed dub poet and journalist. I was shaken to the core and renewed by the reaffirmation of the integral role of performance in stimulating community discourse. His thoughtful, provocative, and humorous performance was profoundly captivating. Devoid of significant gesticulations, stage movements, or vocal manipulations, Mutabaruka's dramatic articulations were underpinned by an intellectually rigorous and creative analysis of the ways in which black people collude with and disrupt asymmetrical systems of power. Part poetry, part prose, part stand-up comedy, Mutabaruka's work astutely

---

> That day, I left the classroom buoyed by what we had accomplished as a group when I relinquished control over what I thought I should know and decide. I was reminded that in a co-constituted learning relationship, triumphs are often tiny and change is incremental. I was also reminded to measure my effectiveness as a teacher against the extent to which I have guided and been guided by students in our creation of a rigorous, imaginative, and intellectual exchange.

---

aligned him with his mostly Rastafarian audience, offering content that affirmed some of their values. A particularly memorable moment was when he endorsed the vegetarian dietary practice of many Rastafarians, describing the white box that KFC comes in as a "coffin" with "dead animals" in it that people pour red "blood" over and eat. Eventually Mutabaruka, himself a Rastafarian, delved into an uncompromising critique of contemporary Rastafari in particular, and black communities in general. Among other things, he lambasted the religion's adoption of a reverence for Christian doctrine, excoriated the omission of a woman in the Holy Trinity, decried the despiritualized use of marijuana and lamented that these trends were counter to Rastafari's roots as a revolutionary faith practice. The organization of his set was impeccable. The transitions were seamless. That evening, I observed an adept artist-intellectual forego facile, familiar analysis of the systemic inequities that plague the status quo and offer, instead, an insightful critique of the oppressive ideologies that multiple black communities in Canada, Jamaica, and beyond have developed and maintained. The response was visceral. The audience was galvanized. Their cacopho-

Keleta-Mae in the classroom: "A co-constituted learning relationship requires constant experimentation with ways to rethink, reshape, and redistribute power."
Photo by Oluwatomisin O. Dipo

nous dissent and support were palpable. I remember clapping my hands and looking for the closest exit sign as I mentally mapped the quickest route out of the building. It was the first (and only) time in my decades of attending performances that my mere applause as an audience member was transformed into an activist statement for critical self-reflexivity. That moment taught me that within the context of public performance, applause can be more than a polite reflex: as in the aforementioned definition of "activist," applause can be an act of advocacy "that undertakes vigorous political or social campaigning." At the end of his performance Mutabaruka announced that he would be at the back of the room selling and signing books, available for conversation.

The days and months of close reflection that followed Mutabaruka's performance, and my performance as his audience member, crystallized for me that the work of those committed to the socially transformative possibilities of imagination in pursuit of social justice cannot hinge on whether or not it is unanimously popular. It also reminded me that it is not enough to provoke thought, but one must also be thoughtful and accountable. Mutabaruka untied some audience members' moorings and made himself available afterwards for discussion. In *Teaching Community: A Pedagogy of Hope,* bell hooks writes, "Dominator culture has tried to keep us all afraid, to make us choose safety instead of risk, sameness instead of diversity. Moving through that fear, finding out what connects us, reveling in our differences; this is the process that brings us closer, that gives us a world of shared values, of meaningful community" (197). These days I measure my effectiveness as an educator against the extent to which I am active in communities committed to civic engagement and grounded in a pedagogy of justice that challenges students, teachers, and our extended communities to be provocative, thoughtful, and accountable. The experience of Mutabaruka's performance deepened my commitment to surround myself with discerning communities of people who challenge my moorings regularly and who profoundly believe in the expansive possibilities of art, pedagogy, and scholarship.

Razack states that, "[a]s long as we see ourselves as not implicated in relations of power, as innocent, we cannot begin to walk the path of social justice and to thread our way through the complexities of power relations" (22). I have been criticized in lectures, workshops, meetings, and elsewhere for the disparity between my capacity to identify injustices and provide solutions. At a conference session called "'The Dilemma of the Black Intellectual': The Threat and Imperative of Blackness in the Canadian University" at the University of Toronto in April 2010, an audience member asked the panel a question that I have been asked many times. He noted that the panel had identified many concerns but had failed to offer pragmatic solutions. What were the panel's solutions, he wanted to know. The irony was that it was the

In a recent classroom exercise illustrating her "pedagogy of justice," Keleta-Mae called out the name of a theorist or artist discussed during class and asked students to write a few words on the blackboard about how that individual interprets blackness.
Photo by Oluwatomisin O. Dipo

first time that a satisfactory answer to that vexing question came to my mind, though I too was an audience member and the question had not been posed to me. Nonetheless I found myself silently chanting to the panel members, "Reframe, reframe"—imploring them to turn the question on its heels. How do we step out of a business management mode that only values the presentation of problems when coupled with solutions? How do we learn to value the work required to clearly identify and articulate problems? How do we then hear that information, allow ourselves to be moved by it and do the work of thinking about how we can individually and collectively contribute to solutions?

I recently assigned a blackboard activity (captured in images here) for my Black Theatre and Performance class. I called out the name of a theorist or artist that we had dis-

Keleta-Mae's blackboard exercise: "The blackboard was full of converging and conflicting ideas."
Photo by Oluwatomisin O. Dipo

cussed during class and asked students to write a few words about how the theorist/artist interprets blackness. Soon the blackboard was full of converging and conflicting ideas from the Combahee River Collective, Andrea Davis, Frantz Fanon, Lorena Gale, Paul Gilroy, bell hooks, Bob Marley, Katherine McKittrick, and Barack Obama. We surveyed our work. I asked enthusiastically, "What do you think?" I was met with a resounding silence, broken only by the raising of a lone voice. A student shared that when she came to the class she thought that the word "black" was negative, one that people used because they had to. "Now I'm confused," she said. The facial expressions of some of her classmates suggested to me that they too were somewhat unmoored. Another student said that she was also unsure what to do with all of this, and how to think about it. "Good," I responded. "That's great." Then I spoke about the work of opening our thought process up long enough to really think about new information, to allow ideas that are new to us to move within us and affect us. I reminded them of the disclaimer that I offered in our first class: that if they left the course thinking that they knew what black theatre and performance was then I had failed as a teacher. I reminded them that black theatre and performance encompasses the cultural production of hundreds of millions of people. How could we possibly have a substantive understanding of such a vast topic after one semester of study? How could we ever know exactly what it is or what it means? If, on the other hand, they left the course with a few analytical skills that they could carefully apply to their thinking about black theatre and performance, then our time together would have been fruitful.

> I reminded them of the disclaimer that I offered in our first class: that if they left the course thinking that they knew what black theatre and performance was then I had failed as a teacher.

A few years ago I presented a lecture called "Art/Life as Social Justice" for the Hamilton-Wentworth Elementary Teachers' union. In conversation with an elementary teacher afterwards, I shared my vivid childhood memory of painting a self-portrait without the paint colours or racial understanding to paint myself accurately. He told me, quite matter-of-factly and somewhat dismissively, that markers and crayons now come in a bevy of hues associated with skin colour so that children can draw themselves and others. Those are the markers and crayons he uses in his class.

Justice, I thought.
One step closer to justice.

Work Cited

hooks, bell. *Teaching Community: A Pedagogy of Hope*. New York: Routledge, 2003. Print.

Johnson Hodari, Ashkari and Yvonne McCalla Sobers. *Lifelines: The Black Book of Proverbs*. New York: Broadway Books, 2009. Print.

Oxford English Dictionary. "Activist." *Oed.com*. N.d. Web. 2 Feb. 2011.

Razack, Sherene H. *Looking White People in the Eye: Gender, Race, and Culture in Courtrooms and Classrooms*. Toronto: U of Toronto P, 1998. Print.

Smiers, Joost. *Arts Under Pressure: Promoting Cultural Diversity in the Age of Globalization*. London: Zed Books, 2003. Print.

Naila Keleta-Mae is an interdisciplinary artist, educator, and scholar. She is a Faculty Advisor (MFA in Interdisciplinary Arts, Goddard College), a PhD candidate (Theatre Studies, York University), recipient of a Canada Graduate Scholarship (SSHRC), and a winner of the IFTR New Scholar Prize (2011). www.nailakeletamae.com.

Making it Up as We Go Along: Improvisation and Environmental Education

by Julia Lane

We promise to uphold the ideals of improvisation: to cooperate with each other, to learn from each other, to commit ourselves to the moment, and, above all, to have a good time!
—Excerpt from The Canadian Improv Games oath

Improvisation is often associated with shows like *Whose Line Is It Anyway?*, where the goal is to make the audience laugh. This paper expands the concept of theatrical improvisation in line with Gary Paul Nabhan's understanding of life on earth as "the Great Improvisation" (9–10). Such a perspective sheds light on the benefits of pairing exercises derived from theatrical improvisation with environmental education (EE). Nabhan's epithet draws attention to the indeterminacy, the interconnection, and the complexity shared by ecosystems and improv troupes. This paper discusses the ways in which theatrical improvisation can encourage cooperation, collaborative learning, commitment to the moment, and enjoyment (all promises in the Canadian Improv Games oath, quoted above) in environmental education. Environmental education demands we cut ties with the sedentary classroom learning so often typical of Western teaching, and improv exercises meet this demand in compelling ways: having students consciously engage in improvisation can aid their understanding of the ways in which we all improvise daily—of the indeterminacy of life. This can help students to see themselves as integral, interconnected parts of "the Great Improvisation," a fundamental goal of environmental education.

As an experienced learner and a new teacher who is starting to combine improv and environmental education in my own contexts, I hope that this article will be beneficial to other new EE teachers looking to enliven their classrooms. More experienced teachers of theatre and environmental education may be inspired by an approach to improvisation which de-emphasizes broad humour (but embraces genuine laughter). I have often heard from friends and colleagues that they felt alienated from improvisation because they were not "the funny kid." The pairing of improvisation with environmental education not only has the potential to enrich EE practices but can also challenge the stigma of improvisation as merely comical.

> I have often heard from friends and colleagues that they felt alienated from improvisation because they were not "the funny kid." The pairing of improvisation with environmental education not only has the potential to enrich EE practices but can also challenge the stigma of improvisation as merely comical.

In October 2010 I attended the Simon Fraser University Education With/out Borders conference in Belcarra Park, Port Moody, British Columbia. This provided me with an opportunity to workshop the exercises included in this paper. For their participation and feedback I would like to thank the graduate students who attended my session. This article is greatly enriched as a result of their insights.

* * *

It is a chilly, grey day but the rain is holding off. I play a Cherokee flute as my colleagues wander into the cabin where my "talk" is supposed to take place. When they have gathered, I ask the participants to write down why they came to this session. What is it about improvisation and environmental education that interests them? As they write, I tell the participants that I have never committed any songs to memory for the flute. Every time I pick it up, I play something different. My flute playing is an important part of my improvisatory practice. I share this to destabilize certain assumptions about what improvisation is and how/where its techniques might be useful. I warn the participants that this will be an interactive session and that we are going to go outside. I invite them, sincerely, to leave if this does not interest them; after all, the day is cold and grey. They all commit to the experience and we venture outside to a relatively flat area surrounded by giant old-growth trees.

Cooperation

Theatrical improvisation is founded on making and receiving "offers," so this is where the workshop begins. After a brief physical warm up to get students "into" their bodies (and to shake off the damp cold), I ask the participants to stand in two parallel lines facing me. I invite the first two (brave) volunteers to step forward. I encourage the participants not to *try* to be funny, but rather to say the first thing that comes to mind. I ask the student to my right to make "an offer"—a statement or a question to which her partner can respond. Let's call this person Student A. Let's say that Student A asks, "Hey, do you want to go skating later?" Student B is then tasked with accepting this offer and adding to it or "plus-ing" it in order to move the scene forward. I tell the participants that it can be useful to begin by saying, "Yes, and" as this ensures that the offer is both accepted (yes) and that something new is added (and). Student B responds "Yes, and afterwards we can have our picture taken with Santa." Student B has therefore provided context for the scene by indicating that it is Christmastime.

"Scatter" hydroglyph, part 3 of 5: a water capture basin for desert wildlife near Moab, Utah. Carved sandstone, 4' × 3' × 3", 1987.
Photo by artist Lynne Hull

Once the participants are comfortable with this initial exercise, I complicate it by encouraging the participants to incorporate an awareness of their surroundings into the offers that they make. Switching it up, I ask Student B to make the initial offer. She steps forward and points upwards, exclaiming, "Look at how tall these trees are!" Now, if Student A were to step forward and say, "There are no trees here, we are in the middle of a clear cut," she would be blocking the advancement of the scene. However, Student A can move the scene forward by saying something like: "What is that on the top branch there?" This is a "yes, and" moment. What is important is that the participants cooperate to build a scene together, rather than attempting to impose their own directions on it.

"Twist" osprey nesting platform: Green River Greenbelt, western Wyoming. Wood, 30' tall, 1993.
Photo by artist Lynne Hull

This introductory improvisation exercise encourages students to become comfortable making and accepting offers spontaneously without pressure to perform or be "funny." My goal in asking the participants to incorporate an awareness of their surroundings into their offers was initially to challenge them to *have* an awareness of their surroundings. In my experience of improvisation I have noticed that performers (and directors) sometimes work very hard to deny the reality of their surroundings. Given that in improv situations, relationships and contexts are created in the moment, I am almost always more satisfied by scenes that accept and use their surroundings, rather than deny them. This is another kind of acceptance—accepting the offer of the place that you are in.

When the participants in my workshop included an awareness of their surroundings, it increased the immediacy of their offers. Suddenly, the trees, the ground, the sounds of birds, the water ten feet away all became fodder for initiating scenes. What's more, these offers grounded in the surroundings immediately allowed me to become more connected with the players because I was in this environment as well. When the participant pointed up at the trees, I too took note of how tall they were. When another participant pointed out the chill in the air, I too took a moment to feel the cold on my skin. The offers were instantaneously becoming more visceral and alive.

I started to think about the ways in which the natural environment itself constantly presents us with offers, with the invitation to become more aware of our surroundings. These offers can range from the minute—the crunching of leaves under foot in the fall—to the large-scale—"natural disasters" such as hurricanes and earthquakes. Thinking about the environment as making offers caused me to question the human response to these offers. Do we even notice them? And when we do, how do we cooperate with our partner (the environment) in order to advance the scene together? The rebuilding of homes along the same fault lines after a natural disaster seems to block the offer.

> When the participants in my workshop included an awareness of their surroundings, it increased the immediacy of their offers. Suddenly, the trees, the ground, the sounds of birds, the water ten feet away all became fodder for initiating scenes. What's more, these offers grounded in the surroundings immediately allowed me to become more connected with the players because I was in this environment as well.

Discussions of the human impact on the environment tend to emphasize the negative. When the discussion does focus on positive human contributions such as reducing energy consumption, I often find that these contributions do not so much "plus" or advance environmental well-being, but serve to mitigate our more harmful impacts. Viewed from the perspective of the cooperative improv scene, perhaps the human/nature relationship can become more collaborative. This perspective asks us not only to pay more attention to the offers made to us by the environments that surround us, but also to be aware of our own contributions to those environments in fresh ways. In this vein the work of eco-artists such as Andy Goldsworthy, whose site-specific art draws attention to the natural features of an environment, and Lynne Hull, whose sculptures create habitats for wildlife, can provide further inspiration.

Genuine laughter in the "Education With/out Borders" Workshop led by Julia Lane.
Photo by Marco Espinoza

Once the workshop participants had the opportunity to make and accept offers with an awareness of their surroundings, I asked them to make and accept offers silently. The first thing that struck me was how much movement was suddenly present in the exercise. When the participants were making and accepting verbal offers their work was primarily stationary. Now that I had invited them to break free from the line structure and work silently, everybody was moving around and engaging their bodies in the exercise. In silence, the participants explored the environment that surrounded them. They bent down to touch the earth, stretched up straight to imitate trees, and mimicked the birds and plants that they saw. At the beginning of the workshop many of the participants indicated that they were nervous and did not have much theatrical experience. Yet in this silent exercise, the students appeared to be remarkably free in their bodies and their expressions as they worked together to make and accept silent offers that included the environment around them.

Standing with a beautiful being—spontaneity and deep contemplation.
Photo by Marco Espinoza

> I started to think about the ways in which the natural environment itself constantly presents us with offers, with the invitation to become more aware of our surroundings. These offers can range from the minute—the crunching of leaves under foot in the fall—to the large-scale—"natural disasters" such as hurricanes and earthquakes. Thinking about the environment as making offers caused me to question the human response to these offers. Do we even notice them? And when we do, how do we cooperate with our partner (the environment) in order to advance the scene together?

Learning from Each Other

The current model of education implies that teachers are those who have earned the right to stand at the front of a classroom and speak. The commitment to "learning from each other" in improvisation can encourage students to see themselves, their teachers, and the environments that surround them as what Lynn Fels and George Belliveau term "co-creators" in the learning/performative moment (230). From the beginning, the workshop participants were committed to an experience of co-created learning because of the conference context; however, it seemed to me that the atmosphere of co-creation was enhanced by moving the workshop outside and encouraging ongoing interaction between the participants, the workshop facilitator, and the environment.

A central improvisation skill is listening. Highly skilled improv teams achieve what can appear to be telepathy. What these teams develop is the ability to listen to each other, not only with their ears, but also with their entire focus. Tewa scholar Gregory Cajete writes about the traditional hunter as a model for ecological learning. As he explains, the traditional hunter worked to foster "complete attentiveness to the moment" (60). Improvisers work toward this same goal. Developing attentiveness allows us to better listen to and thus learn from each other. When our awareness is expanded beyond those who speak, we are able to listen to and learn from the beings and interactions that constantly surround us.

The participants in my workshop emphasized that the experience of being outside and silent was powerful for them. Some shared that this was an opportunity to slow down and really connect with the environment. Others compared the experience of engaging in silent improvisation with meditation—working toward being aware of themselves and their

> Once the workshop participants had the opportunity to make and accept offers with an awareness of their surroundings, I ask them to make and accept offers silently. The first thing that struck me was how much movement was suddenly present in the exercise.

surroundings without imposing words. By asking the participants to be silent I actually invited them to hear the sounds of the (human and more than human) environment. After the workshop one of the participants reflected on the experience of "listening for connections"—of actively working to hear and feel her connection with her partner and with the world around her. The assumption that a lack of human noise is equivalent to silence is akin to the notion that when a teacher is not teaching the students are not learning. The invitation to silence ourselves allowed us to listen for the sounds of the world around us and acknowledge what can be learned from hearing, and accepting, its offers.

Commitment to the Moment

After the workshop I asked the participants to write reflectively about their experiences. One of the participants shared,

> At first, the improv activity was intimidating but as we were engaged in it, I was encouraged to let myself go and experienced the moment. It allowed me to become creative [...], which I don't do in my everyday life.

When we work toward "complete attentiveness to the moment," we allow ourselves to let go of insecurities ("I can't improvise; I'm not funny") and concerns about future possibilities ("what if I look silly?"). As the above participant reflected, this commitment to the moment can foster creativity by allowing us to take risks in a safe space. Environmental issues present us with the unknown; climate change and environmental degradation are changing the geographical realities of the planet in ways that threaten our habitual experience of the world. As Nabhan insists, humans need to be "reminded that nature is not only more complex than we think, it's more complex than we *can* think" (98). Meeting the challenges of a rapidly changing planet demand a human population that is prepared to be creative in the face of the unknown. Engagement in improvisational exercises can provide a training ground for such experiences. To paraphrase Augusto Boal, improvisatory theatre is a rehearsal for the environmental revolution. Teaching and learning are inevitably shaped by the interactions among teachers, learners, and environments. Being aware of, and committed to, each moment of these interactions impacts the content of the interactions and will, very often, result in unexpected learning. Fels and Belliveau remind us that

> Having an itinerary and a destination allows us to take our first steps, but being open to those who travel with us creates a curricular exploration that recognizes learning as a shared journey, one that requires us to be alert and aware of the environment and context through which we are travelling [...] (41)

The natural world changes every moment. By asking for a commitment to the moment, improvisation introduces students to an awareness of indeterminacy and to the feeling of possibility that exists the moment before a change occurs: when anything is possible and something is just about to happen.

> The natural world changes every moment. By asking for a commitment to the moment, improvisation introduces students to an awareness of indeterminacy and to the feeling of possibility that exists the moment before a change occurs: when anything is possible and something is just about to happen.

Having a Good Time

Environmental educators often express concern over depressing and overwhelming lessons that focus on environmental problems. In *Last Child in the Woods*, Richard Louv argues that emphasis on environmental degradation can actually alienate children from the natural world, contributing to what he terms "nature deficit disorder." Introducing improvisation into environmental education allows students to have fun in an area of study that lends itself to depressing, frightening, and overwhelming subjects. Most improv exercises require very little to no materials and thus can be used in almost any setting, including outdoors. Encouraging students to engage in fun activities outside not only draws on students' childhood experiences of outdoor play, but can also increase their positive associations with time spent in, and with, the natural environment. Open-ended artistic outlets such as improvisation also allow students to express and work through challenges and concerns they may encounter in learning about environmental issues.

Conclusion

A good friend who participated in my workshop expressed his concern over what he called a "conditioning to the surface of awareness" in improvisation. Spontaneity and indeterminacy can lend themselves to a perspective wherein only the moment counts. This is counterproductive for the development of long-term environmental ethics. However, the improvisational experiences that I have shared in this article are not geared toward such instant and momentary gratification. Rather, they are exercises intended to increase awareness of the spontaneity and indeterminacy that connect us with the natural world of which we are a part. These experiences can be drawn upon in other lessons in order to increase students' contemplations about the offers that they make toward and accept from the world around them.

> Introducing improvisation into environmental education allows students to have fun in an area of study that lends itself to depressing, frightening, and overwhelming subjects.

The final exercise of the workshop asked participants to find something that they thought was beautiful and to stand with it in stillness. After a moment, I drew the participants' attention to the small movements that they were making even in "stillness." Just as I asked them to become aware of sound in silence, I asked them to become aware of the movement that exists in stillness. This movement connects us to the perpetual rotation of the earth: we can never stand completely still so long as the planet continues to move. I then asked the participants to become aware of the movement of the beautiful being with which they were standing. I asked them to notice how their movements impacted this being and how this being impacted their movements. This exercise is a far cry from *Whose Line is it Anyway?*, and even from the Canadian Improv Games, whose oath provides the structure of this paper. Yet, it is an exercise based in improvisation. It is an exercise that sees indeterminacy and spontaneity as a basis for deep contemplation and connection. It is an exercise that draws attention to The Great Improvisation that connects us with the beauty and the challenges of the life surrounding us.

Improvisation has become an important consideration in my life and my creative practices. Sometimes, a being outside of myself will remind me of the commitment I made, through improvisation, to "the moment." A few months ago I was attempting to find my way around a university campus and was drawn out of my world of maps and meetings by seven or eight giant slugs migrating across a sidewalk. These slugs slowed my pace, silenced my busy thoughts, and reminded me that my day was not comprised of attempts to get from one place to another but of moments, each rich with possibilities and teeming with life.

Works Cited

Cajete, Gregory. *Look to the Mountain: An Ecology of Indigenous Education*. Colorado: Kivaki, 1994. Print.

Fels, Lynn and George Belliveau. *Exploring Curriculum: Performative Inquiry, Role Drama, and Learning*. Vancouver: Pacific Educational, 2008. Print.

Louv, Richard. *Last Child in the Woods: Saving our Children from Nature-Deficit Disorder*. Chapel Hill: Algonquin Books of Chapel Hill, 2006. Print.

Nabhan, Gary P. *Cultures of Habitat*. Washington: Counterpoint, 1997. Print.

Julia Lane is a PhD candidate in Arts Education at Simon Fraser University. Her doctoral work focuses on the pedagogical possibilities of Clown and Trickster figures, particularly in terms of cross-cultural dialogue. Her Master's thesis investigated the intersections between theatre, Indigenous Knowledges, and environmental education.

"A Precise Instrument for Seeing": Remembrance in *Burning Vision* and the Activist Classroom

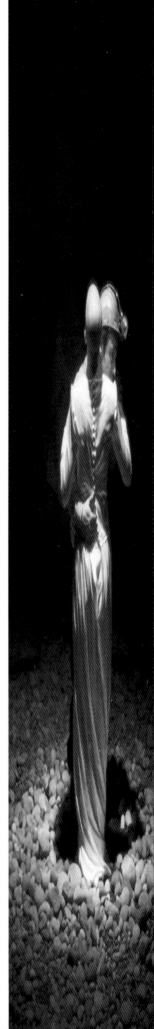

by Allison Hargreaves

On the topic of "political theatre" in Canada, Alan Filewod remarks that, "Canadian playwrights have time and again used the stage as a means of revising received teachings of Canadian history" (vii). And, whereas contemporary Canada is popularly constructed as a model of progressivism, tolerance, and liberal virtue, a recent tradition of political theatre has sought to contest this myth—often by recalling for audiences the social injustices that mark Canada's past. To engage with political theatre in the undergraduate classroom is thus to consider how knowledge of historical injustice and trauma arrives to us in our contemporary moment, and to make as our site of critical inquiry those teachings offered by both "received" and alternative histories. In teaching a course on political theatre in Canada I had hoped to do just that—to make *learning* the "lessons of the past" itself a matter for reflexive analysis and debate where current issues of social justice were concerned (Simon, Rosenberg, and Eppert 3). Yet, in framing our course with a set of questions around the practice of "remembrance" (what it means to recall historical violence and oppression on the stage or in the classroom, and what our critical engagement with the "past" and with remembrance itself might teach us), I sometimes found these very terms to foreclose rather than open-up the possibility of our understanding "historical" injustices as informing those of the present. For example, when reading plays about Canada's history of slavery, or about residential schooling, students often relegated these events and their intergenerational consequences to the past: things were bad *then,* it was often said, but they're not like that *now.*

This was a frequent consolatory refrain, and indeed it seemed confirmed by our very reading of these plays themselves. That we could address ourselves in a university classroom to the practice of witnessing traumatic history from an ostensible position of

The Radium Painter (Erin Wells) and The Miner (Marcus Hondro). The Radium Painter stands with her radium watch-dial painting kit in hand.
Photo by Tim Matheson

Koji (Hiro Kanagawa), a Japanese fisherman, is transported across the world and met by "the Stevadores" (Kevin Loring and Marcus Hondro) tasked with transporting uranium ore by boat.
Photo by Tim Matheson

duced through the very practice of remembrance itself? I wanted to make these questions the very basis of our engagement with political theatre, if not to overturn then at least to undermine the narrative of past harm and present redress through which students seemed so often to approach Canadian history. My goal was to shift the discussion from the facts of historical violence as we witness them today, to the potential violence implicit in our viewing practices. In order to do this, I invited our collaborative reflection on these questions in relation to a play itself—Métis playwright Marie Clements' 2002 play *Burning Vision*.

> By what pedagogies is our present relationship to the past typically expressed? Moreover, how might our class encounter historical violence in Canada as taken up in contemporary political theatre—*not* as a redemptive or consolatory process, but as a means of critically engaging current social injustice as represented, resisted, and sometimes subtly reproduced through the very practice of remembrance itself?

As a play that radically reframes authorized Western histories of World War II and of the atomic bombing of Hiroshima in particular, *Burning Vision* occasioned for me a teaching opportunity in which alternative historiographies of war could be discussed in terms of counter-hegemonic remembrance practices. Whereas received forms of history and remembrance arguably beckon us toward problematic ways of witnessing, a play like Clements' *Burning Vision* challenges us to *see* our relationship with the "past" anew. To teach a text in which we are asked to witness (rather than disavow) the extraordinary complicities of our daily lives with the violence of war, the invasion and occupation of Indigenous land, or the ongoing consequences of ecological destruction—this is indeed a practice intended "not to console but to provoke" (Young 30). What I had already learned in the course, however, is that there is often something consolatory about the moment of provocation, and that as a teacher of "activist" or political theatre, my pedagogy was at risk of trading one kind of redemptive satisfaction for another. No matter my commitment to material politics, and to orchestrating pedagogical encounters with historical memory that necessarily transcend the space of the classroom either metaphorically or in literal fact, the structure and rhythm of the formalized instructive setting seemed to embed the possibility of con-

remove actually affirmed for many students (rather than challenged) the redemptive narrative of Canadian progressivism. It struck me that in order to negotiate this matter more reflexively in the classroom, we would have to do some more thinking aloud about just what "remembrance" entails, and how it intersects with our teaching and learning practices. I wondered: where the teaching of "socially conscious" or "activist" theatre is concerned (Graham 3), and where the "problem of how to tell stories of violence through the medium of theatre" is under explicit debate (Salverson 59), by what pedagogies is our present relationship to the past typically expressed? Moreover, how might our class encounter historical violence in Canada as taken up in contemporary political theatre—*not* as a redemptive or consolatory process, but as a means of critically engaging current social injustice as represented, resisted, and sometimes subtly repro-

The Radium Painter (Erin Wells) and The Miner (Marcus Hondro) waltz to the sound of the Geiger counter.
Photo by Tim Matheson

solatory closure by making into plain intellectual exercise even the most challenging or difficult knowledge. To be profoundly challenged or provoked, as my students and I were when we read and performed *Burning Vision*, was an experience nonetheless amenable to reassuring containment—structured as a finite encounter with history as bound by time, and by the "fourth wall" of the classroom setting itself.

Resisting the pull of received historical memory in a reflexive way thus became the principal focus of my pedagogical engagement with Clements' play. Teaching the text in this way meant meditating in dialogue with my students about the meta-theatrical techniques by which the play deliberately challenges received history. It also involved frank discussion around the interpretive strategies by which we were tempted to re-embed the play within dominant, linear historical frames of reference. Indeed, if we were to defy what had been our class's recourse to normative remembrance, it would be our task to theorize this impulse in "real-time"—that is, as we performed it. In the first place, though, I was concerned to establish for our classroom community the ways in which *Burning Vision* dramatizes the actual historical role that Canada played in supplying the uranium used by the United States during World War II when it developed the first atomic weapon of warfare. Itself a "marginal" and often untold facet of Canadian history (van Wyck 99), this narrative arrives to us in *Burning Vision* not with the promise that by our very process of witnessing, "history will not repeat itself" (Read 23), but rather with the truth that this history—as well as its consequences and casualties—is present among us still. This is true both figuratively, as the traces of such mass violence imprint themselves indelibly, if unevenly, on contemporary daily lives lived in the aftermath of war, and materially—most literally in the health effects of radiation on the Dene community on whose land uranium pitchblende was "discovered," and with whose labour it was mined. In the chain of events leading to the unfathomable act of violence carried out against Japanese civilians by the United States, the Sahtu Dene of Canada's Northwest Territories thus stand at a physical point of origin where the corporate and governmental exploitation of their land and labour positions them as at once responsible for, and civilian victims of, the atomic bomb in its earliest and most elemental form.[1]

> To teach a text in which we are asked to witness (rather than disavow) the extraordinary complicities of our daily lives with the violence of war, the invasion and occupation of Indigenous land, or the ongoing consequences of ecological destruction—this is indeed a practice intended "not to console but to provoke" (Young 30).

This history belies the popular Canadian myth that the violence of war always takes place elsewhere. On the stage, Clements' project is to make manifest the radical contingencies of these "traditionally exclusive histories of Euro-North American, Japanese, and Dene peoples" as they relate to the intergenerational and transnational traumas of war (Whittaker 131). In order to theorize this aspect of Clements' project in the classroom, I asked students to brainstorm the different meta-theatrical means by which these histories are staged in spatial or aural proximity to one another, and to analyze these strategies in terms of their interventions into "received history" and dominant modes of remembrance. Already equipped with a knowledge of the history *Burning Vision* seeks to re-tell, students readily produced an inventory of the play's challenging conventions: Whether by the dramatized, voice-over testimony of the nineteenth century Dene see-er who prophesized the "discovery" of uranium on Dene land (as well as the violent use to which it would ultimately be put), or through the personified embodiment of uranium itself in the character of "Little Boy," *Burning Vision* disrupts any audience attempts to assimilate this history into a realist

---

[1] As Cindy Kenny-Gilday of the Deline Uranium Committee puts it, the Dene were "the first civilian victims of the war" (Nikiforuk).

frame of reference by which the colonial discourse of "discovery," knowledge, and progress could be naturalized. As Robin C. Whittaker recounts, Clements' play "uses the event of the atomic bombing of Hiroshima ... and the fact that the uranium used in that bomb was mined by Dene miners from Dene land, to suggest spiritual, political, and ethical synchronicity at three geographically and culturally distinct locations: Hiroshima, Japan; New Mexico, United States; and Port Radium in the Northwest Territories, Canada" (130–131). Characters from each of these locations speak within and across the geographical and temporal divides that would, in realist drama and normative social memory, keep them discrete. Scenes taking place deep beneath the earth at the Port Radium mining site in the 1930s are staged alongside those featuring an American bomb test dummy (the aptly named Fat Man) ensconced in the comforts of his 1950s living room. Dialogue delivered within these specific but interpenetrating representations of time and space is sometimes critically juxtaposed, and other times performs a call-and-response effect through which "characters and worlds collide" (Clements 109).

The Radium Painter (Erin Wells) and The Miner (Marcus Hondro) in the aftermath of the atomic bomb: "A black dust has settled over everything" (119).
Photo by Tim Matheson

With its undoing of normative temporal and geographical distinctions, then, my students and I found that the play more than performs a synchronicity of times and spaces that would construct an alternative historiography of war; it also asks its audience to witness the ideological means by which we conventionally separate contingent agents and actions as a way of disavowing (even while acknowledging) "others" whose histories appear at first unconnected to our own (Graham 4). The challenge as put to us by this play is to *see* this difficult history and perhaps to be transformed by it, even as so much of it is commonly invisible—taking place, as it does, on the margins of mainstream historiography, and unfolding unseen at the molecular level within the very bodies of its living inheritors. In dominant histories of the atomic bombing, the recourse to the visual is strong: the bomb is known by a blinding flash of light, or a billowing mushroom cloud. *Burning Vision* functions instead as a "precise instrument for seeing" that which normally can't be seen (Clements 102): the long-term material and social effects of the bomb that leave no character (and, by implication, no audience) of this play untouched.

> To be profoundly challenged or provoked, as my students and I were when we read and performed *Burning Vision,* was an experience nonetheless amenable to reassuring containment— structured as a finite encounter with history as bound by time, and by the "fourth wall" of the classroom setting itself.

In this sense, the "burning vision" of this play refers not only to that of the Dene see-er whose vision foretold the mining of uranium on Dene land, but also to our own "vision" as witnesses to (and inheritors of) this history. This was a challenging call to witness, and although our classroom community readily partook in the intellectual exercise of itemizing the strategies by which Clements defamiliarizes World War II history, students nonetheless expressed a profound discomfort with the way *Burning Vision* asked them to see their own investment in the comforts of dominant remembrance. In those contexts with which it is often asso-

---

> The challenge as put to us by this play is to see this difficult history and perhaps to be transformed by it, even as so much of it is commonly invisible.

---

ciated today—for instance, as performed in memory of human loss suffered in war, in genocide, and in other sites of systemic, mass violence—remembrance means more than the solemnized reflection on (or protest of) past events in our present: it commonly presumes an educational end toward which remembering occurs, and a possible future in which "justice and harmonious social relations might [therefore] be secured" (Simon, Rosenberg, and Eppert 4). This play, however, seemed to frustrate the promise of knowledge and understanding as necessarily guarding against the repetition of past traumas in the future. We agreed as a class that *Burning*

Vision deliberately withholds any straightforwardly edifying or redemptive sense of progress as gained through the process of reading or watching the play itself, and yet for many students this was thought to undermine the play's *practical* applications for social justice. What was revealed, for instance, when a selection of scenes were performed and discussed by students in the classroom, was an overwhelming inclination to equate the play's politically transformative potential with its capacity to make known and felt the very historicization of war it critiques.

> We agreed as a class that *Burning Vision* deliberately withholds any straightforwardly edifying or redemptive sense of progress as gained through the process of reading or watching the play itself, and yet for many students this was thought to undermine the play's *practical* applications for social justice.

More than an effort to simply dramatize an untold story of Canadian history, *Burning Vision* is concerned to query the normative, linear conventions of Western social memory. A thoughtful adaptation of Clements' critical intervention, the in-class student performance juxtaposed a series of scenes that were chosen and arranged in part for their disorienting effect with respect to received histories of the war. In this performance "collage" (Clements 94), the discovery of uranium pitchblende ore on Dene land in 1930 was staged in near simultaneity with sound and visual effects representing the bombing of Hiroshima; meanwhile, the character of Rose, a Métis bread-maker working in the North for the Hudson's Bay Store, kneaded fine black dust from the uranium ore into a pale ball of dough while addressing the audience directly: "Where does war start? Does it keep going until it ends in us and when it does, where does it live?" (94). With these provocative scene selections and staging methods, the student performance helped to illustrate for our class how "characters and worlds collide" both in the world of the play and in the performative space (109), while also undermining the normative modes of "timekeeping and mapping" by which the audience could disavow colonial violence in Canada and its material contribution to the making of weapons of war (Whittaker 131). And yet, what the in-class performance of *Burning Vision* refused to give us in terms of linear coherence or narrative closure, students in the audience sought to impose after the fact—anxiously attempting to re-order into more recognizable teleological patterns the performance's decidedly non-linear representation of history. Despite their existing knowledge of the historical events upon which *Burning Vision* is based (acquired throughout that week's lectures on the play), students remarked that the performance itself was "confusing" and frustrating to watch, and that they gained no new, politically "useful" insight into this history as a result of it. Students wanted to know: how could the play be politically resistive or activist, if it did not offer usable "lessons of the past" (Simon, Rosenberg, and Eppert 3)? At stake in these comments was more than a desire to make ordered sense of apparent causes and effects, and to pin down precisely where war starts and ends. Rather, there was implicit in this moment an attempt to re-assemble what the performance had threatened to collapse: a consolatory distance between ourselves and the violence of war.

This was a teachable moment—an opportunity to make student discomfort and resistance the very object of analysis where the play's destabilization of normative remembrance was concerned. What I wanted to highlight was the fact that there may be something violent about our appeal to dominant linear accounts of history, especially where they offer the promise of redemptive solace (that things were bad then, but they're not like that now). One of the ways in which I sought to make this the object of critical consideration in the classroom was in asking students to reflect upon what normatively constitutes a "usable" past in the first place. What seemed so usable about dominant historiographies of war, I argued, was quite possibly the reassurance they offered us. In the realist tradition of Canadian political drama, the

---

> Students wanted to know: how could the play be politically resistive or activist, if it did not offer usable "lessons of the past" (Simon, Rosenberg, and Eppert 3)?

---

imperative to understand and inhabit others across the boundaries of history, subject position, and experience arguably becomes an end in *itself*, rather than a starting point from which to problematize the inherited positions of systematized privilege or disadvantage from which we observe or perform the past in our present. By contrast, in teaching *Burning Vision* I wanted to offer my students an alternative model of critically-engaged witnessing—one that would provide "obstacles to any easy identification" with "a simple or linear story of victims and pain" (Salverson 70), and that would instruct us instead toward more reflexive reckonings with history. Through this process, I hoped we might be productively troubled by our complicities with traumatic history as inherited in the present, rather than pleasurably absolved.

> In teaching *Burning Vision* I wanted to offer my students an alternative model of critically-engaged witnessing—one that would provide "obstacles to any easy identification" with "a simple or linear story of victims and pain" (Salverson 70), and that would instruct us instead toward more reflexive reckonings with history.

Works Cited

Clements, Marie. *Burning Vision*. Vancouver: Talonbooks, 2003. Print.

Filewod, Alan. "Introduction." *New Canadian Drama 5: Political Drama*. Ottawa: Borealis, 1991. Vii–xii. Print.

Graham, Catherine. "Editorial." *Canadian Theatre Review* 117 (2004):3–4. Print.

Nikiforuk, Andrew. "Cancer Killed 14 Uranium Workers: Echoes of the Atomic Age." *Calgary Herald* 14 Mar. 1998. Web. 7 Feb. 2011.

Read, Jennifer. "Marie Clements's Monstrous Visions." *Canadian Theatre Review* 120 (2004): 19–23. Print.

Salverson, Julie. "Anxiety and Contact in Attending to a Play about Land Mines." *Between Hope and Despair: Pedagogy and the Remembrance of Historical Trauma*. Ed. Roger I. Simon, Sharon Rosenberg, and Claudia Eppert. Lanham: Rowman & Littlefield Publishers, 2000. 59–74. Print.

Simon, Roger I., Sharon Rosenberg, and Claudia Eppert. "Between Hope and Despair: The Pedagogical Encounter of Historical Remembrance." *Between Hope and Despair: Pedagogy and the Remembrance of Historical Trauma*. Ed. Roger I. Simon, Sharon Rosenberg, and Claudia Eppert. Lanham: Rowman & Littlefield Publishers, 2000. 1–8. Print.

van Wyck, Peter C. "The Highway of the Atom: Recollections Along a Route." *Topia* 7 (2002): 99–115. Web. 2 Mar. 2010.

Whittaker, Robin C. "Fusing the Nuclear Community: Intercultural Memory, Hiroshima 1945 and the Chronotopic Dramaturgy of Marie Clements' *Burning Vision*." *Theatre Research in Canada* 30.1–2 (2009): 129–151. Print.

Young, James. *The Texture of Memory: Holocaust Memorials and Meaning*. New Haven: Yale UP, 1993. Print.

Allison Hargreaves is an Assistant Professor of English in the Department of Critical Studies at UBC Okanagan where she specializes in Indigenous literatures. Her current research and teaching investigates literary, activist, and policy interventions into gendered colonial violence in Canada.

Creative Copying?: The Pedagogy of Adaptation

by James McKinnon

As a teacher of post-secondary theatre who works in both liberal arts (BA) and vocational (BFA) contexts, I consider it my job to help my students develop both creative and critical skills. Although these abilities are highly prized, few of us perform with confidence in both modes. In theory, a post-secondary drama department should be an ideal place to develop these skills, since both creative process and criticism are taught and practiced there. But in reality, they are often taught and practiced in isolation. By the time I meet them, many or most of my undergraduate drama students have either consciously chosen or unconsciously gravitated toward one specialization or the other. Some see themselves as artists and eschew critical theory and theatre history as useless—or even potentially harmful; others feel they are not blessed with creative genius, and choose to concentrate on becoming skilled researchers, writers, or technical artists. In the drama department where I have done most of my teaching, there are very few students who excel (and several who struggle) in both areas. Recently, inspired by my research on how Canadian playwrights use and abuse "the classics," I have turned to adaptation as a conceptual and practical model for developing critical and creative skills simultaneously. While it may seem counterintuitive to teach creativity through "copying," my experiments suggest that adaptation-based drama teaching is effective, engaging, and highly versatile. As the examples below show, adaptation works in a variety of teaching contexts and serves a number of objectives.

There are many reasons that few of us practice creative and critical thinking with equal confidence, but most are rooted in the very notion that they are distinct and separate. In fact, contemporary creativity research shows that creativity and criticality are not opposed but rather interrelated and interactive processes (Lubart 298; Runco). But we

In the words of Canadian playwright and adaptor Jason Sherman, "Adapt or die!" University of Alberta Drama students Neil Kuefler and Vanessa LaPrairie rehearse a scene from Mark Ravenhill's *Shoot/Get Treasure/Repeat* for a project directed by their classmate Mark Vetsch.
Photo by Mark Vetsch

often approach them separately, and the curricula and institutional practices of drama departments frequently reinforce the conceptual separation of critical and creative processes. Creative and critical skills are often taught and practiced in different courses, by different teachers, and in different buildings: theory and history courses take place in lecture halls and seminar rooms, and focus on reading and writing; while directing, acting, voice, and movement happen in studios and theatre spaces, and focus on kinesthetic, interactive methods. To move from drama history class into scene study class, therefore, is to adopt a different mode of thinking, working, and being, and I have often observed the resulting disconnect as the material learned in one classroom is seemingly checked at the door of the next classroom—even if the topics overlap (e.g., Elizabethan theatre history and Shakespeare scene study).

In addition, as creativity researcher Keith Sawyer has shown, many people still subscribe to the romantic/idealist conception of "creative genius" as a heavenly gift that is essentially impenetrable to rational inquiry. The enduring romantic myth of creativity as an inscrutable gift possessed by solitary geniuses—Caspar Friedrich's 1818 painting *Wanderer Above a Sea of Fog* captures this notion—is subtly consecrated in the curricula of most drama departments. Survey courses are typically oriented around canonical playwrights, defining their work as the "art" of a given era or nation while overlooking the creative contributions of scenographers, actors, and to a lesser extent, directors: the holy text is permanent, while designers (unless their names are Appia or Craig) come and go. The efforts of non-playwrights are treated as supporting creative genius rather than consisting of it. We glorify the creative genius and his (rarely her) masterpieces, treating them as if they suddenly appeared *ex nihilo*, but rarely talk about the lengthy, fundamentally collaborative process that produces such work. Ultimately, this gives the impression that creative genius consists of the ability to sit down at one's desk, pull a quill out of a hollowed-out skull, frown pensively for a moment, and then crank out *Hamlet* in one sitting. Artists are supposed to be blessed with a flair for originality and creativity, and most students feel they aren't blessed in this way. Many feel intimidated by the pressure to just "create" out of thin air. Insofar as creativity and critique are the purview of the artist, "doing theatre," for many students (only a tiny fraction of whom are or aspire to be playwrights), means learning how to support someone else's artistic vision. (Even acting students, though they tend to be confident of their creativity, spend much of their vocational training learning how to take direction.)

> There are many reasons that few of us practice creative and critical thinking with equal confidence, but most are rooted in the very notion that they are distinct and separate.

One productive way to dispel these myths is to define creativity as a function of adaptation, rather than of originality. While contemporary criticism often considers adaptation derivative, parasitic, uncreative, and uncritical, the modern contempt for adaptation is a product of the same romantic myths outlined above. From the classical era through the Renaissance, art was created not through spontaneous invention, but by emulating and adapting the established masters of the form. Shakespeare is a case in point: though often revered for his original genius, his plays, creative though they may be, are all adaptations. In fact, *everything* we do and

Adaptation requires a little finesse. Treating dramatic text as a starting point—rather than an objective or a revered artifact—forces adaptors to consider the importance of context. Instead of asking "How do we do this scene?" adaptors must ask, "What do we want to say about or through this scene?" or "How should we use this scene to suit this audience, in this time and place?"
Photo by Mark Vetsch

say, to the extent that it consists of putting familiar materials to new uses in a new context, is adaptation; adaptation is not the opposite of creativity, but the basis of it.

Adaptation-centred drama pedagogy offers many strategies for challenging false dichotomies and putting both creative and critical talent within the reach of any student. For one thing, studying adaptation reveals and demystifies the *process* of artistic creation. Simply discovering that *Hamlet* is "just" an adaptation helpfully puts the mighty Shakespeare in perspective, particularly for junior students who may have been browbeaten with him throughout their high school years. But the real payoff comes from examining *how* the Hamlet story has been adapted, by Shakespeare and others, tracing its trajectory from an ancient Viking saga to a Jacobean revenge tragedy to contemporary versions based on absurdism (Tom Stoppard's *Rosencrantz and Guildenstern Are Dead*) and carnivalesque parody (Michael O'Brien's *Mad Boy Chronicle*).

Looking at variations on the familiar plot reveals important insights into creativity. For example, the fact that Shakespeare didn't invent the story of the heir who feigns madness to outwit his usurping uncle doesn't make him uncreative. Quite the opposite: his creative process is visible in the adaptations he makes to convert the pagan heroic epic into a revenge tragedy for the Christian era. In "creating" *Hamlet*, Shakespeare's inventive skill, formidable though it may have been, was perhaps less important than his technical expertise: to make a long, narrative romance into a (comparatively) short revenge tragedy, he selected some parts of the lengthy epic plot while omitting others; compressed the time frame; fleshed out the existing characters, invented new ones, and eliminated others; added a number of spectacular elements to hold the attention of the audience; and adjusted the major dramatic question in accordance with the new ethic, changing it from "how will the hero take honourable revenge?" to "how can Hamlet define and realize justice without submitting to the ghost's (un-Christian) demand for murderous vengeance?" Moving forward in history, we can study how Stoppard turns the revenge tragedy into an absurdist comedy by shifting the focus onto two marginal characters, or how Michael O'Brien uses tactics of carnivalesque parody to debase the mythical original and challenge its canonical authority. Investigating what adaptors do with their sources reveals evidence of their creative process, demonstrating how, contrary to popular conceptions, creativity is not manifested in sudden flashes of inspiration but in methodical, persistent labour.

Creative and critical skills are often taught and practiced in different courses, by different teachers, and in different buildings: theory and history courses take place in lecture halls and seminar rooms, and focus on reading and writing; while directing, acting, voice, and movement happen in studios and theatre spaces, and focus on kinesthetic, interactive methods. To move from drama history class into scene study class, therefore, is to adopt a different mode of thinking, working, and being.

Learning adaptive techniques demystifies "originality" by showing students that masterpieces are not suddenly invented out of nothing, but through skills and methods that they too can master. Many students are intimidated by playwriting because it seems highly unlikely that they could simply sit down, suddenly invent a plot and characters, and churn out a play, much less a good play, but studying adaptation empowers students with a sense of their own critical and creative agency, while providing a set of practical tools to exert that agency in adaptations and retellings of their own—which they prove eager to do. This approach often brings out the creative genius in my most unabashedly uncreative students: the non-drama majors who choose "Play Analysis" as their fine arts elective, because it seems least likely of all the available options to require any demonstration of creative ingenuity or personal investment. After introducing them to drama with *Oedipus Tyrannos,* I have them watch an animated film adaptation that retells the Oedipus story in eight minutes (www.oedipusthemovie.com). The film's most notable adaptations include casting vegetables in place of human actors, and showing certain scenes not directly represented by Sophocles, including the fatal duel between Oedipus and Laius (Oedipus, a potato, wields peelers, while Laius, a broccoli, fights with a cleaver), and a sex scene between Oedipus and Jocasta (who is "played by" a tomato).

Some students feel impelled to defend the "original" from this betrayal, and need to be reminded that the film does not replace the alleged "original" but is, like Sophocles', merely one of many co-existing versions of the story. Most find the film hilarious, and it is obvious to everyone that the divergences from the expected plot (whether or not one approves of them) are what create the "interpretive *frisson*" of the adaptation, as Daniel Fischlin has put it (317). So what are those divergences? And how can similar strategies be put to use in other contexts? Students in my last class identified several of the film's adaptive tactics and put them to use in their own adaptations of famous plots and current events, experimenting with the effect of changing the point of attack (What if *Oedipus* opens with the final episode, showing his exile in disgrace, and then gradually reveals his identity to the spectator in flashbacks?), debasing the characters (What if the plot of *Tartuffe* was played out on an elementary school playground?), and so on. Without realizing it, an entire class of students who chose the course specifically to avoid being evaluated on their creative skills became quite comfortable with practicing creative adaptations.

> The fact that Shakespeare didn't invent the story of the heir who feigns madness to outwit his usurping uncle doesn't make him uncreative. Quite the opposite: his creative process is visible in the adaptations he makes to convert the pagan heroic epic into a revenge tragedy for the Christian era.

Adaptation also entails critical insight: adaptors refashion old material because they have something to say about it. So in addition to demystifying creative genius, studying and practicing adaptation overcomes resistance to critical theory by showing how it is not opposed to, but a fundamental aspect of artistic creation. Djanet Sears's *Harlem Duet,* for example, adapts *Othello* by multiplying the protagonist and dislocating him in time and space, so that we see him living in three different epochs of African-American history. Among other things, this shows us not that the "tragedy" of Othello is a unique disruption of the "normal" course of events, as Shakespeare's version suggests, but precisely that, from an African-American perspective, the traumatic experience of miscegenation *is* the normal course of events, repeated over and over again. In addition, Sears invents a new character, Billie, the black wife Othello abandons, to show how the tragedy is experienced by the black community that Othello leaves rather than by the white one that excludes him. Students who see how and why Djanet Sears decentres Shakespeare in history, geography, and action simultaneously learn techniques of plot construction and the utility of post-colonial theory in not only critiquing but also *creating* new art.

> Without realizing it, an entire class of students who chose the course specifically to avoid being evaluated on their creative skills became quite comfortable with practicing creative adaptations.

As Sonia Massai observes in "Stage Over Study," adaptors often anticipate scholars in their critical revisions of classic texts. Massai looks at the works of Edward Bond and Charles Marowitz to show how they creatively critique Shakespeare using methods and perspectives that would only later be described by scholars as "cultural materialism." In the classroom, it often seems as though artists create art and critics criticize it, but adaptations show how "every rewriting is a critical reading and every critical reading is a rewriting" (Massai 255). This perspective is invaluable in a post-secondary creative arts context, where students often identify with either creativity or critical theory and are dismissive of or intimidated by the other. Working with, on, and through adaptations demands critical and creative sensitivity simultaneously. One student in a Dramaturgy course, inspired by the relationship between creative and critical practice, decided to extend Brecht's ideals about active spectatorship beyond the point imagined by Brecht himself, by literally forcing the spectators to influence the action: she proposed adapting *Mother Courage* into a semi-improvised, "choose-your-own-adventure" cabaret in which the actors would stop the action and make the audience vote on a number of possible choices for the characters. When I ran into her two years after the course, she was working on a script.

Adaptation is highly adaptable to a number of different contexts and circumstances: the examples above and below are taken from both lecture-based and practical courses, for both drama majors and non-majors. In a lecture-based environment, I might point out how playwright Michael O'Brien travesties *Hamlet* in *Mad Boy Chronicle* by setting the plot in medieval Denmark and changing the characters to grotesque Vikings (a choice he justifies by claiming to return to the *real* original which Shakespeare adapted); then we might brainstorm a number of other revered stories in our culture, and split into small groups with the goal of debasing a famous masterpiece using similar tactics. In a creative-based course, or where resources allow, I might ask students to take such ideas and develop them further. For example, if we learn about plot structuring by looking at different versions of *Oedipus,* I'll ask the students to experiment with the same variables (point-of-attack, inciting incident, selection and arrangement of story events, etc.) in adaptations of their own.

> Classroom work on adaptations reinforces what researchers and theatre artists already know: first, that creative breakthroughs are not sudden but gradual—much more perspiration than inspiration, as Edison put it—and second, that "creativity is almost never a solitary activity but [rather] fundamentally social and collaborative" (Sawyer 259).

Group projects work especially well, and in doing so they dispel the myth that creative work typically represents the output of a solitary artist, struck by inspiration. Classroom work on adaptations reinforces what researchers and theatre artists already know: first, that creative breakthroughs are not sudden but gradual—much more perspiration than inspiration, as Edison put it—and second, that "creativity is almost never a solitary activity but [rather] fundamentally social and collaborative" (Sawyer 259). These facts, though experienced daily by both theatre artists and scholars, are often obscured in coursework that asks students to admire the finished product of a masterpiece without supplying any insight into the highly collaborative and laborious processes that created it. Contrary to the image of Shakespeare, created by centuries of editorial commentary and tradition, as a unique genius who delivered one masterpiece after another to the comparatively unimportant, anonymous actors at the Globe, the real Shakespeare worked in collaboration with other writers, and probably with actors, and largely by gradually reworking stolen and borrowed plots from existing sources into plays.

Working on collaborative adaptations provides an important impetus to the group performance work that often distinguishes drama from other undergraduate programs. Sometimes, students take it for granted that they will be asked to perform simply because they are in drama (or alternatively, in spite of the fact that they are not actors). Memorizing, rehearsing, and performing a scene from a play just because it's on the course outline doesn't always provide or demand much critical reflection. But adapting a play to suit particular criteria is an exercise that demands and displays creative and critical skills simultaneously. In one course on modernism—which acting and design students typically approach with disdain because to them it is just a waste of time they could be using to learn *real* skills—I asked the students to adapt and perform scenes from the modernist canon, with the intention of investigating the extent to which these now-classic texts still can or should serve to shock, provoke, and break conventions. The more scholarly students in the class enjoyed being able to channel their critical insight into creative products. One such group, having discovered that Beckett forbade casting women in *Waiting for Godot,* did just that, drawing parallels between the play and the existential *ennui* represented in *Desperate Housewives.* Many of the actors, at first thrilled simply by the prospect of performing in a boring "history" class, discovered that they enjoyed the intellectual challenges involved in critical adaptation—one of them went on to write a very modernist manifesto railing against the conventions of realism, the style she had spent the previous several years training to master.

In contrast to the habitual association of adaptation with "copying" and plagiarism, my experience with adaptation suggests that learning to copy is actually an effective way to develop creative skills and foster critical engagement simultaneously—just as the ancients did. (It can also stimulate pro-

> In contrast to the habitual association of adaptation with "copying" and plagiarism, my experience with adaptation suggests that learning to copy is actually an effective way to develop creative skills and foster critical engagement simultaneously.

ductive discussions of intellectual property that go beyond the standard "academic dishonesty" boilerplate in most course outlines.) Notwithstanding the allegiances and assumptions they may have chosen before we meet them, I believe we have a duty to equip students with both critical and creative skills, particularly if they are training for a career in which both are vital. Artists who eschew critical thinking as pedantry are simply robbing themselves of powerful means of creative insight and expression, while even "pure" scholars need creative skills in order to challenge critical orthodoxies and create new knowledge. By working from the premise that adaptation, not originality, is the basis of both creative and critical thinking, one can vanquish false dichotomies and render these intimidating mysteries into a set of practical tools that anyone can appropriate and adapt to suit his or her own ends.

Works Cited

Fischlin, Daniel. "Nation and/as Adaptation: Shakespeare, Canada, and Authenticity." *Shakespeare in Canada: A World Elsewhere?* Ed. Diana Brydon and Irena R. Makaryk. Toronto: U of Toronto P, 2002. 313–338. Print.

Lubart, Todd I. "Models of the Creative Process: Past, Present, and Future." *Journal of Creative Research* 13.3/4 (2000–01): 295–308. Print.

Massai, Sonia. "Stage Over Study: Charles Marowitz, Edward Bond, and Recent Materialist Approaches to Shakespeare." *New Theatre Quarterly* 15.3 (1999): 247–255. Print.

O'Brien, Michael. *Mad Boy Chronicle: From Gesta Danorum by Saxo Grammaticus, c. 1200 A.D. and Hamlet, Prince of Denmark by William Shakespeare, c. 1600 A.D.* Toronto: Playwrights Canada, 1996. Print.

Runco, Mark A. *Critical Creative Processes*. Cresskill, N.J.: Hampton Press, 2003. Print.

Sawyer, R. Keith. *Explaining Creativity: the Science of Human Innovation*. Oxford: Oxford UP, 2006. Print.

Sears, Djanet. *Harlem Duet*. Winnipeg: Scirocco Drama, 1997. Print.

James McKinnon just finished his PhD in Drama at the University of Toronto. His research focuses on how Canadian playwrights use and abuse canonical authors to engage contemporary spectators. He teaches several courses at the University of Alberta Department of Drama and is also a dramaturge, performer, director, and adaptor.

The ICE Approach: Saving the World One Broken Toaster at a Time

By Grahame Renyk and Jenn Stephenson

Developed by Sue Fostaty-Young and Robert J. Wilson, ICE is a tool for assessing student learning. The basic principles are outlined in their co-authored book, *Assessment and Learning: The ICE Approach.* Standing for Ideas, Connections, and Extensions, the ICE model maps the process of skill acquisition as learners move from a first encounter with a new problem to competence and expertise. *Ideas* (I) are the fundamental concepts—vocabulary, definitions, facts. They may be presented as lists, descriptions, or "just information." Once in hand, these basic building blocks are put together by learners into *Connections* (C). Connections involve identifying patterns and relationships between the basic ideas. They may link pieces of information together or they might also link what is newly learned to something the student already knows. Finally, when a learner becomes adept, they might demonstrate *Extensions* (E). Extensions arise when students synthesize what they have learned through the process of making connections to generate new knowledge. Extensions answer questions like "What does this mean?"; "How does this change my view of the world?"; and, as we are now famous for bluntly saying in the classroom: "And so what?"

In its primary form, ICE is intended as a means of measuring student learning, and of determining at what level students are working. However, because ICE sets out a progressive route from Ideas through Connections to the ultimate goal of Extensions, ICE is not just descriptive of an individual's achievement at a particular point in time. It is prescriptive, pressing students to think outside the assignment, outside the course, and outside the academy to ask, "Why does this matter?" In this way, ICE is essentially activist in its philosophical bent.

Book cover from *Assessment and Learning: The ICE Approach* by Sue Fostaty-Young and Robert J. Wilson.

In the drama department at Queen's, we have been team-teaching the first year introductory course DRAM100 in a closely collaborative fashion since September 2007. With an enrollment of 225, DRAM100 draws a diverse group of students from across the university. For some students this is a foundation course for a concentration in Drama; for others this is a first-year elective. The course is certainly introductory, but rather than focus on foundational facts, we have elected to introduce students to the key questions in the field asked by drama scholars and practitioners at all levels. The ICE model has provided the core structure for asking these questions. Working backwards from this ultimate goal in using ICE as a model for thinking about theatre, we incorporate ICE into both assessment and assignment design as we scaffold this process for students, yoking this critical thinking pattern to specific learning tasks.

When teaching students about ICE, we regularly tell a story about a broken toaster. This is what we say (the plot has been frankly stolen from Wilson and Fostaty-Young's book [54]):

Imagine here there is a broken toaster. The first group examines the broken toaster, they point to one particular part that is broken. They say see this bit here is broken. A second group examines the broken toaster. This group sees the broken part and they also note that the reason that the toaster is broken is because the part that is broken is no longer working with another part of the toaster mechanism. They say they know why the toaster is broken. A third group examines the toaster and putting together information from the previous two groups, they see which part is broken, they see how it works together with the rest of the mechanism and ... they fix the broken toaster!

Working at an Ideas level, one can identify the elements that contribute to the malfunction and one can conclude: "Yup, the toaster's broken." Moving to a Connections level, one identifies the relationship between the elements, determining patterns such as cause-and-effect. Here one can say: "Yes, the toaster's broken and here's why." Finally, looking at the broken toaster with an eye for Extensions, one can extrapolate from the relationships already noted and use this information in a new way. Then one may say: "The toaster's broken, here is why, and I know how to fix it." The first time we tell this story at the beginning of our course, the goal is simply to introduce students to the ICE terminology and to give them a concrete example of how this approach works. We tell the story again a second time on the last day of class as a kind of valedictory address. In this version, we conclude by challenging the students, saying "I want you to be the kind of people who go out into the world and fix broken toasters!"

When teaching students about ICE, we regularly tell a story about a broken toaster.

But what does it mean to fix broken toasters in the context of the activist classroom? Perhaps the best way to explain how ICE leads to a more activist approach to learning is to discuss how we have started to apply the ICE progression to assignment design in DRAM100.

The simplest assignments are those geared primarily towards assessing Ideas-based learning, but convergent assignments that are looking for "right" answers can only go so far. In a post-secondary theatre-as-a-liberal-art classroom, where students may go on to become professional theatre practitioners, or to postgraduate work in the theatre and performance studies, or to a myriad of other career paths where their main contact with theatre will be as audience members,

DRAM100: *Introduction to the Study of Drama*

ICE *Assessment Rubric for Production Critique*

	Ideas	**Connections**	**Extensions**
Critical Thinking	• Proposes a general topic for discussion • Accurately describes content of the production • Identifies elements for analysis or contrast • Sequences observations	• Proposes a relationship between production elements to be evaluated and a theme or attitude • Illustrates patterns and connections • Formulates generalizations based on evidence	• Suggests significance or purpose for an identified relationship • Extrapolates from comparisons or applications to create new knowledge or awareness • Extends thinking beyond the confines of the specific production
Reasoning	• Assembles evidence relevant to general topic	• Evidence is linked directly to claims • Connections between claims, evidence and conclusions are logically sound	• Evaluates alternative or opposing viewpoints • Validates conclusions
Communication	• Uses clear, direct, and conventional language • Uses paragraphs to sequence distinct ideas • Uses words in accordance with their correct meaning • Errors of grammar or spelling do not detract from readability	• Uses language to build bridges between concepts • Use of language contributes to the interest of the reader and enhances the presentation of ideas.	• Modifies language and structure to reflect the structure of the argument • Uses language to communicate personal relevance

Source of assessment model format: Fostaty-Young, Sue and Robert J. Wilson. *Assessment and Learning: The ICE Approach.* Winnipeg: Portage and Main P, 2000.

An example of an ICE rubric distributed to students for a production analysis assignment.

students are (hopefully) being encouraged to contribute a new and deeper understanding of their field and indeed the world. The goal for the activist classroom is to propel students towards precisely this sort of divergent Extensions-level thought. In our experience, ICE has provided a valuable roadmap for designing assignments that facilitate this sort of creative critical engagement.

In DRAM100, we use ICE-based rubrics to design and evaluate assignments, assessing skills according to where they fall along the progression from Ideas to Extensions. However, we also use discussions of the ICE model itself to encourage a meta-cognitive understanding of the learning process in our students. The simplicity of ICE's three-part framework has been invaluable in helping students to, basically, learn how they learn. Indeed, in modeling the thought process as a simple progression from Ideas, through Connections, to Extensions, Fostaty-Young and Wilson have provided a potent conceptual metaphor for discussing the learning process with students, and an excellent starting point for concretely explaining to them how they can more readily arrive at complex Extensions-level critical thought in their work.

ICE was created partly in response to the limitations of some of the more well-worn behaviourist models of learning that arose out of the 1950s and 1960s, perhaps best represented by Bloom's Taxonomy. Such taxonomies, note Fostaty-Young and Wilson, "emphasized the products of learning ... in the behaviourist model, it was not important what the learner was doing during the process, only what the outcomes looked like" (6). They go on to note that:

> in the almost half century since the publication of this and like taxonomies, cognitive psychologists have come a long way in understanding the mechanisms people use to move from little knowledge to a lot. Some learners, for example, habitually use "surface" approaches to learning, content with attempting to match their learning to the specific demands of the task. Often, schools unintentionally support such learning approaches by a too-heavy reliance on multiple choice and completion-type assessments. (6)

An office talisman: the quintessential broken toaster.
Photo by Jenn Stephenson

CONNECTIONS RESPONSE ASSIGNMENT:

Choose either *A Doll's House, Mother Courage*, or *Krapp's Last Tape* and complete the following:

Find a "piece of storytelling" from outside of what we've studied in DRAM100 that you feel is working in a similar artistic tradition as your chosen play. This "piece of storytelling" can be a movie, a television show, a theatrical work, a novel, or a short story.

Start with a brief description of your example. Then convince me that your example is working in a similar artistic tradition as your chosen play by making specific links between the two. (Hint: you can look for links in terms of style, the way that the story is being told, and/or the world-view that might be behind the storytelling).

500 word maximum

The activist classroom seeks to develop students beyond a task-oriented, "surface" approach to learning. The point is not only to gather knowledge, but also to process and challenge it. Similarly, ICE seeks to promote a pedagogical approach that "emphasizes depth of learning more than coverage" (6), making it ideally suited to a Humanities classroom.

Core to the ICE approach is the notion that learning is a cognitive process occurring in each individual student. Conceptually, this invites a shift in how we think about learning, especially in terms of *where* that learning happens. Teaching comes from the instructor, but learning comes from the student. By describing learning as coming from the student, we are not talking simply about student effort and attention; rather, we are talking about the actual cognitive work of transforming information into knowledge. For information to become knowledge, it needs to be cognitively processed and incorporated into the context of prior knowledge by the learner. That process can only occur within the student.

Because it is modelled specifically as a *progression*, ICE has proven particularly helpful in designing assignments that locate learning in the student. Inherent in the model is the notion that critical engagement and deep learning (i.e. Extensions-level thinking) arise out of Connections. In DRAM100, we have been experimenting with several assignments designed to encourage Extensions-level engagement according to this progression. One of the most successful is a simple Connections-based assignment that invites students towards Extensions by asking them to establish and describe a specific connection between a concept covered in class and some aspect of their own prior knowledge. In its design, this assignment cuts to the very core of the ICE approach to learning. The assignment appears as follows:

Here, a connection is proposed between a play studied in the course and a "piece of storytelling" from the student's prior experience. The assignment design provides the student with a structural template for the response while leaving the choice of discussion material somewhat open. The firm structure helps abate the anxiety created by a blank slate assignment. It offers a clear starting point, and it initiates thought and analysis by forcing students to juxtapose two ideas, thus jump-starting the cognitive exploration of each concept. However, while the students are forced to make the connection itself, they are given some freedom as to what to connect. This allows them to bring their own prior knowledge into the discussion and to process course materials on their "home turf," thus locating the learning process in their own individual cognitive frameworks.

An important caveat to this assignment is that students must be encouraged to go beyond simply making a superficial connection between two concepts. While the initial connection is important, it is in the exploration of the specific and varied links between concepts that the extended learning usually occurs. Take one student's response to the Connections Assignment described above:

> We also use discussions of the ICE model itself to encourage a meta-cognitive understanding of the learning process in our students. The simplicity of ICE's three-part framework has been invaluable in helping students to, basically, learn how they learn.

> Bertolt Brecht's play *Mother Courage and Her Children* effectively parallels the modern TLC reality show *Jon and Kate Plus Eight* ... [e]ssentially, both stories discuss how societal structures, specifically capitalism, persuade people to behave in ways that are contrary to their inherent nature. *Jon and Kate Plus Eight* documents the life of the Gosselin family, including parents Jon and Kate, along with their eight children, a pair of twins and sextuplets. Originally the series allowed viewers to observe the struggles associated with raising eight young children, all around the same age on a modest income. However, as the popularity of the show rapidly increased, the focus shifted to filming the Gosselins' acquired material wealth resulting in the demise of Jon and Kate's seemingly stable marriage.
>
> ... the characters in *Mother Courage* and *Jon and Kate* fall victim to the capitalist environment that surrounds them. Mother Courage and Kate Gosselin attempt to financially and emotionally provide the best life for their families in the confines of their society. Both mothers are extremely resilient, yet ultimately they fall victim to this ingrained societal value, which results in their demise. These women must go against their inherent instinct to protect their family from outside forces in order to satisfy the financial obligation to their family. Mother Courage, for example, denies aiding her son in order to help the remaining family survive. Kate Gosselin compromises her children's health and happiness by alienating them from a life without television cameras. There is a social convention that dictates that families must produce a sufficient income to feel secure. Profit factors into each decision these women make and subsequently, is the main reason for conflict. In the case of Kate Gosselin, her seemingly happy family is subsequently torn apart by a nasty divorce, a byproduct of her decision to do a reality show. Mother Courage's children each die while she is haggling; ironically, a decision she feels is necessary to provide for them ... exploitation is a common element between both stories. Mother Courage and the Gosselins willingly use their children for economic gain.
>
> *Reprinted with kind permission of Grace Johnson.*

Admittedly, at first glance the connection between Courage and Gosselin seems specious. The temptation for the instructor is to read on with a roll of the eyes and the usual "kids-these-days" lament about the oversaturation of trash culture. However, a closer look reveals that the student has begun to cut to the heart of *Mother Courage*. In drawing specific links to Courage, the student begins to see Kate Gosselin in the context of the economic and political forces that create and subsume her. The student is beginning to make sense of Brecht's

A still from the archival video of DRAM100 Lab H's 2009 mash-up of *A Dream Play* by August Strindberg and *Love and Human Remains* by Brad Fraser.
Video by Grahame Renyk

play by using a contemporary pop culture reference; however, she is also making sense of contemporary pop culture by referring back to Brecht. For the student, and indeed, for everyone in the course (since we discussed this response in class), new understandings of both Brecht and the contemporary world arose out of this tiny little assignment—something that would certainly delight Mr. B. Is it a sophisticated Marxist reading of Kate Gosselin? Not as of yet. However, the student is now ready to encounter Marx in a whole new way since, before being told about his ideas, she has discovered some of them for herself.

What is most important is the fact that the realizations arrived at in this response arose from within the student, and did not come directly from the instructors. We may have facilitated the realization, but we did not create it. This is what opens the potential for the activist classroom. The student has generated her own understanding; she has begun to

---

In modeling the thought process as a simple progression from Ideas, through Connections, to Extensions, Fostaty-Young and Wilson have provided a potent conceptual metaphor for discussing the learning process with students, and an excellent starting point for concretely explaining to them how they can more readily arrive at complex Extensions-level critical thought in their work.

A still from the archival video of DRAM100 Lab C's 2009 mash-up of Timothy Findley's *Elizabeth Rex* and Sophocles' *Antigone*.
Video by Grahame Renyk

A still from the archival video of DRAM100 Lab H's 2009 mash-up of *A Dream Play* by August Strindberg and *Love and Human Remains* by Brad Fraser.
Video by Grahame Renyk

engage critically and creatively with the world of her own accord. Indeed, we believe that this is the goal of the twenty-first century activist classroom—not to deliver information, nor to indoctrinate students into a single mode of thinking, but rather to prepare students to be critical questioners as they engage with a complex, information-saturated world.

In another DRAM100 assignment, students, working in lab groups of twelve to fifteen members, are asked to take two scripts from our course anthology and "mash" them together to create a new devised performance piece. As with the Connections assignment discussed above, an initial structural framework is forced upon the students, and they are driven to respond by finding connections and relationships between the distinct plays. The structure helps foster learning by providing students with something to push against. As they make connections between the plays, our hope is that new ideas and approaches will shake loose.

One recent mash-up combined Sophocles' *Antigone* with *Elizabeth Rex* by Timothy Findley. In performance, the group in charge set up two parallel worlds: *Antigone* costumed in greens and *Elizabeth Rex* in reds. With a single female figure shuttling between the two worlds, the group staged short alternating fragments from each with a shared motif or repeated word triggering the transition from one to the other. The connections generated across the two play worlds were especially rich, linking Antigone to Elizabeth, of course, but also linking the rulers Creon and Elizabeth, the executed Antigone to Essex, and—amusingly—Tardy, the near-blind seamstress, to Tiresias. The new play drew on key themes from the seed texts to reconfigure core questions about the burdens of leadership and the performance of self. Ultimately, the two worlds collapsed into self-reflexivity as Elizabeth/Antigone rejected being written by Shakespeare/the mechanism of tragedy and instead decided to write her own self.

> The activist classroom seeks to develop students beyond a task-oriented, "surface" approach to learning. The point is not only to gather knowledge, but also to process and challenge it.

Another group's mash-up introduced Indra's Daughter from Strindberg's *A Dream Play* into the central action of *Love and Human Remains* by Brad Fraser. One of the restrictions of the assignment is that the scenes can only use original language from the two seed plays. Here the chanted threnody "Skin. Blood. Breasts. Feet. Hands." from Fraser's play beautifully depicted bodily transformation as the deity figure of Indra's Daughter became corporeal. The new understanding developed by the lab group for the mash-up argued that it is impossible to remain innocent in a world that is not. So, to support that perspective, instead of simply being disappointed at the suffering of humans, this Daughter, in the end, suffers a "mental break" and in a violent rampage kills everyone.

These two projects are typical of the best work that emerges from this challenging assignment. With such an

> Core to the ICE approach is the notion that learning is a cognitive process occurring in each individual student. Conceptually, this invites a shift in how we think about learning, especially in terms of *where* that learning happens.

Stills from the archival video of DRAM100 Lab C's 2009 mash-up of Timothy Findley's *Elizabeth Rex* and Sophocles' *Antigone*.
Video by Grahame Renyk

open-ended task the results are wide-ranging and wonderfully unexpected. Beyond the dramaturgical and scenographic choices made by the groups in support of their core understandings, we try to further encourage students to extend their thinking into the world around them by asking them to explain how their mash-up will be relevant to their current social and historical context. We ask them to answer the questions: "Why Here? Why Now?" with their presentation. As with the Connections Response, we strongly encourage students to move beyond pat answers and superficial connections towards drawing specific links between what they have created and where they are situated as spectators and creative artists.

In our experience, the use of ICE in both assessment and assignment design promotes a learning-based, rather than teaching-based, approach to pedagogy. Ultimately, it responds to the question: Are we teaching, or are we fostering learning? The simple formulation of Ideas-Connections-Extensions, when put into practice, helps remind the instructor that the learning process ultimately needs to be located inside the student. Information can be thrown at the student, but until that student chooses to actively internalize and process that information, there is no learning happening. ICE provides a useful tool for engaging the twenty-first century learner, and for preventing his or her learning from being lost amid all the other noise our contemporary culture produces.

> In our experience, the use of ICE in both assessment and assignment design promotes a learning-based, rather than teaching-based, approach to pedagogy. Ultimately, it responds to the question: Are we teaching, or are we fostering learning?

Works Cited

Fostaty-Young, Sue and Robert J. Wilson. *Assessment and Learning: The ICE Approach*. Winnipeg: Portage and Main, 2000. Print.

Grahame Renyk and Jenn Stephenson teach in the drama department at Queen's University. Renyk is the recipient of the 2010 Frank Knox Teaching Award presented by Queen's University's Alma Mater Society. Stephenson is a two-time recipient of the Drama Department's Teaching Excellence Award (2005 and 2009). Both are infamous for their obsession with ICE.

"Elder up!": A Mentor/Mentee Memoir

by Tara Beagan

When I was three years old, my sister left me for kindergarten. I felt entirely abandoned. I could not see why I wasn't allowed to go with her. As a sort of consolation, she would return home and pass on her lessons learned. She taught me the alphabet and how to write. When I arrived at kindergarten, I could spell her name, my name, our surname, and "I love you." This is my first memory of looking up to someone who was teaching me—she was, in essence, my first mentor.

Fast-forward twenty-five years.

At twenty-eight, I wrote my first full-length play. It created enough of a din to catch the attention of the Artistic Director of the oldest and most reputable indigenous theatre company in North America, Native Earth Performing Arts (NEPA). Yvette Nolan would become my artistic mentor, in a relationship that is very much influenced by a traditional way of teaching—she is a mentor to me regarding work, in all that affects the work, and in all that is affected by the work. Namely, well ... everything.

Yvette and I share a common background. We are both playwrights via acting—she is a director and I began learning, with my first main stage gig at her side, as her assistant. We come from similar families, with First Nations mothers and Irish Canadian fathers—"shamrock and tomahawk." A major difference between us, though, is that I had the good fortune of coming into being while she, an artist with so many serendipitously comparable parallels to my life, was already on the scene.

This is not to say that there haven't been such artists bringing ideas to fruition for some time.

Theatre on this continent pre-dates those widely hallowed theatre greats of Ancient Greece by a few thousand years. Unlike the tradition in Ancient Greece, though, our

Dreary and Izzy premiere, 2005. (l-r); Michaela Washburn and Lesley Faulkner.
Photo by Nir Baraket, www.nirbareket.com

tradition of performing stories of humans, nature, and deities within a ritualized practice was not documented in a manner that has become the foundation for formalized education throughout the world. That is to say, it wasn't written down. There are no clay pots or parchments that have depictions of how our theatrical culture was practiced. This difference—and the culture clash that occurred at contact—means that many details of our age-old folkways have been lost. It also quite likely means there has been a high level of evolution within pan-indigenous, North American theatre culture. Arguably, when a people's history is oral, said people are more amenable to maintaining an active dialogue around what is tradition and why. Traditions among First Nations have always evolved with time and the needs of the natural world. This evolution is sometimes responsive to internal change, but often it occurs as a result of external forces.

The evolution of our performative traditions post-contact largely reflects the relationship between First Nations and non-First Nations. The fundamentalist, reactionary outlawing of the potlatch and of any social, political, and/or spiritual gatherings among Natives in Canada in the early twentieth century meant that the First Nations had to make big changes in a damn hurry, or they would lose everything. Venues changed, artists worked in secret, and scenes enacting cannibal spirits took on a more imminently threatening, prescient quality, which would influence the artists carving the masks involved in such scenarios, as well as those performing them.

> Theatre on this continent pre-dates those widely hallowed theatre greats of Ancient Greece by a few thousand years. Unlike the tradition in Ancient Greece, though, our tradition of performing stories of humans, nature, and deities within a ritualized practice was not documented in a manner that has become the foundation for formalized education throughout the world. That is to say, it wasn't written down.

Artistic traditions that come from traditional First Nations culture can still be seen in contemporary indigenous works. There are many schools of thought around this: on one end of the spectrum, you have people (often those who have had little experience interacting with present-day Aboriginal folks) who think a project isn't legitimately indigenous if there isn't a direct usage of a traditional performative element such as drumming or vocable singing. On the other end, you have artists who refuse to incorporate any traditional elements in their work in overt ways, believing that they would be contributing to the propagation of stereotypes that detract from the diverse artistry of our many peoples. The spectrum's middle parts are where the riskiest, most challenging work lives.

Take, as an example, one emerging playwright with whom I have had the honour of working: Waawaate Fobister. Waawaate began his artistic career as a traditional grass dancer, and his beautiful, brave play, *Agokwe* (whose premiere production won multiple Doras) tells part of this story. Waawaate and I were paired by Yvette at a Young Voices meeting after the success of his debut play. He began his writing as a NEPA Young Voices member and then returned after *Agokwe* took the stage by storm. The reasons for this were many.

Waawaate had worked, with varying degrees of compatibility, outside of his FN artist community. While *Agokwe* was housed by a few developmental programs, its final evolution with Ed Roy proved that one need not work with an indigenous dramaturg/director if one is an indigenous playwright. Waawaate's second play, *Medicine Boy*, focuses on a gifted

Outgoing and incoming NEPA Artistic Directors Tara Beagan and Yvette Nolan at the Weesageechak Festival XXIII, January 2011.
Photo by Nir Baraket, www.nirbaraket.com

young man accepting the path to becoming an elder. Waawaate was commissioned and well supported by the Vancouver Playhouse for *Medicine Boy*, hitting the ground running. The work's first phase was a success; he then butted up against difficulties. Fortunately, Waawaate's grounding in his values, and in the mentorship he had received from Roy, from Buddies in Bad Times Theatre in Toronto, and from Native Earth, enabled him to walk away from a dramaturg who could not see the profound importance of the text's use of Ojibwe.

When Waawaate returned to Native Earth, I was a playwright-in-residence and working with the Young Voices Program. Yvette had raised me into a viable dramaturg for new playwrights, and I have enough skill in my own writing now to recognize when I can be of use to a play and its writer. The day Waawaate arrived at our session with his re-worked pages, I was lit up by what he was doing. I felt quite sure I could see what he wanted to achieve. We were paired up, and he has since demonstrated great faith in our work together, acquiring his own funding to give us a week in a rehearsal hall with actors. Although I am, in many ways, Waawaate's mentor on this project, his example has inspired my own confidence in my ability to contribute to new plays and to help foster new playwrights. I have since encouraged several new writers to embrace their impulses to use their mother tongues, their culturally specific colloquialisms, and their own unique methods of indigenizing their work. This lesson I learned from Waawaate.

While I, myself, don't have the Ntlakapamux language, I do hold its culture, and I aspire to learn more as I grow into myself. Further, I hold my Irish culture near and dear. In fact, it was a celebration of my Irish ties that first led me to embrace my Indian, and my Elder, with Native Earth and Yvette's assistance.

In *Thy Neighbour's Wife* (UnSpun Theatre, 2004), I played an Irish woman. We managed to earn some rave reviews; this brought three prominent First Nations theatre artists out to see the play, and they in turn brought my work to Yvette's attention. Shortly after Yvette came to see the play, I met with her at Native Earth HQ. I had applied to the company's annual new works festival, *Weesageechak Begins to Dance*, and the play I had submitted had been declined. Yvette asked me whether I had any other scripts on the go. I pitched the storyline for a screenplay I had in the works. She was intrigued. As a result of ignorance and enthusiasm, I promised her a first draft by month's end.

Young voices: Waawaate Fobister and Yvette Nolan, 2007.
Photo courtesy of Native Earth Performing Arts

The script was featured in the 2004 festival and went on to be programmed in the winter of 2005. My ties to NEPA were formalized with this work, and I could not have been happier. In early 2005, I was hired as Community Liaison for the company—partially on my perceived merits as an artist, and largely (I imagine) due to my driving desire to figure out how to make good within the role. I did the best I could. I failed on many counts, but I also learned heaps, as, I think, did Yvette. It was during this time that I began to refer to Yvette as my mentor.

Indigenous artistic leads at the inaugural Matariki Theatre Festival, Tawata Productions, 2010.
Photo courtesy of Native Earth Performing Arts

During my time inside NEPA's office, I wrote my first commission and I was handed my first dramaturgical gig. The playwright was thirty years my senior. I was terrified. I did not know why I was being trusted to contribute to his growth in some way. Yvette was convinced that I could do the job. Her faith helped me find my way.

> During my time inside NEPA's office, I wrote my first commission and I was handed my first dramaturgical gig. The playwright was thirty years my senior. I was terrified. I did not know why I was being trusted to contribute to his growth in some way.

Larry Guno showed up in Toronto (he was from Terrace, B.C., and Nisga'a) with a profound commitment to improving his powerful play, and a face that conjured up male relations on my mother's side. Picture Chief Dan George with a smile, a freshly barbered shave and haircut, and dark blue jeans. We sat in a café and spoke around his play. He told me his stories and when he slowed, I asked him questions that may or may not have related to his play. He responded with generosity and warmth. We laughed like family, and established a shorthand quickly. He was determined to write the strongest play he could, and by the time our hot chocolates were drained, he had promised to return to Toronto for *Dreary and Izzy*, set to hit the stage that winter. Larry passed away before winter and sadly before he had the chance to tackle his rewrites. I'm pretty sure he would've laughed when, many years later, I was able to joke that our dramaturgical session—riddled with my clumsy attempts at competency—contributed to his early end.

During 2005, I made and lost a new friend. I also found and temporarily lost a mentor. I failed in a number of my goals as NEPA's Community Liaison, and made several foolish choices in my relations with NEPA and the larger community during production of *Dreary and Izzy*. I didn't understand the importance of loyalty to an entity that was investing in my growth, nor did I demonstrate adequate appreciation for how difficult an undertaking it is to walk within the role of Mentor. A cavernous rift was cloven between Yvette and I; 2005 was a busy year, a rough year.

> I didn't understand the importance of loyalty to an entity that was investing in my growth, nor did I demonstrate adequate appreciation for how difficult an undertaking it is to walk within the role of Mentor.

Native Earth operates on seven traditional principles; variations on them exist among several nations whose roots are in what is now Ontario. NEPA maintains that these tenets exist, in some form, within most cultures worldwide. These tenets are: Patience, Humility, Wisdom, Tolerance, Strength of Character, Courage, and Generosity. When listing them, I always seem to name first the one I am thinking of the most, and forget the one of which I am most in need. While Yvette and I were sore with one another, courage was on my mind, and humility was tricky to come by. Eventually, I humbled myself, gathered what little courage I had lurking in the drawers of my oft-used writing desk, and set myself before a nervous Nolan.

I knew—after nearly six months—that the gift of her presence in my life was rare and vital to my grounding in the work. I had felt all along that my personal well being was impacted by her feelings towards me, but I lacked the humility to admit it. Suppose she didn't see me as a worthwhile investment after all of the difficulties we had been through? The only thing more awful than that prospect was the thought of losing her guidance and friendship altogether. We met, at my timorous behest. We spoke openly and found our way—over many years and tricky bumps in the road—into a relationship that is strong and open to evolution.

I've been lucky enough to find a mentor who knows that we all have to be willing to make big changes in a damn hurry, or lose everything. We've had far too many years with voices silenced to stop talking to one another.

Our reparations have been slow and laboured—but well worth it. Our struggle back to one another has been supported by our community. Our ties are stronger now, and we have undertaken some mutually courageous endeavours. Yvette took me on as an Assistant Director of a new play in 2008. She then invited me to apply to the Canada Council for the Arts for a playwrighting residency with NEPA in the 2009/10 season. This residency concluded with a trip to Aotearoa (New Zealand) where we worked as one creative pairing on the inaugural Matariki festival of new works for the contemporary Maori theatre company Tawata Productions. Yvette had me on as dramaturg for her play, *Two Old Women*.

I've been lucky enough to find a mentor who knows that we all have to be willing to make big changes in a damn hurry, or lose everything. We've had far too many years with voices silenced to stop talking to one another.

It was in Wellington, NZ that Yvette's early elderhood truly came to light for me. Yvette was programmed to address our Maori cousins as a featured artist on the first day of Tawata's Matariki festival. As soon as she saw that scheduling note, she let me know that she'd prefer to have me sitting before our hosts alongside her, thereby encouraging more of a conversation, rather than an address. She also noted that she would like me to speak to my experience, having come through NEPA as a new playwright, and arriving at the place where I was in residence as a full-time playwright. I was humbled, I was honoured, and I was nervous as hell.

Hone Kouka, the much-lauded trailblazer and sublimely talented playwright, hosted the festival with the brilliant young upstart, Miria George. Yvette and I sat side-by-side on the day of her session and we introduced ourselves and one another to our Maori colleagues. Yvette quickly opened the room up to questions, and therefore to conversation. It became clear that both Kouka and Yvette search their home countries for promising talent and take the risk of putting well-stretched funds behind young artists. Many theatre companies in Canada (and in Aotearoa) foster emerging artists. Few have as great a history of persecution to overcome—on their home soil—as do Native Earth and Tawata. The need for our stories, as told by our own, is pressing enough to beg hope of our leaders. Fortunately for me and my multitude of peers—both at home and in Aotearoa—neither Yvette nor Kouka see any other way of being.

It was during this open forum that I heard Yvette speak of the reason why she most treasures the relationship NEPA has with Tawata. Kouka is the only other indigenous artist known to her who shares her degree of commitment to developing artists through the work. Yvette has to travel across the globe to be in company with such a peer.

I work with a number of artists who serve as role models—actively and accidentally. Many of my peers have worked in youth mentoring programs, and many of them wear multiple hats. Only recently did I take that inventory. Quite recently, I was charged—as Artistic Associate of NEPA—to gather prospective candidates to apply for the position of Artistic Director. It was this task that led me to look at my community through a different lens.

After eight years of innovative leadership with Yvette, Native Earth was seeking a new leader. (Yvette has received funding to begin work on what is sure to be the definitive book about the history of indigenous theatre in Canada.) The search inspired a roundtable with artists invested in the company. With more than a dozen people in attendance, the circle's topics ranged from the perceived definition of the job to Yvette's personal experience when applying for it. And the circle demonstrated the breadth of the company's influence—an influence that quite literally spanned the continent.

Whether we like it or not, those of us in the First Nations artist world are mentors. As soon as we work in a public forum, we are teaching our own society about what we do and who we are today.

I, personally, was determined not to consider applying for the position unless Yvette herself suggested as much. That day came, and I was shortly thinking up creative means to put off writing my letter of interest. When, finally, the day of the deadline dawned, I typed the final revisions to my wee missive. It was brief, heartfelt, and one of the most difficult pages I have ever forced myself to write. I submitted my application to Yvette, though she was not on the hiring committee. I don't know if she read it. I did, however, want to leave its submission up to her. In a way, I wanted to make sure that she wanted me to be considered to sit in the chair she had occupied so gracefully for eight years.

Eight years ago, I had yet to write a play. Back in 2003, I was still reluctant to claim my ancestry, having grown up off-reserve, pale, freckled, and curly-haired. During those eight years, the more I worked among FN artists, the more certain I became that I belonged among them. The more

I am told by some self-important individual that I "don't look Native," the more certain I am about how wrong such people are.

Whether we like it or not, those of us in the First Nations artist world are mentors. As soon as we work in a public forum, we are teaching our own society about what we do and who we are today. I have been assigned the title "Mentor" by multiple programs: Project One Generation with Big Soul Productions, the AMY Project, Cahoots Theatre Projects' Crossing Gibraltar, Native Earth's Young Voices, as an instructor at the Centre for Indigenous Theatre, as a facilitator at the Tsatsikisapo'op Middle School, and by Diaspora Dialogues. Emerging artists I have worked with range from a teenaged Burmese girl to a Cree playwright in his twenties to a British woman in her forties. Have I earned these mentorships? I don't know. I do know, however, that the old adage about a teacher learning from her students is truer than anyone can describe to anyone who has not braved the possible failure of putting herself before a learning artist.

During my interview before the NEPA AD hiring committee, I often found myself admitting "I don't know." I have a lot to learn—that I know. I am increasingly invested in engaging our young indigenous population in artistic expression. That I know. I will go to Yvette Nolan and hope for guidance as long as she will receive me. That I know.

During my interview before the NEPA AD hiring committee, I often found myself admitting "I don't know." I have a lot to learn—that I know. I am increasingly invested in engaging our young indigenous population in artistic expression. That I know. I will go to Yvette Nolan and hope for guidance as long as she will receive me. That I know.

Tara Beagan is a proud Ntlakapamux and Irish Canadian playwright. Beagan is a Dora Award-winning playwright and Dora and Betty Mitchell Award-nominated actor. She has worked with UnSpun, Cahoots, Urban Curvz, Tarragon, Nightwood, Factory, Crate Productions, Caravan Farm, Theatre North West, Theatrefront, and Kick Theatre. She serves as a mentor to emerging artists and has recently begun work as Artistic Director at Native Earth Performing Arts.

Elephants in the Classroom: A Forum on Performance Pedagogy

Organized and edited by Marlis Schweitzer and Laura Levin
Transcription by Cassandra Dee Ball and Megan Macdonald

Workshop participants:

Natalie Alvarez
Allan Boss
Barry Freeman
Catherine Graham
Nelson Gray
Nicholas Hanson
Andy Houston
Erin Hurley
Stephen Johnson
Aida Jordão
Laura Levin

Megan Macdonald
James McKinnon
Mia Perry
Monica Prendergast
Marlis Schweitzer
Annie Smith
Kim Solga
Jenn Stephenson
Richie Wilcox
Lydia Wilkinson

In recent years, educators at all levels have enthusiastically discussed the value of incorporating metacognitive practices into the classroom.[1] By asking students to stop and think about not only what they are learning but *how* they are learning—and perhaps more importantly, how they are *not* learning—teachers are equipping students with the tools to understand and take greater responsibility for their education. At the same time, teachers are also learning about how they themselves might become better educators. But these pedagogical discoveries are often solo discoveries, made in the middle of a classroom exercise, on the commute home, or in the study at night. In the interest of bringing these discoveries into a communal setting, we organized a three-hour workshop for the 2010 annual meeting of the Canadian Association for Theatre Research/Association canadienne de la recherche théâtrale. Taking up the conference theme of "Interconnected Knowledge," we aimed to harness the collective knowledge and experience of the CATR membership to address real-world pedagogical issues (the "elephants" that lurk in the classroom) and build teaching networks through discussion and creative engagement.

We divided the workshop process into four stages. In stage one, we sent out a call for workshop participants over the CANDRAMA listserv. We were delighted to receive responses from a broad range of theatre educators (graduate students, postdoctoral fellows, and professors at all levels of their careers) from small and large campuses across Canada. In stage two, we asked the workshop participants to e-mail us a list of two to three pedagogical challenges that they had encountered at some point in their teaching. We explained that these challenges could include such things as: student resistance to certain theories or political perspectives (i.e. feminism); student reliance on "bad" online sources; racist, classist, or sexist comments in essays or in the classroom; student expectations for "A" grades, or faculty feuding over pedagogical approaches. Once we had received responses from everyone, we compiled a list of the four "top" challenges, which we planned to use as the basis for small group discussion and creative engagement during the workshop. To that end, we organized the workshop participants into four groups and assigned one of the pedagogical challenges to each. Group One (Nicholas Hanson, Barry Freeman, Lydia Wilkinson, Catherine Graham) took up the challenge of incorporating performance practice into the classroom. Group Two (Allan Boss, Erin Hurley, Annie Smith, James McKinnon, Jenn Stephenson) explored issues related to the development of critical thinking. Group Three (Monica Prendergast, Stephen Johnson, Natalie Alvarez, Nelson Gray, Richie Wilcox) discussed strategies for approaching cultural difference in the post-identity politics classroom. And Group Four (Andy Houston, Mia Perry, Kim Solga, Aida Jordão, Megan Macdonald) looked at assessment of student work.

In stage three—the actual workshop—we began by asking each of the groups to first discuss the particular pedagogical challenge they had been assigned and then develop an assignment or activity that not only addressed that challenge, but might be used in an actual classroom setting. We then brought all of the groups together to present a brief summary of their activity before opening up the floor to discussion.

The transcript of that discussion follows here, representing stage four of the workshop process: sharing our collective metacognitive exploration with the readers of *Canadian Theatre Review*. It is our hope that this document serves as a springboard for further discussion, reflection, and innovation so that the conversation does not end on the printed page.

* * *

The workshop participants.
Photo by Marlis Schweitzer

(The session began with presentations of the assignments generated by each of the groups.)

Nicholas Hanson: Our group was looking at practice and theory in the performance classroom and bridging that divide. Here is the context of the type of class situation that we were addressing. We were imagining a class of forty to sixty students—like a second, third, or fourth year class—where a professor lectures on a topic on Monday and Wednesday, and then maybe on Friday, or every other Friday, a small group of four students or so, presents a scene that reflects the lecture. So let's say this is the theatre history model: I lecture about Classical Greek theatre for four classes, and on the second Friday a group does a scene from *Oedipus Rex*.

We identified multiple problems with this format, but the two primary issues were: first, when the emphasis on *the show* overtook the learning or the challenges intrinsic to the theatrical style that was being explored in the class [i.e. Classical Greek theatre], and when students became very anxious about performing—particularly students in an English/Drama divided kind of class. Conversely, the drama-oriented students, who are using this as an outlet for their performance aspirations, make their presentation a big spectacle, and this goes against the professor's intention that this be a small performance for the purpose of illustrating a theatrical style. Second, this format tends to show a lack of respect for the craft of performance. It's fairly illogical to say, "I have given you two fifty-minute lectures on Noh theatre, thus you four eighteen-year-olds are empowered to present a five-minute piece of Noh theatre, which honours all of the traditions and ideas inherent in that art form." Perhaps, we're pushing our students towards superficiality and shallowness; anxious about authentically producing this kind of

Nelson Gray listens as Monica Prendergast shares her thoughts on how to get students to engage with questions of race when thinking about such things as casting.
Photo by Marlis Schweitzer

work, students tend to resort to a superficial, silly parody of the format as a self-conscious crutch, instead of being vulnerable to other students by speaking very slowly for five minutes in a scene.

So here's the concept that we collectively devised to reframe this assignment and address these problems. Again, let's say we're teaching a theatre history class. This whole class is going to present a theatre festival, and this is a theatre festival that will feature historical works. We create a few groups, and each is responsible for making a submission to the theatre festival. Over the course of the semester, the class as a whole acts as a jury whose responsibility will be to select three of the twelve pieces most suitable for this theatre festival. So groups would be required to make a presentation to the class, demonstrating the value of their submission based upon criteria which the instructor sets—for instance, things like artistic merit, relevance in 2010, connection to the contemporary world, and impact on a community. As well, each group would submit a written response to the instructor, which digs into these ideas in more detail and with more coherence perhaps. Finally, each group presents a two-to-five minute scene, but this time, instead of it being all about a virtuosic presentation, the notion is that they are developing a preliminary rehearsal version. If accepted into this theatre festival, the group would expand this version into a fuller work. So it's conceding that "this is not finished. We're just getting our feet wet; we are not masters of this yet, but with your support in this theatre festival, we would develop this into a greater idea." At some point, perhaps midway or logically at the end of the semester, the class meets and has a discussion as a jury about which three of the applications are ideal for this festival. This involves, then, critical thinking as people have to match the criteria that have been outlined in the festival submission guide with what was actually presented. And then perhaps the individual students in the class will have to write an individual response outlining which three they thought were most effective. This could take the form of a class discussion, an individual writing assignment, or it could be a combination of both.

There are many ways that the teacher could flex this: if this was a Canadian theatre class, you could simply say that it's a festival of contemporary Canadian plays, and groups are assigned a region or a playwright. You could also change the number of students per group, the number of minutes per scene, whether or not the jury discussion is live (it could be on a blog), all depending on preference/structure/ bias/ familiarity. But that was our idea for keeping a format that is pretty inherent in a lot of curricula—that method of lecture and demonstration—but spinning it so that we could get away from it being about the show, so that we can respect the craft of theatre production as something that you don't just learn in two days and then slap together. The assignment respects the theory, it respects the practice, and it integrates the two together.

Nelson Gray: Our group was looking at cultural difference and how to overcome some of the resistance that we all experience in trying to discuss gender, sexual orientation, race, ethnicity, etc. in the contemporary classroom. Our idea was to develop a casting exercise where students are given a problem to solve in terms of cultural difference. It would be designed so that the students have to cast a traditional play and contend with the problems of cultural difference that the play presents. For example, students might be asked to cast *The Importance of Being Earnest* and highlight the fact that Oscar Wilde was a gay playwright through their casting choices. The assignment could be adapted by using a different text or by bringing forward different identity problems that the play presents. The casting exercise would be followed by a discussion and writing assignment exploring the issues it raised. It could be preceded by or paired with teaching historical case studies of casting that engage with cultural difference—for instance, the photonegative version of *Othello* where Patrick Stewart was cast as a white Othello and the rest of the cast was black or The Wooster Group's use of blackface to deconstruct classic texts.

Monica Prendergast: Just to tag on to that, another issue that kept coming up in our group was how to deal with young people who don't want to acknowledge race, don't want to acknowledge sexual difference, and don't want to acknowledge feminism or queer theory. They adopt the "we're all the same" kind of post-racial mythologizing. How do we address that attitude in productive ways?

In the field of Drama Education, there are obviously lots of games for actors and non-actors that help deal with this, but a very simple one is called "The Line-up," which is when you reach a point in a group where the conversation feels very frozen and there is a lot of tension in the room: how do you break through that? The Line-Up is a very simple, physical way to take a stand on a position. So the example we were talking about is if you have a class that is very resistant to a feminist or queer analysis of a play, and nobody is willing to move. Then let us literally move. Let's get on our feet. Here is the continuum: people at one extreme of the issue stand on one side and people who feel the other way about it stand on the other end. Students have to find their place on the continuum and stand there. Where do you stand? Take a stand! Students are asked to talk to the people who are standing close to them, and then identify someone on the line who is really far away from them, and talk to them. It's a way to break down a conversation that has hit a wall, have the students talk to each other, and then hopefully, the conversation can then continue forward.

Laura Levin: This is a standard drama education exercise, rather than one generated for this session, yes?

Prendergast: Yes, that's just one simple drama education exercise that can be adapted in the range of classes that we teach, classes that may not traditionally use drama education techniques. It is a helpful exercise when you hit a wall with issues of cultural diversity.

Jenn Stephenson: I am speaking on behalf of the critical thinking group. We created two short exercises, and I'll give you the background on each. The first one related to the problem of "in-class discussion," and the feedback we frequently get where students say, "I just want to hear you talk, Jenn, I don't want to waste time hearing what my peers have to say." As we talked around that, we saw that one of the challenges is how to encourage and teach students to discuss fruitfully, effectively, so that discussion does become rich and interesting, because we have all been in discussions that go off track into anecdote and where students are speaking only to get participation marks.

We thought about how to teach students to make effective critical comments, and we created a little game that we're calling "PAS." Very briefly, "PAS" stands for Paraphrase, Application, and Spiral. We talked about how a good comment might have three steps: the first is paraphrase ("Yes I heard what you are saying, this is what I hear you saying"); the second step would be to apply ("I can apply what you just said to this other thing") and perhaps could be quite limited to the text in question, or could be something broad but at the discretion of the professor; and the third step is spiral ("and now I wonder if this might also do something else"), which would move the discussion outwards from that initial application.

So this is what we are trying to encourage, and the way the exercise works is that we would begin with a short text of some kind: it be could a scene, it could be a paragraph of theory, it could be a video, it could be whatever you want to discuss. So it begins with a short text, and someone begins by saying, "This is what I think the text is saying, here is how it applies to another section of the text, and I wonder if it might also be applied or do this other thing." And then the student passes it along to the next person who says, "What I hear you saying is this, here's how it might apply to something else, and I wonder if it might also do something else," and then they pass along the ball. The ball—practicing how to make a discussion—would go around the group. We like that we have the ball—or something tangible like a stick or a coffee cup or a mitten—as the idea is that some physical thing goes around. And we did consider the very reasonable possibility that some students might stall. We would hope that people would be able to paraphrase, "yes I heard what you said," and hopefully make a preliminary application, "well that reminds me of," but this third step of spiralling on might be a place where people get stuck. And we think that it would be acceptable in the exercise to say, "Okay, that's fine," and maybe the individual can throw the third step back to the group. So you can open up at that point to the group, and then keep going. And the idea is that they practice, and really lay it out in steps so eventually it would be natural, and as the course goes on you can have these kinds of rich discussions.

The second question we tackled was how to get students to develop their own research questions. This might happen when students are working from scratch, or when they are given a topic for an essay and need to develop a question. Some struggle with: "How do I go from a topic, to a question to be investigated?" So the approach that we took was an exercise—a take-home assignment—where students are asked to reverse engineer the question. They would be given a text of some kind; it could be a play or a piece of theory, like if they were asked to do Schiller: "What is a question that Schiller is trying to answer in this essay? What is a question that Strindberg is trying to ask in this play?" The student would then have to trace the things that the text is doing in an effort to answer the question. So we try to deconstruct the play or text, and then finally ask "Well, then, what question does this raise for you?" So it's a question back in response to the play's question. Again, we are demonstrating *how* to ask a question.

Mia Perry: Our group explored "evaluation assessment." We were looking at *what* to evaluate in student work and how we can look at meaning-making when a student's writing is possibly incomprehensible. So we have come up with a sort of tool. The tool is a flexible method of assessment and also provides a method of developing and analyzing writing practices. It was inspired by this notion of "thinking-writing," or using performance to think about and evaluate writing, as opposed to the other way around. And we think some of the core goals of the exercise are to expose the process of meaning-making, expose the intention of the student, and push students to evaluate the clarity of their ideas.

The exercise involves groups of three to five students, and each group is working collaboratively on evaluating their own essay writing. The students stand in a group with their backs to the circle. One student stands apart and reads the first and last sentence of their own work out loud to the others.

Aida Jordão: Then the student counts down, "three, two, one" and everyone has to turn into the circle to create an image of what those sentences suggest to them. When you hear the sentences what does it suggest to you physically?

(The group gets up and does a short demonstration of generating an embodied image in response to two sentences from a student essay.)

Kim Solga: The key at this point is that you need a facilitator to take the students through the images that have been created, and you've got to set a goal in advance. If you are reading the first and last sentences of the paragraph, then what you are probably looking for is cohesion. Does the first sentence support the last sentence in some way? Where is the emphasis? Do the people doing this exercise seem to connect more to the first sentence or the last sentence? Is that what your intention was? What does the embodiment of this language tell you about what you have and haven't communicated in these sentences? And then the idea is that by going through this process in the classroom in small groups, students will then be provoked to go back and say "Let's think again about how we have communicated what we want in this case, and let's try writing these sentences again to see if we can gain greater clarity"—if clarity is the goal. Even though it's a flexible model, there has to be a clear framework. If you are working on what makes an effective introduction, maybe the person reads the entire introduction, and everyone is asked to take the one image that stands out to them. Maybe everyone gets the same thing, or maybe the introduction is super unclear, and nobody gets anything. And then the student sees, "Okay, I didn't communicate anything like what I thought I was communicating, so now let's go back and use what we learned in this exercise and try writing again." That was the basic idea.

Perry: One of the strengths of the flexibility of the exercise is that it can work even if you weren't trying to create a linear cohesive interpretation. For example, some of us are doing devised work where this isn't the goal. Here, you can still use the exercise because it's about exposing meaning making. And you might look at your group of four or five and see that they have all come back to you with the very same interpretation, and you might see that as a failing, so it really depends on the context. And the other thing that it introduces for us is the fact that it's taking the student—the writer or the creator—into a thought process about their own meaning making, about their own writing, and about how their audience is making meaning.

Catherine Graham and Barry Freeman discuss the challenge of incorporating performance practice into the classroom.
Photo by Marlis Schweitzer

Solga: And it's worth noting here that we thought about the steps in this process and Mia suggested that it could be a template for an entire class that you might call "Think/Write/Perform/Write/Think." Or it could be the framework for an essay writing development day: "We are all going to work on introductions today and we are going to use performance to do that, and after you go away you are going to have a better sense of how your writing connects or disconnects once you put it down on paper. You are going to actually physically see the strengths and weaknesses of your writing." Ultimately the exercise is the beginning of a process that gets you back to a better-crafted sentence. So it's a lot like comparing your writing in the classroom, but doing it in an embodied way.

Marlis Schweitzer: Thank you. We've now all shared all of our exercises. At this point, we would like to open the conversation up to the room. Let's begin by addressing questions to certain groups or by offering thoughts about additional applications.

Gray: First, I want to respond to Nicholas and his group's terrific festival idea. Having done many assessments for the Canada Council, and having learned so much from going through the assessment process, I think that is another benefit of the exercise. When you are forced to choose which performance is going to get funded—or in your case which shows will be selected for a festival—you gain valuable insight into real world theatre practices.

Schweitzer: I just want to ask a question about the written responses that you suggested students would submit to the instructor. Would the rest of the class read the written submissions? If so, would that be a nice way of doing an overview of the whole year, perhaps in preparation for the exam?

Barry Freeman: I like the idea of the responses being more public because, in my own experience, if students have to show one another their writing they tend to put more time into it. So I've used a blog in the class, and a blog is one thing that could accompany this and it collectively pools their ideas together in one spot. They can all review those to do maybe a longer writing assignment that is their justification of which two or three productions they would choose at the end of the course. But having all that material in one place where they can go through it is a great idea.

Hanson: Nelson, that's an interesting point about the Canada Council because that is actually how we started on this, and then somebody came up with this festival idea, and we thought the Canada Council might seem a bit too bureaucratic to students. We were also talking about game shows and reality shows and about injecting an element of fun that makes this exercise dynamic and spirited. This festival idea seemed to be the best of both worlds. It was kind of gimmick-free. It didn't have like "There are four dragons with this much money and ...." (*Laughter.*) But it also has more live action, instead of a straight-up, written, bureaucratic type of application. We were thinking of a second year class as the site for this assignment as the festival idea may be grounded more in their immediate interests and passions. But I think certainly it could easily be adapted to explore the process of grant applications.

Prendergast: I think it's a great model and, as Nelson said, it's a real world application. I just want to add a possible extension or maybe a layer, which is coming out of Neil Freeman's work around the purpose of teaching as a subversive activity, which argues that education should function as a counterbalance to society rather than a replication of it. So as somebody who is currently writing about utopian performative pedagogy, I might inject into this model the question: Do we have to support a competitive model of doing theatre? Or is there another way? Is there a utopian vision of what this theatre festival might look like, one that has the same elements but doesn't necessarily have to function in a competitive, capitalistic, consumer-driven manner? So that's just a question, and it comes from critical pedagogy, but I think it might move the model in a slightly different direction.

Perry: I was just going to say, building on what Monica started, why not use our ideals of what we wish it was like when you are before an arts council? Instead of making it a judgment or a win, we could make it appear like a feedback process. So the process has a peer jury, but instead of choosing and eliminating, it's about developing. It's about getting feedback from a jury but you are also always going to be accepted, always going to be worthy of pursuing. You are getting your peers to assess it according to *your* criteria or objectives, to feed back into a process that is recursive.

Stephenson: Do the winners get to perform their pieces at the end or is the festival purely hypothetical?

Hanson: I think in our context it was purely hypothetical.

Stephenson: In a course we teach at Queen's in first year, the students are in lab groups that run parallel to the lectures. At the end of the first semester they present what we are calling "trailers." They do little trailers for the play they've been assigned. They are short, they are punchy, and they tell us everything we need to know about a particular play in three minutes. And then in the second semester, there are extended presentations by each of the groups, which take place in the last four weeks of the course. And I love the idea of adding this kind of analysis component onto that, where other students are being asked as a jury to evaluate what they have seen in the first part and to write about it.

Catherine Graham: I would actually like to respond to both of those comments. In our group, we talked about the whole problem of competition. One option we considered was that maybe it's not *our* festival. It's *a* festival outside us. We are "Team Thirty-three" and we are trying to put forward our best three players. We felt one of the keys is that the instructor set very clear criteria for the festival so we're not just doing a popularity contest. But I think the other side of that, and where the pedagogy can be subversive, is if something is not getting selected, there is the possibility of stopping to say "Okay, maybe we need to question these criteria" if we're seeing that a piece we thought was valuable is not getting chosen.

The other thing I wanted to raise in relation to Jenn's comment is the problem that in some of these (particularly first year) classes, we are trying to do everything in one class. Maybe they don't need to do the full-out production in *this* class. But how do we start thinking about making links between different classes? This might require more communication among professors than always happens. And it's a much bigger problem for people who are teaching sessionally, who aren't necessarily well integrated, and I think that's something for us to think about. How do we make sure that when that sessional instructor goes back to finish their doctorate we don't lose everything that went on in that room?

Solga: Catherine, other issues that might come up in that context are—well for me—having very few other people in my program who are willing to buy into this kind of work. Ensuring continuity might be easier in a dedicated theatre department where, presumably, you have a bunch of people who are willing. But I think you are absolutely right that it is worth our labour, however we might do it, to start breaking down boundaries between professors and sessional instructors because students need that continuity, and they are always telling us that, and when they don't get it they are frustrated and angry.

Stephenson: I just want to speak briefly to Catherine's point about departmental curriculum integration. I'm sure many of you have heard this but there's a move, certainly in Ontario, coming down from the Ontario Council of Academic Vice-Presidents to develop UUDLE (University Undergraduate Degree Level Expectations).[2] You need to show how you meet six criteria in order to demonstrate that your degree is viable. We have started this in our department in a really preliminary way by doing UUDLE analyses of individual courses, starting at the bottom. So how does Drama 100 fill some of these UUDLE requirements, and which ones are left unfilled? Of course, there is the expectation that upper-year courses will then take up other UUDLEs with the idea that, when you get to the top, the whole program will be UUDLE'd. But this is coming down from the government, to standardize undergraduate degrees, to say "Yes, our degree actually does x, y, z." It's a great moment to, you know, take the bull by the horns and try to integrate courses, because people are really reluctant to say, "My course does this but not that. Does your course do this?" It is a great idea but it's a really difficult discussion to have.

Jordão: This group said that they envision doing the festival exercise with a class of forty to sixty students. I'm just wondering about the physical line-up exercise and the pass the ball exercise. What do you envision in terms of numbers for these activities?

Stephen Johnson: I think one of the issues we had was: What kinds of classes are we talking about here? If you have a small acting class you may want to discuss a certain project, but if you have a theatre history class of forty to sixty people, let's say, can you have people standing up and moving around? That is a long line with, as I envision it, everyone bunched at one end, and then some brave soul waaaaay at the other end of the room. Then you start dialoguing … maybe.

We had particular issues with what you do depending on the nature of the class. And I think also, moving a little bit beyond your question, we had issues with how much you can ask students to do without personalizing what becomes very personal, very quickly. So we talked about sending students out to speak to someone who is *other* than themselves. It could be someone five years older or younger—just someone not in their world. And then you can move on from there to a variety of other worlds, and then come back and perform that, speak to that, describe that, perhaps have a short transcript of that or talk about the casting of that. And use someone like Anna Deavere Smith or *The Laramie Project* or other instances of transcription theatre to frame the experience. And perhaps move then into the idea of profiling, typing, and self-reflection. Our group didn't present this exercise because the question I asked, being the bureaucrat I am, was: "Gee, do you have to go through the ethics review board to be able to send your undergraduate class out to interview somebody for fifteen minutes?" That takes a while.

Perry: But they are in your own classrooms. The *others* are all there.

Prendergast: You could do interviews within the class, which might solve that problem. It is a performance ethnography project, really a mini one, and the results would vary from institution to institution. In our Applied Theatre Program at the University of Victoria, we do this all the time, and institutional review doesn't seem to be an issue. We sort of have blanket coverage because we are an established program. But I can see in other settings it would be problematic.

Levin: Are there any questions about the casting exercise that you put forward at the beginning of the session? My guess is that we could spend two hours discussing the ethics of the interesting interview assignment that you just talked about!

Johnson: One of the reasons for the casting assignment was an attempt to depersonalize and to give examples of how other people have dealt with this kind of problem of cultural difference in a theatrical setting. And then say, "Okay now you do it," and do something radical.

Natalie Alvarez: Just to elaborate on the exercise as a group member, what is key for me if I were to adopt this exercise in, say, a theatre history class would be to get students to talk about the implications and mechanics behind representation. So what happens semiotically, what happens to meaning-making, when you do this kind of casting? Because the impasse I reach during class discussions is that students are absolutely resistant to looking at representational issues in the text when they imply queer readings or racialized readings. That's how I could see myself adopting that exercise.

Perry: Just very quickly, my question is whether it is possible to depersonalize this, and if so, why would you want to do that if you are dealing with diversity in the classroom, or even in casting?

Alvarez: The issue for me when teaching at Brock is that I see a sea of white and then maybe three visible minority students. And what I have found is that it gets personal very quickly and then you make the non-white students the object of the discussion, or at least they feel that way because they are in such a minority. If I was teaching at the University of Toronto, which I have in the past, I probably wouldn't feel concerned because the class is so diverse. So that's my only hesitation.

Perry: But isn't it just as personal for the "sea of white"?

Alvarez: I feel that the problem with the performance ethnography exercises is that they need to challenge the unidirectional optics. They can't just be about, "let me find someone who is different from me." They need to go back to a self-reflexive "How am I racialized?" or "How am I gendered?" or "How do I read?" or "How am I constituted by that person I encounter?" Because I find that these questions can get to the problem of white privilege, of "I can't see race" … in other words, because "I don't need to see it." How do you bring discussion back to the personal so that the "sea of white" can become cognizant of the way in which they too are inscribed and racialized? So we can resist the colonizing gaze and instead see ourselves as always determined by something other than ourselves. That's the question that lingers, for me, after our discussion.

Levin: Stephen, when you say "depersonalizing," then, you don't mean that you ultimately want to depersonalize, to have the students dismiss their own connection with the racial content. Instead, could we say that you are using a strategy that is deliberately task-based? You are crafting an assignment that is oriented towards analyzing a cultural text or play and then that text leads students into the personal, rather than starting with the intensely personal ("Who am I?") which can be alienating if that's the opening frame.

Johnson: There would be too much pushback and antagonism in the classroom immediately if you didn't provide some kind of intermediary question or object that they can focus on. It's just some kind of critical distance to begin with, and then they can start to apply it to themselves.

Levin: Right.

Graham: I would like to name it differently. I'm not sure I would call it "depersonalizing," and as I'm listening to you talk about it I actually really like this idea for a couple of reasons. To me it's "contextualizing," so that you understand that you are not the first person who has ever thought about this, and you don't have to think about it only on the basis of your personal experience in life or in this classroom. There have been numerous historical attempts to solve this problem. I'm not sure that we really empower students when we ask them to revert to only what they have been able to know about their own lives. And, if we do that, then why are they coming to university? I mean if you can figure all of this out by just looking at your own lives, why pay the tuition? It's expensive. I like to be in a position sometimes to say, "Oh, okay, so *you* would take the Laurence Olivier solution, whereas *you* would prefer the Anna Deveare Smith solution." And this contextualizing approach allows students also to start to understand that the personal position you have come to has been conditioned by culture. I think that kind of exercise allows them to see this isn't exclusively about your personal morality. If you come to see the world this way it's because you have grown up in a culture that has led you to see the world this way, and here is how other people have grappled with the culture. Otherwise, I find this discussion comes back really quickly to "Who is a good person?" and "Who is not a good person?" It goes nowhere when you are on that track.

Solga: I just wanted to say that doing stuff like that makes it a thousand times easier for the students in the class to push their own thinking. Because when you say "You would prefer the Olivier model and you'd prefer the Smith model," then a student can put up his or her hand and say "Yeah, but the problem with the Olivier model is…." If it's personal, they are not going to want to do that. So the students are empowered to push their own discourse by looking at it through those frameworks. The student who proposed the Olivier framework is probably going to be a little hurt, but it's not going to deteriorate nearly as much as it would from "Well, I actually think that John is completely wrong and totally racist." And I've had that happen in the classroom and that's alarming … and then you stop and deal with that for forty-five minutes.

Schweitzer: Just in the interest of moving us forward, I have a question for Jenn's group. I really liked that ball exercise. I think it's really useful and wanted to suggest that another "S" word could be "synthesis"—you know if you wanted to have PASS (paraphrase, application, synthesis, spiral) or something like that to have the correct spelling!
[Laughter]

I have a question, though, about flow. If the class becomes acclimatized to a certain format of discussion, it's nice because everyone is familiar and comfortable with it and we are able to push the analysis forward. But on the flipside, does it interrupt other kinds of flow? Do you predetermine a kind of structure to the conversation with PAS, and if so, how might you get around that? Maybe it's about "Here's the ball and I'm going to throw it across the room." How would you do that?

Gray: So what I hear Marlis saying is …
[Laughter]

Stephenson: That's a really great question and may need a little bit of clarification. The actual passing of the ball around the circle is a training exercise in which you would not normally do that.

Schweitzer: I understand that, but what happens if that's the training, and then what if they are so well trained—

Levin:—What is the next step? How do you get it to flow after that?

Stephenson: That's a great question because this "one, two, three" process might not be always what you want. You might want some other kind of response.

Allan Boss: When I was teaching a graduate level research methods class, I brought in somebody to talk about the scientific method because I wanted the students to be exposed to the very rigid methodology that exists in the scientific world. The scientists very clearly said, after they explained the method, "But generally we throw this away." So it's about learning the rules and then getting rid of them.

Gray: Can I just say that I really support the paraphrase idea, because I find that in research papers, students just cut and paste quotations in a list instead of paraphrasing. And it's in the paraphrase that the actual essay gets written. So developing that skill orally is useful and you can tell students that this is something they can work with in their papers.

Stephenson: The "paraphrase" was something Erin [Hurley] laid on the table first, and what I particularly like about it is that students have to listen. They actually have to listen to what the other person is saying. You can't just have your say that is unconnected with anything that has gone before, which is, again, quite typical. So there is respectful listening built into the process.

Levin: Just to return to Marlis's point about how you can get a conversation to flow again after doing the exercise—I have two thoughts. One is that there are a couple of dialogic conventions that aren't contained in PAS that appear in good conversations—for example, one you brought up in your second exercise, "the question." Sometimes a good intervention is to say, "I think that's really interesting. Can I ask you more about your point?" This would be based on a paraphrase, "I just heard what you said. That was really interesting to me." But then the question extends it, "Is this what you mean, Natalie, when you say x?" I bring this up because you could do a day or two of the PAS and then you could add another kind of critical intervention like the question. And I'm sure there are many possible add-ons we could think of. Then it becomes a game and you keep adding to it to make it more dynamic and allow the structure of the dialogue to change and flow. My other thought is that in order to get students to really appreciate conversation we might actually take students to a conference or expose them to sites where they have to listen to people have good conversations. Then you could ask them, "Why was that a strong dialogue?" and "What are the elements of that script?"

Prendergast: I'm riffing off Laura's idea here because you could discuss these skills using plays like *Oleanna* or *I'm Not Rappaport* where dialogue between two characters is really at the heart of the text. I think that young people are not very skilled at good conversation and that our culture has in fact de-skilled conversation. So I really think a crucial pedagogical question that we need to ask across our field, across education in general, is how do we get young people to talk effectively to each other? We have the advantage of having plays available that show that happening. So that's another layer to this process that could be really exciting.

Alvarez: I like how the ball passes to everyone so everyone is obliged to participate in this conversation. I just want to know what everyone's opinion on this is. I've been continuously exposed to fellow colleagues that try to come up with alternative assignments for those people who aren't comfortable speaking in a group. I'm wondering what you think about that because I'm of the mind that we should teach students to engage critically in discussion face-to-face because everything in society has a way of disabling that. But this exercise, I imagine, puts people in a situation where they have to talk whether they want to or not, and is that coercive? What about those people who are not comfortable speaking and do we enable that? Do we allow them to refrain?

Stephenson: My own sense of it is—and I'm sure there are twenty-four other opinions on it—that being able to speak is an important skill. That said, it's incumbent on the instructor and the students in the room from the outset to create a safe environment. So there have to be structures in place to say, "This is a room where we have a community. These are the kinds of things that may be said and these are the kinds of things that are not appropriate." We have to set up that safe space to speak from the beginning, and then I think you can require people to speak within those structures, within that kind of safety zone.

Erin Hurley: Our idea for the format of the exercise was that even shy students—which I was and still am—would have something to fall back on so that there is a pattern, which gives them a launching point. So they would have key phrases like, "What I hear you saying is …," "I would like to apply it to …," or "That reminds me of …." It just gives them a start. And there's nothing saying that others can't help, that they can't say, "I'm stuck at A," and then we work as a group. We talked about having a box with keywords in it that could start another set of questions or something like other prompts that would enable them to talk.

Graham: I agree with Erin. I think what makes the space safe is the passing of the ball. The fact that everyone has to speak turns it into a game because it has really rigid rules. So it takes the pressure off the individual: "I just have to roll the dice and move six spaces. I just have to finish these sentences that are pre-given for me." But I also suspect that many people are very shy about speaking because they are afraid they won't be listened to. And the other thing about any kind of talking object is it creates a space where they can be listened to, and they can make their comments as long or as short as they like. So I feel like I am accommodating them, but I'm not *not* requiring them to do the exercise. They have to get over the bar, but I am providing the step stool to help them do that.

Solga: The other thing you can do easily is set up context beforehand. We talked a lot in our group about how important it is to have clear objectives, a clear context, and a clear mandate. To set it up you say, "This is the exercise we are doing, these are the skills that I hope are going to result from this, these skills are essential to the work you are going to do in this class. I completely respect any fear you might have about this, but you are going to have to do it because it's an essential component of the class and that's that." If you set that up at the outset, students can perceive it as an expectation of them, rather than something they can immediately grieve and say "Oh, but it's not fair that …." You have just told them exactly why it's fair and why it's an expectation, and you've just made things really nice and clear. In my experience, when you do that, students are like, "Oh, okay I get it and I am willing to give it a shot."

Schweitzer: I think Natalie's question about format and addressing different student needs is important as well. Perhaps another way of using this exercise would be online. You could very easily use PAS in writing. So you could say, "Over the next week I want each of your blog posts to directly respond to the previous person who was posting." Shy students, who may have really amazing ideas, can then do that, and then the instructor can even build on the comments later in the classroom, like "This is where we were online; let's continue and pass the ball in the real world." Connections like that could be a really helpful way of encouraging more students.

Stephen Johnson (foreground) and Richie Wilcox listen attentively to a group member talk about ways to approach racially charged subject matter in a classroom environment.
Photo by Marlis Schweitzer

Levin: Are there any follow-up questions for the last group?

Hurley: So in your evaluation exercise you read the first sentence of the introduction to the paper and then you read the last sentence of the introduction, and then the people make an image in the circle. I wonder if that ends up producing writing that is then oralized, that is not written. Of course, we write conference papers differently than we write articles because people have to sit there for twenty minutes and listen to you, but I wonder what that transfer is. It may be less of an issue in an introductory course because you just want to be sure they understand what they are communicating.

Megan Macdonald: It came from an exercise that I have done with my students for the last five years, and it was only the first and last sentences. It wasn't introductory paragraphs, conclusions, or anything like that. I did get my students—after the first essay in the first four to six weeks of the course—to bring their essays in and, sitting in pairs, read out their first and last sentences for every paragraph. The person across from you then tells you what they think your essay was about. And it worked. They then went back

(l to r): Megan Macdonald, Mia Perry, Kim Solga, Aida Jordão, and Andy Houston discuss strategies for assessing student work.
Photo by Marlis Schweitzer

than text—into an image—you could do it sitting down. You could also do it in a way that differs from the kind of conventional performance format; you could draw an image that comes to mind.

Stephenson: But you still need a student who is able to see that image.

Solga: The idea is transforming the text into something performative—I used the term "performative writing" at one point—and then, turning it back again. And this addresses Erin's point. I think that you are absolutely right that you start getting hung up on "Okay, what did I understand when I heard it?" So then one of the things you want to do when you are turning it back into text is to focus on clarity, clarity of image. Even when we read, it's wonderful to be able to see the image, and cognitive science tells us that we

and, by the next essay, their paragraphs were starting to come together. That was one tiny idea that we used to drive this forward. Because it was one-on-one there wasn't a lot of oralizing of the whole idea and the entire essay, but I see that this depends on how you facilitate it.

Jordão: If you are worried about the communication being done orally by someone reading out loud instead of reading to themselves, you could always have the text written down on slips of paper and given to the people who are standing in the circle: "Here is the first and last sentence. Read it, scrunch it, throw it away, and do your image." You can introduce lots of variables. This is just one way of doing it. The idea is to get the physicalization, to move it to a different level of communication, as an experiment. And as Kim was saying, you explain your hypothesis, and see if it works.

Stephenson: This is just sort of an aside, and this applies particularly to what you guys have done because it's physical and performance-based, and it applies generally in many cases. Over the last two years of teaching I have become increasingly aware of students with significant disabilities. I have seen, in my classes and in my department, blind students, students who are deaf, and students with significant mobility issues. And all of these exercises, everything you plan, require us to constantly think about accommodation. Your particular exercise makes me think, "I can see what the barriers are." And then I have to start thinking about "How would I accommodate particular students in that?" It's been a constant challenge recently and it's on my mind.

Solga: I think you are totally right Jenn, and there are two things I want to emphasize about this. First of all, because it's about turning something text-based into something other

The workshop began with four groups of five to six participants talking about specific pedagogical challenges and then transitioned to brainstorming activities that addressed these challenges.
Photo by Marlis Schweitzer

read by creating images. It's that process of going from thinking to text to image and performance, then back to text, then back to thinking, and teaching students that performance isn't just this cool thing we do just because ... but it is a tool for cognitive work. It's a tool for understanding; it's a tool for writing. And again, the mandate has to be clear at the outset of the class: "We are going to work today using this tool. Our goal is to make your writing clearer. Does your intention match up with what happened?"

Schweitzer: I think we're at time so we have to stop for today. We'd like to say thank you. This has been incredibly inspiring and I'm excited to go and revise all of my syllabi with the new assignments! But we also wanted to pose a challenge. Given what we have heard today, I know there are definitely ideas that I would want to take up in my classes. So we would like this not to be a one-time only event, and if there are those of you who thought, "I definitely want to explore this idea," then keep in touch, and we might be able to reconvene either next year or at a future date, and say, "You know we brainstormed all these ideas. We had some really concrete assignments. How did they work? Did they go over? Did the students resist them? What was your adaptation?" In this way we might continue the discussion.

Notes

1. See, for example, Monkie Moseki and Salome Schulze, "Promoting self-regulated learning to improve achievement: A study in higher education." *Africa Education Review* 7.2 (Oct. 2010): 356–375; Christine Goh and Ysnita Taib, "Metacognitive instruction in listening for young learners." *ELT Journal: English Language Teachers Journal* 60.3 (July 2006): 222–232; and Regin Boulware-Gooden et al., "Instruction of metacognitive strategies enhances reading comprehension and vocabulary achievement of third-grade students." *Reading Teacher* 61.1 (September 2007): 70–77.

2. Information on this initiative is available from OCAV's website: http://www.cou.on.ca/Issues-Resources/Student-Resources/Publications/Reports/PDFs/University-Undergraduate-Degree-Level-Expectations.aspx. Many universities are developing guidelines for instructors as well. For a representative example, see http://cte.uwaterloo.ca/teaching_resources/OCAV/index.html.

3. Natalie and Stephen discuss student resistance to discussions of identity politics in an article included in this issue of *CTR* ("Minstrels in the Classroom: Teaching, Race, and Blackface", 31–37).

Laura Levin and Marlis Schweitzer teach in the Department of Theatre at York University.

Accountable and Theatrical Acts of Witness: Queen's University DRAM 476 Testimonial Project Pieces 2010

Introduced and curated by Kalanthe Khaiat

Brett Payette, Emily Herczeg, Catriona Graveson, and Alyssa Bignell perform *Choice?* on 24 November 2010.
Photo courtesy of Emily Herczeg

Caution: Copyright Marissa Nascimben, Katherine MacNeill, Isabel Winson, Jacqueline Andrade, Lauren Jackson, Stephanie Russell, Sean Ogle, Ruth Goodwin, Austin Schaeffer, Jon Hallis, Katie Muzyka, Mark Rochford, Anja Zeljkovic, Brett Payette, Emily Herczeg, Catriona Graveson, Alyssa Bignell, Jennie Appleby, Kathleen Jerome, Blythe Hubbard, and Alain Richer. These scripts are protected under the copyright laws of Canada and all other countries of the Copyright Union. Changes to the script are forbidden without the written consent of the authors. Rights to produce, film, or record in any medium, in any language, by any group, are retained by the authors. The moral right of the authors has been asserted. For performance rights, contact the authors through Kalanthe Khaiat, 373 Union Street, Kingston, ON, K7L 2R4.

General Introduction

In my most recent cover letters for upcoming summer theatre festival work I described the kind of theatre I hoped to collaborate in creating as "socially conscious, engaging, thought-provoking, and formally innovative." Conceiving of theatre—and of artistic creation, more broadly speaking—in these terms, and prioritizing these particular qualities, I attribute to having been a student in Professor Julie Salverson's DRAM 476 class in 2009.

The title of the course is "Cultures of Theatre: Ethics and Performance, Facing History in a 'Tragic Culture.'" Julie's course provokes students to think not just about how or why we make theatre, but also how to do so while respecting and harnessing theatre's power as a medium of socio-historical—and profoundly personal—representation, retelling, and commentary. Building on Peter Brooks' challenge to those of us who create and produce art "to consider all of our actions public, communal and witnessed," the course is designed to "explore how to think about what is at stake for artists and educators as translators of stories of public violence" (Salverson, "DRAM 476"). In 2009 we referred to our work in the class as dealing with how to tell "difficult stories." DRAM 476 demands intellectual and *emotional* engagement with some of the realities of the world that are most difficult to talk about.

These conversations do not happen often in Queen's Drama, partly because students tend to be so widely and heavily involved (theatrically and otherwise) that most time spent together is devoted to accomplishing a specific project. Drama feels different from Gender Studies (where I did the other part of my undergraduate work), and Cultural Studies (where I am pursuing my MA). Although every course in Drama demands passion for studying and participating in the creation of theatre, only DRAM 476 (cross listed to Cultural Studies) explicitly asks us as students to be accountable in our theatrical work. The forms of accountability the course demands are: to our individual aesthetic and ethical values; to the well-being of everyone participating in the discussions; and, for the Testimony Performance Project, specifically to the people whose stories form the basis for each piece.

Julie's assignment sheet describes the project that created the following short plays as "an exercise in performing testimony and exploring vocabularies of representation," and defines a Testimony Performance as "an act of witness within the confines of a culture of spectacle" (Salverson, "Testimony" 1). One of the bases for this project is to consider ourselves as potential witnesses of any and all crises around the world, past and present. The culture of spectacle manifests most obviously in contemporary Western mass media, in which moments of trauma from across the globe are represented for the consumption of a Euro-American public. One way to understand what the course calls our "tragic culture" is as an obsession with showing, telling, and receiving stories of violence that are not our own. By participating in this culture, we unconsciously become witnesses to violence, no matter how far removed from us in time and space the specific violations may be. The Testimony Performance Project asks students first to be conscious of their positionality (who they are as witnesses) and then to perform theatrical testimony from this acknowledged (and fluid) standpoint.

Two key questions immediately strike me regarding this assignment. Why is the focus on other people's "difficult stories" when students may well have their own? And, how can we avoid speaking for those others in a way that silences their voices, giving voice instead to us, as privileged Queen's students? Focusing on other people's stories reproduces the potential for voyeurism (implicit in mass media coverage), and for fetishizing an Other and her or his experience on the basis of her or his difference. This project, however, urges students to engage with other people (not Others!) and their stories in a completely different mode: not as passive consumers, but as active witnesses and retellers who recognize and respect the individuality and agency of the people directly involved in their chosen crisis.

Topics with personal connections must be explicitly connected to a broader social issue (this speaks to my second question). One of the ways to create a testimonial for a specific traumatic event that does not silence anyone is to incorporate the voices of a variety of people who were directly involved, as both victims and witnesses. A danger emerges when "difficult stories" are reduced to single-perspective narratives. (And yet, in this class, simply presenting a selection of viewpoints on the topic would not constitute an effective Testimonial Performance either.) To paraphrase Julie's response to a question about the extent to which these pieces could or should take a stance on their topic: *witnesses, when providing testimony, are responsible for being aware of their assumptions and biases, not for being disinterested in what happened.* They should incorporate those biases openly into their testimony. Doing so is part of what ensures that the witness's voice does not subsume other important voices, or hide behind others as though the witness was not also a significant part of the story. In developing a Testimony Performance, then, students are accountable as witnesses to the specific moment within their chosen event, and as witnesses to their own thoughts and feelings while researching the topic. Likewise, each piece below encourages readers or audience members to consider their own accountability as witnesses.

I want to extend my deepest thanks to Julie for inviting me to participate in this project, and to all the students of DRAM 476 for being so open to having me work with them during the process of creating the pieces below. I also want to congratulate each group on work that is socially conscious, engaging, thought-provoking, and formally innovative.

One last note: The order of the five pieces below does not reflect the order of performance; it is the sequence that I believe affords the most interesting read.

Just a Number

By Marissa Nascimben, Katherine MacNeill, Isabel Winson, and Jacqueline Andrade

Curator's Introduction

Nothing in any of my discussions with this group prepared me for the visceral uneasiness they created by having Robert Pickton speak through a severed pig's head mounted on a human body. Combined with the fairy makeup they chose for the Victims, they achieved precisely the surreal, carnivalesque sense of horror they described to me in our first meeting. I shared with them a statistic I had learned from a presentation on the status of women in Canada, delivered by Professor Kathleen Lahey at the Kingston Interval House 2010 annual general meeting. The Canadian federal govern-

David Epstein (Pickton), Marissa Nascimben, Katherine MacNeill, Isabel Winson, and Jacqueline Andrade (Victims) enter the playing space for *Just a Number*, 26 November 2010.
Photo courtesy of Katherine MacNeill

ment allocates almost three times as much money per hog as it does per woman in Canada ($3.57 per hog, compared to $1.21 per woman). *Just a Number* renders the combination of absurdity and horror in that fact into theatrical language.

Together with knowing they wanted to develop a movement-heavy piece, the group was concerned about moving away from the media's uneven representation of Pickton as an individual monster to be reviled and the women he murdered as a collective of victims to be pitied. They wanted to find a way to give a voice to the victims as individuals—without speaking for them. This piece resists and reverses the prevalent discourse surrounding the case that makes the murderer central. In *Just a Number*, the murderer becomes of peripheral interest to the four bodies that represent the murdered women. These victims are aware of their public status, each being no more than "just a number." They transcend this status, morphing between functioning as a collective and as individuals, and presenting the audience with glimpses of those who knew them as loved ones whose lives and stories have been taken. The victims never identify themselves as prostitutes or sex workers. Even the newspaper clipping incorporated into the piece refers to them as "women." Although some of the murdered women's stories have received media coverage, this group chose to do more than simply translate the available information from page to stage. Michelle's story, told by her mother through the body of a fellow murdered woman, is not privileged by virtue of being known. Juxtaposing it with E. E. Cummings' "anyone lived in a pretty how town," the authors challenge the audience to recognize that each of the murdered women have life stories which will never become widely known. The violence inflicted upon them by Pickton is part of a broader, systematic erasure of the identity of the poorest and most stigmatized people. Each is the "anyone" of "anyone lived in a pretty how town," brutally transformed into a "noone," but here, asserting herself as someone nevertheless.

Just a Number

(The Voice of PICKTON speaks as the women enter.)

PICKTON: I my-self am not from this world, but I am born into this world through my earthly mother and if I had to change any-thing I would not, for I have done no wrong. My earthly mother found a boy lying unconscious by the side of the road and she hauled him into a nearby ditch, where he drowned.

(All VICTIMS are clumped together. They are all facing inwards with their heads together.)

VICTIMS *(The following evidence contains graphic information.)*

(VICTIM ONE breaks out of the group and walks towards a newspaper lying on the floor. She picks it up and reads.)

VICTIM ONE: The Pickton farm in Port Coquitlam, B.C., in 2002. In a massive police investigation, forensic experts—including 102 anthropologists—spent two years sifting through 370,000 cubic yards of mud and pig manure, looking for pieces of missing women.

VICTIM ONE *(turns to the group.)*

VICTIM ONE: Did we know?

VICTIMS: When we weep, we weep alone.

VICTIM ONE: Did we weep? Can we mourn?

(The other VICTIMS bring her back into the group and they all come together, tightly.)

VICTIMS: *(Some parts are spoken individually and some along with the rest of the group.)*

My sister has been missing for seven years.

That looks like Dave Pickton, the brother.

Robert Pickton is charged with killing fifteen women.

Fifteen?

Five?

Twenty-six?

Fifty?

He said he wanted it to be an even fifty.

But sixty-three have disappeared.

What number am I?

What number are we?

What's my name?

Pickton, age fifty-four, ran an unlicensed slaughterhouse.

Human remains mixed with pigs remain there.

Teeth, bone fragments—a purse?

VICTIMS (break out into a line facing one way.)

VICTIM ONE: Where are you from?

VICTIMS (turn one by one towards the other.)

VICTIM TWO: These blocks—bloodstains, crack vials, used condoms.

VICTIM ONE: "Low track."

VICTIM THREE: Canada's poorest postal code.

VICTIM FOUR: I can go for $10.00, $15.00, $20.00?

VICTIMS: He seemed like a totally nice guy.

VICTIM ONE: He had lots of dope.

VICTIMS: Before we even got to his place,

VICTIM TWO: Before we even left downtown,

VICTIM FOUR: We probably smoked a little under a gram of crack.

VICTIMS: His stash of drugs was bottomless.

VICTIM THREE: He was kind of picky with the girls.

VICTIMS: He picked—

VICTIM ONE: One

VICTIM TWO: Twenty-two

VICTIM THREE: Fifteen

VICTIM FOUR: Fifty-two?

VICTIMS: Numbered. Together. We are.

> VICTIMS *(roll together on the ground. One steps out representing a worried MOTHER.)*

MOTHER: My Michelle, my dear Michelle, where are you? Do you remember when I would take you to Stanley Park in your pretty pink dress and feed the squirrels? Remember how we would sit at a coffee shop sipping chocolate milk from fancy glasses and seeing who could make the most bubbles? To me you are my beautiful daughter, so full of smiles after a full day falling asleep as we watched a silly movie. I would brush your blonde hair away from your forehead as you were always so warm when you slept, sometimes you would pat my hand, others times you would whisper something. I never could hear what you would whisper and now I would give my life to have you whisper it. How I wish I could protect you and brush the hair away from your forehead, just to watch you sleep—God, what would that take? What can I give to bring my Michelle back to me? I have given you buckets of tears, screams of anguish, a million prayers, please take me to where she is, I need to hear her whisper. I love you, I miss you.

> *(Another woman emerges from the group as a FAMILY MEMBER.)*

FAMILY MEMBER: Willy Pickton knows what he has done. There has been DNA found on the farm of some missing women and no charges laid for whatever reason. Why doesn't this guy just fess up? When he is convicted of the grisly crimes he won't see the light of day anyway. Why not just fess up to all he knows and let us put our loved ones to rest. Let us have closure.

> *(The other two VICTIMS approach the MOTHER and FAMILY MEMBER and console them with an embrace. This turns into a struggle. They push and pull each other until they are finally defeated, on the floor. They rise slowly while reciting a poem: "anyone lived in a pretty how town" by E. E. Cummings.)*

anyone lived in a pretty how town

(with up so floating many bells down)

spring summer autumn winter

he sang his didn't he danced his did

Women and men (both little and small)

cared for anyone not at all

they sowed their isn't they reaped their same

sun moon stars rain

children guessed (but only a few

and down they forgot as up they grew

autumn winter spring summer)

that noone loved him more by more

when by now and tree by leaf

she laughed his joy she cried his grief

bird by snow and stir by still

anyone's any was all to her

someones married their everyones

laughed their cryings and did their dance

(sleep wake hope and then) they

said their nevers they slept their dream

stars rain sun moon

(and only the snow can begin to explain

how children are apt to forget to remember

with up so floating many bells down)

one day anyone died i guess

(and noone stooped to kiss his face)

busy folk buried them side by side

little by little and was by was

all by all and deep by deep

and more by more they dream their sleep

noone and anyone earth by april

wish by spirit and if by yes.

Women and men (both dong and ding)

summer autumn winter spring

reaped their sowing and went their came

sun moon stars rain

> *(The VICTIMS stand facing forwards. They close their eyes and reach out for each other. If they find contact with each other they pull together quickly.)*

* * *

Bloody Sunday

By Lauren Jackson, Stephanie Russell, Sean Ogle, Ruth Goodwin, and Austin Schaeffer

Curator's Introduction

This group focused on the publication of the Saville Report on 15 June 2010[1] and UK Prime Minister David Cameron's subsequent apology to the British people for the actions of British paratroopers on Bloody Sunday (30 January 1972). In early discussions they explained that they wanted to explore the significance of an official apology as a retroactive, performative gesture. The final product explores how this official apology, decades after the fact, is part of the larger process of creating a historical narrative by remembering a moment from a certain perspective. By juxtaposing various points of view, the BBC project performed in this piece uses the figures of the victim, the Protestant child witness, the soldier who opened fire, the outraged militant, and the bereaved partner to construct one specific way of remembering the incident. This singular narrative shapes the stories of the imagined individuals under the guise of testimony. The Stage Manager's focus on getting everything to look, sound, and feel right for the screen emphasizes the performed disregard for complexity in this narrative. Even David Cameron, as represented, is not allowed to speak in his own, readily available words in delivering his apology. The Prime Minister in this documentary must embody the deep conflict that the government preceding his by almost forty years must have felt. What appears on every "cue card labeled BBC" is, as the Cameraperson interjects, "such bullshit." This dissident voice is forcibly silenced.

Bloody Sunday also addresses discursive violence at work in Prime Minister David Cameron's apology. The play suggests that this apology frames the people gunned down by armed forces, and by extension all people in Northern Ireland who advocate(d) for separation from the UK, as perpetual victims. Locking them in this identity denies any progress made in the thirty years separating the act from the apology. The Cameraperson's outburst, "I'm not scared to talk about what happened ... I'm scared that nobody will listen!" succinctly addresses the challenge in discussing "difficult stories."

The treatment of the audience for this piece also concerns ways of remembering. Audience members are separated according to no particular criteria, and made to experience the piece under forced comfort or forced discomfort. On a literal level, this device makes the experience of segregation and arbitrary treatment by authority figures real for the audience, echoing everyday experience in Ireland during the Troubles. As staged for the class presentation, it also allowed one half of the audience to watch the performance from a removed space (the Rotunda balcony). Although these audience members must endure the Security Guard's bullying, they are physically removed from complicity in the official narrative being constructed on the stage floor.

Bloody Sunday

Cast List

STAGE MANAGER, *Lauren Jackson*

CAMERAPERSON, *Stephanie Russell*

ACTOR NUMBER ONE, *Sean Ogle*

ACTOR NUMBER TWO, *Ruth Goodwin*

SECURITY GUARD, *Austin Schaeffer*

> *(The audience is separated into Catholics and Protestants. Half the audience is greeted nicely by the ACTORS, who invite them to sit comfortably up near the stage. The rest are shoved upstairs by a SECURITY GUARD and told to be quiet. This "event" is hosted by the BBC production company commissioned by the British Government, for a filming of Bloody Sunday. All the shots of the ACTORS are projected as live feed onto the stage behind the scene at hand. The two ACTORS hand out candy while a CAMERAPERSON sets up the equipment on stage. There is a STAGE MANAGER getting ready onstage, preparing cue cards and warming up.)*

STAGE MANAGER: *(Standing at a podium marked "BBC.")* Welcome everyone. The British Broadcasting Corporation would like to thank you all for your participation this afternoon. We've been working on this project for months now and your involvement is greatly important. Before we start is everyone comfortable? Great. As you know, Bloody Sunday was a terrible travesty and we here at BBC are committed to exposing the truth of that day's events, and the inquiry that followed. We all know that the British Army is the best in the world …

ACTORS: Here HERE!

STAGE MANAGER: We want you to know that we care …

SECURITY GUARD: (*Shouts at guarded audience.*) SHUT UP!

STAGE MANAGER: Let me introduce to you the artistic team. Our camera operator, long time BBC contributor, Patty O'Something … Returning from their long run on the Broadway stage, Jane and Jon, who will be performing on camera. Great, let's have our first screen test—Victim Number One.

(*STAGE MANAGER hands Actor Number One a cue card labelled "BBC."*)

ACTOR NUMBER ONE: I'll give it a try …

(*Reads monologue.*) Oh the troubles we had that day, I didn't ever think it would come to that, really, I tried to get to safety, I crawled, crawled, gripping the gravel road that lay beneath me, Oh my …

my gut, oh my gut

the blood, yes, I was

shot and left and

after thirty-one short years

my body lay,

now lay to rest beneath the soil

January 30, 1972,

I took my last six breaths

STAGE MANAGER: (*During monologue.*) That's good, get right in there, how about a nice close up of the anguish. Do you think you could cry? A few tears to really hit it home? (*Goes to get a cup of water and places tears on his face.*) GREAT, that's enough of that. NEXT. Let's see … Ahhh yess: the child's perspective.

(*STAGE MANAGER hands Actor NUMBER TWO a cue card labelled "BBC."*)

ACTOR NUMBER TWO: I'll gladly take that on.

(*Reads monologue*) Today is an exciting day. The helicopters are out today and I love when the helicopters are out. Sometimes we play helicopter pilots and we shoot down all the Protestant people in the streets of Derry. (*Making helicopter noises.*) Neeeeeeeeeeeeeeerrrrrrrrrrrr BOOM! It's the best because sometimes dad joins in and usually dad is too busy to play ever. I don't like anyone who is a Protestant. I've never talked to one before, I see them everyday on my walk to school with dad and they always look so cross and sometimes they throw stuff at us and then dad starts swearing at them and frightening me. And you know what they do when you are unsuspecting? They sneak up and attack you from behind because they can become invisible.

STAGE MANAGER: How about a lisp young lady, really sell it! We need to boost the youth audience. Now take a seat, let's get back to the important people. AHHH here's a good one: a soldier!

(*STAGE MANAGER hands Actor Number One another cue card labelled "BBC."*)

SECURITY GUARD: (*To audience on balcony.*) Stand up and shut up!

ACTOR NUMBER ONE: (*Reading monologue.*) My vision of that day is still quite foggy but we heard fires coming out of the south side and we reacted, like I said, we did what we were trained to do. Trouble was expected. Yes, trouble from the PIRA and the Stickies and we were told this, so we were ready. None of firing lasted very long, perhaps fifteen minutes or so. We were well aware that people went down. Yes. And to be perfectly honest we thought at the time the people killed were the IRA. We never expected they be innocent civilians. For me, now looking back on the Bloody Sunday, I did not carry out the shooting on that day and I know now that I am more than thankful of this. There were and are so many moments of sorrow. Sorry for the innocent deaths, sorry for us soldiers, sorry for those who were just doing their job, sorry for the families, sorry that things had to cast this spell over my dear Northern Ireland.

STAGE MANAGER: (*During the monologue.*) Can we have him standing on some sort of platform, make the camera look up to him, like we owe him our lives. How about you standing on that chair?

(*After the monologue.*) Whoa there, don't go saying anything you don't mean! I'll be sure to send that one priority to the editing room. NEXT.

(*STAGE MANAGER hands Actor Number Two several cue cards labelled "BBC."*)

ACTOR NUMBER TWO: (*Reading the monologue.*) January 31, 1972. The day after Bloody Sunday. That was the day I became a member of the IRA—Provisional, I should say. A member of the provisional IRA. That's a dirty word for most in Northern Ireland. Provisional. To them, that word represents something that they are afraid to do themselves. Use force.

STAGE MANAGER: Okay that's enough of that. Who else have you got?

ACTOR NUMBER TWO: (*Reading from another card.*) The guns are silent, my wounds have healed

But fourteen new crosses lie planted in the field.

My love I can remember when you were taken away

And how the tears streamed down my cheek, on Bloody Sunday.

STAGE MANAGER: (*During monologue.*) Have you ever heard of Shakespeare? Really SELL IT!

(*After monologue.*) And that's definitely enough of that! NEXT. Finally! Someone with credentials, Prime Minister David Cameron—let's get some good lighting going on here. How about you have a seat in front of our audience, shake some hands!

(*STAGE MANAGER hands Actor Number One a cue card labelled "BBC."*)

ACTOR NUMBER ONE: (*Shaking the hands of the seated audience members, reading.*) You think it's all mothers and nephews mourning a loss—what about the terror groups? You can't win—it's a trap you see. So what did we do? We created a virtual tour of Bloody Sunday and we showed them what happened. No tears, no theories, and certainly no authority. We brought the streets of Londonderry to life only to stain them in Technicolor for the victims of testimony. And we're fucked; only now we've paid. For every soldier I have exposed to their conduct, there are thousands of "I told you so's" ringing throughout the UK. I'm the prime minister—I have to believe in what makes us great is also what makes us vulnerable.

STAGE MANAGER: Maybe we will lay some music over top of that one, maybe a few shots of him shaking hands and kissing babies ... Well, thank you so much for being here today. That's a wrap. God Bless.

CAMERAPERSON: Such Bullshit!

STAGE MANAGER: Excuse me? I'm sorry, what's your name again? You film the footage, and your turn off the camera—there are plenty of people who would appreciate your job.

CAMERAPERSON: I don't want to talk about Bloody Sunday, I don't want to think about Bloody Sunday and I'm sick and tired of Ireland using those victims as poster boys! Jesus! When I watch programs about the inquiry on the news all I hear is money and politics and disappointment. I'm not scared to talk about what happened. I'm scared that nobody will listen—we have to start listening to each other. We got our apology, are you going to accept it or not?

STAGE MANAGER: You're fired.

* * *

THE PITCH

By Jon Hallis, Katie Muzyka, Mark Rochford, and Anja Zeljkovic

Authors' Introduction

Starting in the summer of 2010, thousands of Roma—commonly referred to as "gypsies"—were deported from their settlements in France. The French government, under President Nicolas Sarkozy, justified its actions by claiming that the Roma are residing in the country illegally and pose a threat to national security. Despite the European Union's criticism of France's actions and the public outcry regarding the plight of the Roma, the government continues with its deportations, and the Roma, both in France and elsewhere in Europe, remain highly vulnerable.

Most of us came to this project with limited knowledge of the subject matter. Poet Carolyn Smart visited the class in September and talked about the Roma deportations, after which Anja pitched the topic as the starting point for creating a piece of theatre. The rest of us gravitated to the idea out of curiosity. At the start of the process we tried as best as we could to unload our pre-conceived notions and identify any baggage or beliefs that would get in the way of being as objective, fair, and humane as possible in our research, writing, and performance. We then set out to create a theatrical interpretation of the situation, both on the microcosmic level of personal relationships between characters, and on a larger level in which we examine the loss or reinvention of culture and identity within a discourse between cultures.

Intrigued by the parallel Domnica Radulescu draws in "Performing the Female 'Gypsy': *Commedia dell'arte*'s 'Tricks' for Finding Freedom" between Roma women and the European actresses who performed in *Commedia dell'arte* troupes, we decided we would conflate Gypsy stereotypes and *commedia* stock characters, and see what happens when a band of travellers arrives at Nicolas Sarkozy's front door. The resulting script makes use of the power of masks to both reveal and obscure identities.

The Pitch

Characters

NICOLAS SARKOZY, *current President of France, elected 2007*

ARLECCHINO, *a trickster and acrobat wearing the traditional commedia Arlecchino mask; Rom.*

FEMALE DOTTORE, *an unqualified doctor who pretends to know more than she does, wears the traditional Dottore commedia mask; Rom.*

COLUMBINA, *the sweet but naïve accomplice to ARLECCHINO's tricks, wears the traditional columbina Commedia mask; Rom.*

Setting
(*The entrance hall or foyer of the state home of the President of France. The audience sits on the staircase, leaving an aisle down the middle. Originally staged on site in the front entrance of Theological Hall, Queen's University, Kingston, Ontario.*)

Part One
(*Loud, rhythmic knocking at the door. Sarkozy enters and comes down the stairs.*)

SARKOZY: Qui est-ce?

(*More rhythmic knocking at the door.*)

SARKOZY: Who is it?

(*A Gypsy violin melody is heard at the door.*)

SARKOZY: I'm not letting you in until you tell me who you are!

(*The doors swing open with music and drum rhythm to reveal the Roma characters in full commedia mask who immediately barge into the foyer. They are ARLECCHINO, COLUMBINA, FEMALE DOTTORE. They each have their hand on a large, white sheet gathered into a sack. They let go, and their merchandise is revealed, lying out on the sheet.*)

ARLECCHINO: (*Sing-song voice along to the melody.*) Buy a pot! Buy a pan! Finest plungers in town!

DOTTORE: Famous cure-all! Works in seconds! Only chance, you won't regret it!

ARLECCHINO: Well you might! (*He laughs; DOTTORE hits ARLECCHINO.*)

SARKOZY: How did you get past security?

ARLECCHINO: The guards loved her dancing. Show him Columbina!

(*COLUMBINA starts dancing around him in a circle, shaking a tambourine.*)

ARLECCHINO: You can buy her too! Half price with the plunger!

SARKOZY: This! This is what I'm talking about! (*He grabs COLUMBINA and swings her to his side.*) How dare she be exploited in this way! Poor, young girl. Is she educated? Is she healthy? What kind of example does she set for the Roma youth of tomorrow? This kind of situation is exactly what this government is trying to remedy. Roma children live in squalor, fostering exploitation by drug lords, thieves, and human traffickers. Don't you want to protect your children? Give them access to education, sanitation, job prospects, a better life?

ARLECCHINO: What, you don't want to buy us?

DOTTORE: (*To ARLECCHINO.*) You idiot!
(*To SARKOZY.*) I want my money.
(*To ARLECCHINO.*) You owe me 300€!

SARKOZY: If you want money, food, stability, a home for your family, a chance to contribute to society—settling down is the way to accomplish these things. Not moving from country to country, with no papers, no job, and no accommodations. The money we give you for, re-homing, is an incentive to start a new life in your country of origin.

ARLECCHINO: What country is that?

COLUMBINA: Spain! (*Flamenco snaps.*)

DOTTORE: Romania!

ARLECCHINO: Bulgaria!

COLUMBINA: No, papa was from Greece!

SARKOZY: All fine, fine countries! And you shall go back to your respective homelands and prosper in their cultural richness. You may use your financial incentive to acquire skills and give back to your community. Maybe one day you'll return to France and—

ARLECCHINO: Wait, so you don't want to buy a knife sharpener?

(*A sales pitch ensues. ARLECCHINO and DOTTORE display each of the items they are selling. During the following COLUMBINA sneaks down to untie SARKOZY's shoelaces.*)

DOTTORE: Surely you need something! Spatulas!

ARLECCHINO: Blenders!

DOTTORE: Toasters!

ARLECCHINO: '94 Dell computer, like new!

SARKOZY: Hey, what are you doing down there?

ARLECCHINO: Baby!

(*ARLECCHINO throws a life-size baby doll wrapped in a blanket in SARKOZY's direction. SARKOZY catches the baby, which distracts him from COLUMBINA. COLUMBINA takes SARKOZY's wallet out of his pocket, removes 100€ from it and returns it to his pocket.*)

COLUMBINA: Here we go, one baby, 100€!

SARKOZY: No, no, no! That's not what I meant!

DOTTORE: You meant, we went and 300€!

SARKOZY: Please, take your child. (*He gives the baby to DOTTORE.*) The point is not that we undervalue the Roma people and their culture. Where we draw the line is at illegal camps set up in urban areas that pose a threat to national security. We need to know who is in our country and where they are living to ensure the safety of immigrants and citizens alike. We can only extend social programs to those in need who have taken the time to properly register their citizenship.

(*ARLECCHINO, DOTTORE, and COLUMBINA all stand feigning interest for a few moments. At first they utter a few suppressed grunts and laughs. Then, they all break into laughter. DOTTORE plays a joyous violin melody and ARLECCHINO begins a jig.*)

COLUMBINA: Aww, is Monsieur Sarkozy sad?

ARLECCHINO: Oh, the world's saddest song for the saddest man in the world!

(*ARLECCHINO conducts DOTTORE in a plaintive melody.*)

DOTTORE: (*Grabs Pantalone mask from the pile of goods.*) Here, why don't you join in! Try this on for size. See, looks good on me, looks good on you! (*Places mask on SARKOZY's face.*)

ARLECCHINO: Come with us and have some fun!

SARKOZY: (*Now wearing Pantalone mask.*) Get out of here you Gypsy scum!

(*SARKOZY pushes ARLECCHINO, who stumbles back into DOTTORE and COLUMBINA, knocking them down to the ground. ARLECCHINO, DOTTORE, and COLUMBINA's masks are knocked off during the fall, revealing their faces.*)

Part II

ARLECCHINO: Goods for sale, good sir! Take your pick. Finest quality for the best prices.

SARKOZY: You're in my house trying to sell me garbage you stole off the streets! Have you no shame?

DOTTORE: No, no, no not stolen. Guaranteed in working condition.

COLUMBINA: Hand-made baskets, only 10€! Present for the wife?

SARKOZY: You're trespassing! If you don't remove yourselves from my property immediately I will call the police.

COLUMBINA: Okay, okay, 8€! But I won't go any lower. I have children to feed.

ARLECCHINO: A man understands the needs of another man. I've got what you're looking for. Every self-respecting man needs a new set of golf clubs. Now, this will get me in trouble with the missus but I'll let them go for 50€. You and me, we understand each other.

SARKOZY: Typical gypsy! Are you deaf? Are you dumb? Both, probably. You're bringing France to ruin with your barbaric way of life! When the police get here, you'll be deported immediately, sent back to where you came from!

(ARLECCHINO takes a step towards SARKOZY's stairs to calm him.)

SARKOZY: This is breaking and entering. What makes you think you have the right to come into my home!

ARLECCHINO: Let's be reasonable. (He puts his hand on SARKOZY's shoulder.)

SARKOZY: Get your filthy hands away from me!

DOTTORE: Something less expensive. Tiffany lamp only 20€!

SARKOZY: I don't want your stolen shit!

COLUMBINA: Please sir, we have mouths to feed!

SARKOZY: I'm not in the business of feeding children who will learn to steal before they can read! I don't want your scarves, your stolen laptops or eggs, you voodoo Gypsy slut!

COLUMBINA: Oh, wouldn't you just love that!

SARKOZY: Well, how much would that cost?

(ARLECCHINO, DOTTORE, and COLUMBINA glance at each other, acknowledging the possibility of profit at last. ARLECCHINO reaches to receive the wallet, but DOTTORE swipes his hand away disapprovingly.)

DOTTORE: You know, if you're not satisfied in that department, we have an array of potions that will work on any woman you desire.

COLUMBINA: Special Gypsy formulations, passed down through the ages. Only Dottore has the mystical power to lure the rare crimson widow beetle so that she can extract its essential oils. That's the secret ingredient.

(COLUMBINA gives ARLECCHINO a pressing look; he doesn't clue in.)

DOTTORE: Yes, I brew it by moonlight to capture the aura of the Luna spirit.

ARLECCHINO: Yes, Dottore knows her stuff—I used the potion just the other night, and let me tell you, it was quite the experience!

COLUMBINA: How much would you pay for something like that?

SARKOZY: Well, for that, 5€. I'll give it a try.

(The ROMA exchange glances as if to say "that's really low," nonetheless they accept the offer. DOTTORE discreetly pours cola into a fancy-looking bottle and hands it to SARKOZY. He pays them in cash. SARKOZY tries to drink from the bottle, but can't because of his mask. He takes the mask off, looks at the potion and refuses to drink it.)

SARKOZY: (Looking at the ROMA with disdain.) The police will be here any minute now!

DOTTORE: I guess we'll have to get by somehow.

(The ROMA pack their goods up in the sheet and hightail it out the door.)

* * *

CHOICE?

By Brett Payette, Emily Herczeg, Catriona Graveson, and Alyssa Bignell

Brett Payette, Emily Herczeg, Catriona Graveson, and Alyssa Bignell perform *Choice?* on 24 November 2010.
Photo courtesy of Emily Herczeg

Authors' Introduction

At the outset of this process, our research covered the broad issue of decriminalizing prostitution. As the ruling of *Bedford v. Canada* had just been released,[2] there was a great deal of discussion on the topic and many opposing viewpoints were being debated in the media. During our preliminary discussions, we noted that all four of us were very clear in our stance of being pro-decriminalization. However, as we learned more about the sex work industry we quickly realized how many different valid perspectives there are on both decriminalization and the sex work industry itself.

Our research plan began to evolve and our interest became centred on the individuals involved in the sex work industry and on how decriminalization would impact different people. It was important to us to learn about as many viewpoints as possible, and to hear personal stories from those within the sex work industry. We attended a panel discussion ("Should Prostitution Be Legal?") in response to the *Bedford v. Canada* ruling held at Queen's University which was an integral part of our research process.[3] Multiple conflicting yet also overlapping perspectives were presented during the discussion, and we were exposed to ideas about sex work in a new light. Although there was little agreement on whether or not we should move towards decriminalization, the one topic that kept coming up was that of choice. We then began exploring questions such as: "when is entry into the sex work industry a true choice?"; "is staying in the industry a choice?"; "who is capable of making a choice?"; and "what happens when a choice is made for the wrong reasons?"

We wanted to represent as many people and ideas as possible, but given our time constraints, we decided it was best to create four distinct characters who could demonstrate the difficulties surrounding choice in the sex work industry. The contrasts between the empowered sex worker vs. the battered woman, the drug-addicted vs. the sober, the independent worker vs. the pimped, and the indoor vs. the outdoor worker were all important perspectives to acknowledge, and we were able to work these into the back stories of our four women. We attempted to portray the contradictory nature of the women's perspectives, and to show our audience that no perspective was more valid or less valid than the others. Translating our research from the page to the stage was the most difficult aspect of the entire process. We did not want our performance to sound like a public service announcement, nor like a clichéd set of monologues. It was important for us to show that each woman's story was legitimate in its own way, and to highlight the vast differences of opinion within the sex work industry itself.

Curator's Note

As this piece was being developed, I was in a class exploring philosophical perspectives on sex work, had become close friends with some people involved in the sex industry, and was peripherally involved in it myself as a dancer in an emerging burlesque dance troupe. When the group members shared their concern with me about having no connection to sex work themselves, I privately offered to put them in touch with a friend of mine who works in the industry. This friend is typically cynical of Queen's students' unconscious exercise of their privilege, so I was thrilled when she reported that she was very impressed with the sensitive, open-minded, and respectful way in which the four students approached their meeting with her. Through their self-awareness and accountability to all the stances in a hugely complex debate (that was never simplified to suit any agenda), this group has created a powerful pro-choice piece.

Choice?

Characters

KRISTEN, *is sixteen. She is dressed in skinny jeans, sneakers, a tank top, and a hooded cardigan. Her outfit is made to look like it was purchased from a low-end teen store (e.g., "Stitches").*

DIANE, *is twenty-four. She is dressed in thigh-high black boots, jeans, a tank top, and a blazer. She looks sexy, but also classy and confident.*

CANDICE, *is thirty-six. She is dressed in a black skirt, very high heels, and a white stretch button-down shirt. Her business suit is made to look slightly cheap, as if it were purchased at a low-end clothing store (e.g., "Suzy Shier").*

JESSICA, *is twenty. She is dressed in leggings, an oversized men's dress shirt, UGG boots, pearl earrings, and a hair band. She is made to look like a quintessential student.*

Setting

(The stage is set in a minimalist fashion. There are four chairs in a row, centre stage. The shoes of the four characters have been set in front of each chair respectively.)

("Beauty" by Shaye plays for fifty-nine seconds and fades out while the four women enter in a choreographed walk. They approach their chairs [glancing at each pair of shoes as they enter] and put on their shoes. The music fades out.)

KRISTEN: I wanted to be free.

CANDICE: I wish I had known.

JESSICA: I needed to stay.

DIANE: I made myself a life.

The four sex workers' shoes, arranged for *Choice?* on 24 November 2010.
Photo by Emily Herczeg

KRISTEN: You don't choose your parents. I would never have chosen mine. By the age of twelve, I didn't want to be at home … by the age of fifteen, I knew I couldn't be at home. Parents are supposed to protect you, reassure you, support you. My parents attacked everything about me. It was pretty fucking obvious they didn't want me. The morning my mom hit me, I chose to leave. I didn't take anything. *(Beat.)* Anything and anywhere else was better.

CANDICE: I'm going to tell you what people don't want to tell you. People who haven't seen it, lived through it, and survived it, don't understand it. Brutal violence and the sex industry are inseparable.

JESSICA: Our fourth anniversary was last week. He was high, I was working. Somebody has to pay the rent … that's why I started working in the first place. Well, sort of. Last year I realized I was in more debt than I would legitimately be able to get myself out of. I started with the goal of just paying off my student loans and then being done. *(Beat.)* That was about the same time that I moved in with Adam.

DIANE: Not everyone can do what I do. It takes a certain kind of woman. I admit I didn't get into it for the right reasons—I hate that. I feel like it undermines what I do now. But I was young, I was naïve, and I was addicted.

ALL: What choice did I have?

CANDICE: Take choice out of the equation. It doesn't exist. When you don't know what else to do, and you don't know how to get out, the option isn't there. There is no choice. I can see it now. I was living a life of luxury with a man who said he loved me. I thought it was what I wanted. *(Pause.)* He loved me, so he set up tricks … he loved me, so he locked me away … he loved me, so he managed my money. He loved me, so when he raped me it didn't matter.

KRISTEN: If I'm a prostitute, can I be raped? What does that word mean anymore?

(DIANE, CANDICE, and JESSICA turn to look at audience.)

JESSICA: Things were going so well. Adam and I moved in together about a year ago. It made the most sense. But since then, things have changed. He's been going through a really rough time … and he lost his job. I was so close to paying off my loans but without Adam working, I had to cover rent. So I called the agency and asked them to double my tricks. *(Beat.)* We love each other so much. I needed to do it. But … sometimes when I come home extra late and I'm tired … he can't control himself when he's high. I know this isn't really him, I know him. He loves me.

(DIANE, KRISTEN, and CANDICE turn to look at JESSICA.)

CANDICE: Asking a prostitute if it's her choice is like asking a battered woman if she loves him, and if she wants to stay. The answer is yes.

KRISTEN: So I spent a little time on the street. I learned a lot. But I found a place to stay with this really cool guy. He knew a bunch of the girls on the strip and heard that I needed a place. He only takes a small cut of what I make, doesn't ask questions, and I get to stay there for free. It's a pretty fuckin' sweet deal. Yeah, I guess this isn't exactly what I pictured myself doing, and your first time probably isn't supposed to be with a john, but fuck it, I have a ton of friends that had a way worse first time and didn't get fuckin' paid for it. I'd choose this over home any day. This shit is easy.

CANDICE: I had no idea what I was getting into. But when you're eighteen, wearing Manolos and driving a Lexus, you think you're living the dream. But bottom line—you're sucking dick for money and if you need to scream you better fucking hope someone can hear you.

KRISTEN: It is work, it's real work.

ALL: No one can deny that it's work.

CANDICE: But it's not healthy work. How can you even think of decriminalizing something that is hurting so many women?

DIANE: After working for a year I finally got clean. I realized that I had been so close to finishing high school and that with no education I would get stuck in the industry. So I got out and went back to school. Graduated that year and got a really good job as an admin assistant. But I wasn't fulfilled ... I sat at a desk all day, helping no one, going home at the end of the day having accomplished nothing. *(Pause.)* There is something so inherently gratifying about sex work that people don't realize – just knowing that for the short time that I spend with my clients I've given them what they need. Half of the people I service think that they're here to fulfill some kinky fantasy, but truth is most just need someone to talk to. I'm in a position now where I run my own successful business. I work independently, screen all of my own clients, and I manage the classiest boudoir this city has ever seen. Business is good, and if we finally get these laws off the books I'll be able to hire some staff and start to help other girls work in a fair and safe environment. I love what I do. I chose what I do, and I'm proud of it.

JESSICA: It's one year. One year of hard work and putting up with shit at home. For three good years in the past, and hopefully many more in the future, isn't that worth it?

KRISTEN: You never know what life's gonna throw your way and you have to play the cards you've been dealt. Getting away from home has been the best thing for me and if this is what I have to do, so be it.

CANDICE: I don't care how many women say that they like what they're doing. If they honestly knew what life was like on the other side, I can promise you they wouldn't be in it.

DIANE: Sex work isn't for everyone, but neither is desk work. What I do fulfills me and helps other people. *(Beat.)* I'm a service provider.

KRISTEN: I'm a prostitute.

CANDICE: I was a whore.

JESSICA: I am a sex worker.

(Beat. The following lines are spoken simultaneously.)

KRISTEN: I made the right choice.

JESSICA: This is my choice.

CANDICE: There is no choice.

DIANE: My life is my choice.

(Blackout.)

* * *

Hold The Boat
(Or, The Canadian Way)

By Jennie Appleby, Kathleen Jerome, Blythe Hubbard, and Alain Richer

Jennie Appleby (Lawyer), Kathleen Jerome (Officer), and Blythe Hubbard (Refugee) perform *Hold the Boat (or, The Canadian Way)*, 26 November 2010.
Photo by Katherine MacNeill

Authors' Introduction

When we began writing this script we wanted to focus on the Tamil people from Sri Lanka who arrived on the shores of British Columbia in summer 2010. However, when we came across an article, "The Immigrant Theme on the American Stage," we realized the extent of the issues we would face as we tried to depict these refugees. The article examines how, throughout the history of immigration to North America, the theatre has often presented non-white people as stock character-types, including the various figures in minstrel shows, the rouge-faced drunken Irishman, or the Jewish miser. In opposition to this racist history in performance and representation, we decided to make the Refugee in our piece a symbolic figure, standing for a variety of individual people and experiences. (Even these we decided to keep vague, to avoid representing specific individual immigrants to Canada whose stories may have been sensationalized.)

We also started thinking about Canadians and their opinions and feelings towards refugees and immigration. Canada, like many nations, has a "brand" identity: it is seen as an all-welcoming country willing to accept one and all—an overly-generalized image we wanted to challenge.

We have drawn on the historical moment of the interrogation of the Tamil refugees to create an interrogation scene that emphasizes the performative nature of such a process.

The Interrogation Officer (symbolized by an officer's hat) will enter the stage, followed by a Lawyer (symbolized by a briefcase), and a Refugee (symbolized by a stick with a bundle tied to the end). By having three actors shift through all three roles over the course of the piece, the script does not impose a set identity on any figure. This arrangement also emphasizes how arbitrary it is for an individual to be born into one country rather than another.

Hold The Boat (or, The Canadian Way)

Characters

OFFICER ONE, *Goofy*

REFUGEE ONE, *Thankful/Compliant*

LAWYER ONE

OFFICER TWO, *Serious/Rule-stickler*

REFUGEE TWO, *Frustrated/Impatient*

LAWYER TWO

OFFICER THREE, *Meek/Shy*

REFUGEE THREE, *Skeptical/Cynical*

LAWYER THREE

Doubling in the performance for DRAM 476:

OFFICER ONE, LAWYER TWO, and REFUGEE THREE were played by Kathleen Jerome

LAWYER ONE, REFUGEE TWO, and OFFICER THREE were played by Jennie Appleby

REFUGEE ONE, OFFICER TWO, and LAWYER THREE were played by Blythe Hubbard

Setting

Note
The e-mail address set up for the OFFICER is canboardercontrol_gov_ca@gmail.com.

(Lights up. OFFICER 1 enters. Uses chalk and draws the straight line. Goes to desk, standing.)

OFFICER ONE: Next!

(REFUGEE 1 enters.)

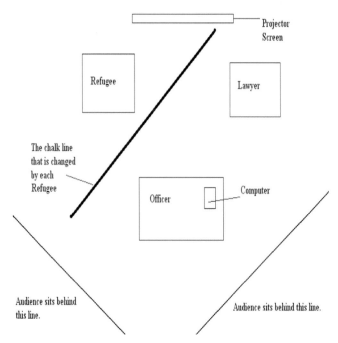

Stage configuration for *Hold the Boat*, Queen's University, November 2010.
Design by Jennie Appleby, Kathleen Jerome, Blythe Hubbard, and Alain Richer

OFFICER ONE: So number 476, oh, there you are, stand here. *(Points at the line.)* I just need to start up my GMAIL. *(While speaking, logs on to GMAIL account, projected onto screen.)* Oh, you know: Government Moderated Answer Inquiry Legitimator. So, ah been on any good trips lately? Ahahaha, just teasing, just teasing.

REFUGEE ONE: Sorry to bother you, I don't want to inconvenience anyone, um, but do you know when I might be getting my belongings back?

OFFICER ONE: All in good time. Your belongings are going through UHAUL testing.

REFUGEE ONE: Pardon me?

OFFICER ONE: Oh, sorry, Unnecessary Hoarding of All Unidentified Luggage, jeez, the Government, and their acronyms. It's a very intense and rigorous process.

REFUGEE ONE: Oh, okay, I can wait.

OFFICER ONE: *(Looking over REFUGEE ONE.)* You seem very nice. Just breathe, relax, and let's get started here. It won't take long, just keep calm. Alright so the first question is from Sceptical Anderson from Fort George, BC *(stands up and draws a box with chalk around the Refugee off the set line)* and he wants to know, "Are you a terrorist?"

(LAWYER ONE barges in.)

LAWYER ONE: You don't have to answer that!!! Bill, how many days have we been doing this? I'm always here at 9 a.m. and you always try to start without me. *(To REFUGEE ONE)* Oh hi, I'm from the Canadian Human Rights Agency and I am here to answer anything you can't or shouldn't.

OFFICER ONE: Karen, I told you I start at 8:55 and this question has been approved. I always start with this one, gets them thinking, *I'm warming up the crowd.*

LAWYER ONE: *(Under breath, simultaneously with OFFICER ONE's line.)* Stupid Pig.

REFUGEE ONE: *(Cutting in, on top of OFFICER ONE's and LAWYER ONE's lines.)* I'm not a terrorist. I'm happy to be here. I've come because this is a country of ... generosity and I promise to abide by your laws. *(While talking, REFUGEE ONE is smudging out part of the line.)*

(Scene transition. Lights down, spots on each place. REFUGEE moves to OFFICER's place, OFFICER moves to LAWYER's place, and LAWYER moves to REFUGEE's place.)

OFFICER TWO (formerly REFUGEE ONE): Sit down please. I have a series of questions from Francois Jutras, Montreal, QC. Answer them as quickly as you can. First what is the capital of Canada?

REFUGEE TWO (formerly LAWYER ONE): Ott—

OFFICER TWO: No answer. What is the population of Canada?

REFUGEE TWO: As of 2010 it's —

OFFICER TWO: Don't know? Next, how many people are currently unemployed?

REFUGEE TWO: *(Makes a sound of interjection.)*

OFFICER TWO: How do immigrants *normally* enter our country?

REFUGEE TWO: Look! How am I supposed to prove myself when you won't even let me answer the questions? You're being unreasonable, let me speak!!

LAWYER TWO (formerly OFFICER ONE): Now calm down. Canadians are polite and compliant. You're not going to help your cause if you get all riled up. You want the Officer to like you, don't you?

OFFICER TWO: No time for pep talks, next question. This one is from Ruthanne from Saskatoon. She asks, "Why should we support you line skipping freeloaders? Why did you pay so much to come here illegally when you could have used that money to immigrate the proper way?"

LAWYER TWO: When people are forced out of their country due to violence, they are then classified as refugees. According to Canadian law their immediate need is our priority. They aren't actually jumping any lines, these "lines" don't apply to them.

OFFICER TWO: Yeah, our reports say that you paid $50,000 to come here. Do you know what that means? That single boat of refugees made somebody 25 million dollars. That's crazy!

LAWYER TWO: It's called human smuggling.

(During the following dialogue REFUGEE TWO draws a jagged line across the straight line past the previously drawn box.)

REFUGEE TWO: What would you do if you were being victimized by your government? If the safety of your family was always a question? You would do what I did. I thought that Canada would offer a better life.

(Scene transition. Lights down, spots on each place. REFUGEE moves to OFFICER's place, OFFICER moves to LAWYER's place, and LAWYER moves to REFUGEE's place.)

OFFICE THREE (formerly REFUGEE TWO): Hello, how are you this morning?

Refugee THREE (formerly LAWYER TWO): How do you think I am?

OFFICE THREE: Well, yes, I guess you're right. Um well let's just move along here, it shouldn't take too long.

REFUGEE THREE: I hope not; I've been waiting to see you for a month.

OFFICE THREE: Yes, well we have to be thorough you know. The safety of Canadians is our first priority here at Border Patrol. We can't always tell who you people are, you could be ... *(Head down to screen.)* Margaret from New Brunswick wants to know ummm, "How are you going to contribute to our country? Are you just going to soak up welfare and steal my taxes?" Oh, that's not a very nice one. Let's skip it.

LAWYER THREE (formerly OFFICER TWO): That question is not relevant; it's too early to determine what this person could contribute, and *why* should that even matter when a human life is in need?

OFFICE THREE: Yes, well let's just move on. This is from Andrew, oh he lives in Toronto. He's wondering where you want to live. "People always say that Canada is so big, and that there is tons of room for immigrants—so why the hell do they all want to live in Toronto!? Quit crowding my city!" Well I hope you get nicer neighbours.

REFUGEE THREE: Are you skipping this question too? It sort of seems that Canadians aren't as welcoming as their Government makes them out to be.

OFFICE THREE: Well now, that's not true, some people really care. What about Kim Phillips here, she is asking things like, aren't you happy to be here? Don't be scared. What was the boat ride like? Do you need help learning English? Did you have clean water and food?

(During the following dialogue REFUGEE THREE draws an outward growing swirl breaching off from the jagged line.)

REFUGEE THREE: Ha! This is insulting! I'm not some weak, starving, incompetent refugee. I made a choice to come here to save myself and my family. We're here to build an independent new life. The last thing we need is to have a disabling stereotype forced upon us.

(Scene transition. Lights down, spots on each place. REFUGEE moves to OFFICER'S place, OFFICER moves to LAWYER'S place, and LAWYER moves to REFUGEE'S place, so now people are back to their original places.)

LAWYER ONE (formerly OFFICE THREE): Well Bill, I can't think of anything we haven't covered. Honestly do we really need to go through her childhood again?

OFFICER ONE (formerly REFUGEE THREE): No, I just liked the part about tricking her grandma into kissing the dog, man that's a good one.

REFUGEE ONE (formerly LAWYER THREE): If I could just be told where I could pick up my bags …

OFFICER ONE: Oh I wouldn't worry about that now, Miss … Ponnambalam (*Says it wrong.*)

REFUGEE ONE: Ponnambalam, actually.

OFFICER ONE: Hahah, you had better get used to people saying your name wrong!

REFUGEE ONE: What do you mean?

OFFICER ONE: No one here in Canada can say these crazy names! Hahah!

REFUGEE ONE: No I mean, do you mean I passed? Do I get to stay?

OFFICER ONE: Oh yeah! Well I knew from the minute I saw you you'd fit right in here, there's a bunch of your kind around these days. Some say there's too many of you, but then what would happen to my job?

LAWYER ONE: Okay so just to finish this, sign here, and here, and initial here, and Bill I need you to witness this, and a … sign here. Oh and, Bill can you stamp this, you forgot to last time.

OFFICER ONE: Oh wait, I've got one last question here. *(REFUGEE ONE and LAWYER ONE stop abruptly.)* It's from this real nice lady in Toronto, basically there is a cultural centre that she wants you to come to for support and she wants to learn more about you. Yea, you should get in contact with her, Sherri Cornfield.

REFUGEE ONE: Thank you.

LAWYER ONE: The stamp, Bill.

OFFICER ONE: Oh yes. *(Stamps, paper on desk.)*

LAWYER ONE: Alright, well 9 a.m. tomorrow Bill, not 8:55. Good luck Miss Ponnambalam. *(Says it wrong.)*

(REFUGEE ONE and LAWYER ONE shake hands. LAWYER ONE exits. OFFICER ONE erases part of line that lets REFUGEE ONE leave the chalk box.)

REFUGEE ONE: Thank you, so much. *(Exits.)*

(OFFICER ONE shuts down computer, erases chalk line that has been altered and draws a new straight one.)

Notes

1. The Saville Report is the document produced at the end of the Bloody Sunday Inquiry, initiated by former UK Prime Minister Tony Blair in a Resolution of the House of Commons and of the House of Lords in January through February, 1998. Following its release, current UK Prime Minister David Cameron issued an official apology on 16 June 2010, in which he publicly acknowledged the UK government as responsible for the British Armed Forces firing on protesters in a demonstration in Derry/Londonderry on 30 January 1972, killing fourteen civilians. A full text of the Report and full details regarding the Inquiry can be found on the Bloody Sunday Inquiry's homepage: http://www.bloody-sunday-inquiry.org/.

2. *Bedford v. Canada* is a constitutional challenge for the decriminalization of sex work, brought forward by Sex Professionals of Canada (SPOC) members Jean Bedford, Amy Lebovitch,

and Valerie Scott. The appellants, represented by Alan Young, Ron Marzel, and Stacey Nichols, contended that four sections of the Criminal Code of Canada dealing with sex work only made the conditions of sex work more dangerous for workers. On 28 September 2010, Ontario Superior Court Justice Susan Himel ruled in favour of striking three of the four sections: S.210 that prohibited bawdy houses, S.212 (1j) that criminalized living off the avails of prostitution, and S.213 (1c) that criminalized communication for the purposes of prostitution. Following the decision, the federal Crown moved for a stay to delay the decriminalization's implementation. On 2 December 2010, Ontario Court of Appeal Justice Mark Rosenberg granted a stay until April 2011—meaning that until then, the three sections of the Criminal Code would continue to be enforced. A detailed summary of the case, ruling, and subsequent stay (including links to Justice Himel's ruling and Justice Rosenberg's stay decision) can be found on SPOC's website: http://www.spoc.ca/index.html.

3   "Should Prostitution Be Legalized?" was a panel discussion organized by the Queen's Law and Public Policy Club, held in Ellis Hall at Queen's on 15 November 2010. The panelists were Alan Young of the *Bedford v. Canada* legal team, Professor Sheila McIntyre from the University of Ottawa Faculty of Common Law, Professors Margaret Little and Christina Marciano from the Queen's Department of Political Science, and Natasha Falle, Executive Director of Sex Trade 101. All these details are available on the Queen's Faculty of Law website: http://law.queensu.ca.

Works Cited

Radulescu, Domnica. "Performing the Female 'Gypsy': *Commedia dell'arte's* 'Tricks' for Finding Freedom." Ed. Valentina Glajor and Dominica Radulescu. *"Gypsies" in European Literature and Culture*. New York: Palgrave Macmillan, 2008. 193–215. Print.

Salverson, Julie. "DRAM 476: Cultures of Theatre: 'Ethics and Performance, Facing History in a Tragic Culture.'" *Queen's University Department of Drama: Current Fall/Winter Courses. Queensu.ca*. Aug. 2010. Web. 28 Dec. 2010.

———. "Testimony Performance Project." DRAM 476 Assignment Sheet. Kingston: Queen's University, October 2010. Print.

Wittke, Carl. "The Immigrant Theme on the American Stage." *The Mississippi Valley Historical Review* 39.2 (1952): 211–32. Organization of American Historians. Web. November 2010.

Kalanthe Khaiat is an MA candidate in Cultural Studies and SGPS Equity Coordinator at Queen's University. Her thesis explores the gendered construction of the stage manager in contemporary Canadian theatre culture. Her research interests include the constructive discourses of sex, gender, and other individual/social identities, and the theory-practice relationship in social justice initiatives.

Views and Reviews

by Views and Reviews Editor Natalie Alvarez

This issue's Views and Reviews constellates performance events from Vancouver to Edmonton and Toronto to Montreal, each of which, in differing ways, calls into question the politics of visibility—and invisibility—in performance. As Natalie Rewa's piece on *Tu vois ce que je veux dire?* reminds us, we often take for granted performance's privileging of the ocular and with it, the delicate movement that is always at play in performance between visibility and invisibility, retrieval and obscurity, exposure and concealment.

In a review that profitably examines two shows in conjunction with one another—Bruce Ruddell's *Beyond Eden* and Marie Clements' *The Edward Curtis Project* in Vancouver—Beverly Yhap examines how both shows perform "a kind of exhumation," bringing into view "received ideas of culture and privilege—of who occupies and creates any given artistic 'canon.'" But these shows also examine the problematics of "preservationist strategies" and the kinds of erasure that can result in the museum's or the anthropologist's desire to plunder cultures "in the name of conservation." Yhap's response to a particularly powerful stage image in *The Edward Curtis Project* points to a potential hazard the work of the preservationist shares with that of artistic representation: "how to assert visibility against [the] sweeping panorama of seductive nostalgia"?

The question of "how to assert visibility" also pervades Scott Sharplin's view piece, which documents the recent emergence of a new multidisciplinary company in Edmonton, Alberta devoted to Aboriginal arts—Alberta Aboriginal Arts (AAA). As the province with the highest Aboriginal population density, Sharplin asks why "the hearty, complex stew" of Aboriginal arts "somehow still remains invisible" in Alberta. AAA co-founders Christine Sokaymoh Frederick and Ryan Cunningham aim to foster and make visible Canada's "fastest growing and least visible cultures on both a national scale," as Sharplin concludes, "and right on their very own block."

Like Yhap, Barry Freeman places two productions in dialogue with one another, Project: Humanity's *The Middle Place* and Cahoots Theatre Company's *A Taste of Empire*, both in Toronto. In *The Middle Place,* the company brings into view the often imperceptible problem of youth homelessness through verbatim theatre, comprised of transcribed interviews with residents of Toronto's Youth Without Shelter. In *A Taste of Empire,* the obscured material relations behind the food we eat are made distressingly and, at times, squeamishly transparent in the form of a cooking show in which sous-chef Jovanni prepares a traditional Filipino dish called *rellenong bangus* for his audience. As the fish is gutted and stuffed with a "foreign mixture," the audience is taken through a history of not only Spanish colonialism in the Philippines, but also of the impacts, as Freeman says, of "the new imperialism of globalization" that now undergirds "systems of food production." After this visceral lesson on cooking, imperialism, and globalized food production, the audience is placed in a profound ethical quandary when they are invited to sample the fruits of Jovanni's labour: what is worse, to eat or not eat the fish?

The spectator is made similarly visible and, at times, complicit in our final two views/reviews, which take us to Montreal's 2010 Festival TransAmériques. Both of the shows under examination deal with the politics—and poetics—of visibility. In their analysis of the *Roman Tragedies,* an intermedial adaptation of Shakespeare's *Coriolanus, Julius Caesar,* and *Antony and Cleopatra* by Amsterdam's Toneelgroep, Natalie Corbett and Keren Zaiontz examine the "dynamic of constant visibility" created by an "aesthetic of surveillance." Through a glut of media technologies, the *mise-en-scène* situates Shakespeare's tragedies "in an era of globalized accessibility [and] digital reproduction" which, for these reviewers, raises questions about the "kinds of engagement" that are possible in these cultural conditions. Corbett and Zaiontz's examination focuses on the "spatial complicity and visible passivity" of the audience who, in a flow of movement between auditorium and stage, are made "visible, yet silent observers" of political intrigues and the formation of political personas generated by the media they, in turn, appropriate.

As in the *Roman Tragedies,* participants of *Tu vois ce que je veux dire?* also become the spectated though, in this case, because their sight is taken from them. Participants are blindfolded and guided through a series of public and domestic spaces, which unfold in the form of an "interiorized" scenography imagined in the mind's eye while they themselves become a site of curiosity for passersby. As Rewa notes, "the title is playfully ambiguous because what you are told is very minimal and what you 'see' in the mind's eye is immensely more than what is told." Rewa's piece is its own *dérive,* taking the reader vicariously through a series of vividly imagined *scenarii,* which structure what she calls "an urban dance of the *seen* rather than *seeing* body." In its poetic interplay of the seen and unseen, *Tu vois ce que je veux dire?* reminds us of the limitations and trappings of performance's ocular-centrism, inviting us to think beyond what is merely "seen," present, material, and legible in the enterprise of theatrical looking.

Unclassified and Controvertible: *The Edward Curtis Project* and *Beyond Eden* in Vancouver, 2010

by Beverly Yhap

Odd, unintended refractions can happen when cultural events are staged against high-profile international sports extravaganzas. It's tempting to find tenuous links between the dramas of competitive ranking in wintry settings with parallel cultural efforts to challenge artistic hierarchies. Such was the case around the 2010 Winter Games in Vancouver when *Beyond Eden,* co-produced by the Vancouver Playhouse and Theatre Calgary, and *The Edward Curtis Project,* produced by Presentation House Theatre, examined the uneasy legacy of two would-be apologists for Aboriginal culture.

In Bruce Ruddell's *Beyond Eden,* a conflicted anthropologist journeys to the Queen Charlotte Islands in 1957 to rescue priceless Aboriginal artifacts. In Marie Clements' *The Edward Curtis Project,* a contemporary Aboriginal woman's journey morphs into a river of parallel inquiries. One of these is Rita Leistner's photo exhibit of contemporary First Nations individuals and communities. The images of the exhibition form a contemporary record of resistance to Curtis' historic monument to "vanishing peoples." At the outset of the project's inception—taking on the work and influence of a prodigious image-maker like Curtis—Clements involved a like-minded artist with a contemporary lens. The results of each form of enquiry—Clements' drama and Leistner's photographic exhibit—bear the title of *The Edward Curtis Project,* which in turn also enfolds both shows within one named experience.[1]

Complementary exchange and overlap occurred between the creators of both stage productions: Bruce Ruddell composed *The Edward Curtis Project*'s score,[2] while Marie Clements developed the Watchman role eventually performed by Tom Jackson in *Beyond Eden.* (During the final week of January—with productions running concurrently—it was possible to compare shared and divergent approaches.) Each company acknowledged the stagings on traditional First Nations territory: explicitly as welcome ceremony at the opening of *The Edward Curtis Project,* implicitly in *Beyond Eden*'s staging of floating Haida war canoes among the audience. Moreover, each show tackled preservationist strategies: in *Beyond Eden,* the museum's right to plunder tribal cultures in the name of

Prelude, *The Edward Curtis Project:* the modern picture story unfolds in snapshot introductions. Tamara Podemski (Angeline) standing.
Photo by Tim Matheson

conservation formed the crux of Lewis Wilson's dilemma. In *The Edward Curtis Project,* the calcifying gaze of Curtis' monumental photographic project was set against a contemporary Aboriginal woman's trauma. To some extent, each show enacted a kind of exhumation: received ideas of culture and privilege—of who occupies and creates any given artistic "canon"—were brought to light and held up to account.

Set in 1957, *Beyond Eden* takes a critical yet not unsympathetic view of white preservationist rationale. The show's germination began with composer Bruce Ruddell's friendship with Haida legend Bill Reid. Through Reid, Ruddell learned of anthropologist Wilson Duff and the two friends' life-altering journey to Haida Gwaii in 1957. His attempts to dramatize their momentous voyage consumed the better part of two decades.

Originally conceived and performed as an opera at UBC's Museum of Anthropology in the late 1990s, *Beyond Eden*'s present form as music theatre portrays its fact-based story in broadly fictionalized, schematic strokes. Lewis Wilson, Duff's stand-in (played by Spirit of the West's John Mann), leads an expedition up the West Coast to remove the last extant totem poles from the deserted Haida village of Ninstints. Predictably, he faces not inconsiderable odds. The challenges of the voyage—treacherous seafaring conditions no less than the reluctant cooperation of Aboriginal guides—are bluntly conveyed largely in song. Having been "adopted" by the Haida during a potlach ceremony, Wilson ("Yaatzexaadee") understands the profound cultural tensions aroused by the expedition. By contrast, Wilson's fellow archeologists—self-avowed "grave-robbers"—tout conventional acquisition rationale against the two Aboriginal guides' warnings of supernatural reprisal. Caught in between are Wilson's wife and son and mixed-race photographer Max Tomson, the Bill Reid stand-in.

In a prelude to the physical journey, we meet Wilson enacting a ritual dance using a traditional mask whose power he summons without grasping its significance. The Watchman, an embodiment of Haida culture played by Tom Jackson, appears and relates a cautionary tale of contact between Raven, Eagle, and the explorer Perez. It's a tale he recounts several times for Wilson's benefit. However different in intention, Wilson's expedition threatens the same disastrous impact as Perez' encounter. This fact is brought home viscerally in the second act's climatic confrontation with the Watchman. Wilson's mask of expertise is stripped away as he witnesses what contact with white civilization has really cost the Haida. And what it could cost him. Despite his observance of cultural traditions and proprieties, Wilson remains a privileged outsider.

As with *The Edward Curtis Project*'s Clara, the mixed-race character Max Tomson comes in for abuse from all sides. On board as expedition photographer, Tomson is Wilson's counterpart, a trusted confidant straddling the divide between the ship's white crew and wary Aboriginal guides. As he comes in contact with the poles, Tomson reconnects with his Haida heritage. He is able to lay claim to the poles that Wilson can only amputate and remove. When Wilson prepares to jettison the whole expedition, Tomson argues for a new rationale of preservation from within Haida culture. Against Wilson's overwrought anguish, Tomson speaks to the right of removal, itself a privilege of custodial ownership. He tells Wilson, "The decision to return with them is a sacred decision of responsibility to the future of my people. So you see Lewis the decision to take these poles is not yours to make." Where Wilson proceeds to hack away at a pole in despondent frenzy—caught up in the action's evident brutality—Tomson sidesteps him and calmly fells the pole, taking his place.

The effect of Wilson's and Tomson's actions carry momentous import; unfortunately, their brief enactment and stilted exchanges (of decidedly latter-day sentiments) provide unsatisfactory glimpses of their characters' more unruly inner lives. Given the show's extensive treatment of Wilson's dilemma, it's disappointing that Tomson's crucial journey to his own identity is only sketchily delineated. The turning point—sung to lyrics taken from Reid's spoken recollections—revolves around Tomson's, not Wilson's, action and perception. For all the arguments for and against removal of cultural artifacts, the decisive moment of transformation in *Beyond Eden* comes through visual and tactile means. The

Act One, Flotilla in *Beyond Eden:* canoes surround the ship in the Watchman's tale of Raven, Eagle, and Perez. (l-r): John Mann (Lewis Wilson) and Tom Jackson (Watchman).
Photo by David Cooper

Act Two, Longhouse in *Beyond Eden:* unmasked, Lewis witnesses the devastating legacy of past trespass. (l-r): Tom Jackson (Watchman) and John Mann (Lewis Wilson).
Photo by David Cooper

Act Two, Rainstorm in *Beyond Eden:* Max explains why he's there. (l-r): John Mann (Lewis Wilson) and Cameron Macduffee (Max Tomson).
Photo by David Cooper

Act Two, Ninstints in *Beyond Eden:* the totem poles reveal themselves. (l-r): Jennifer Lines (Sal Wilson), Andrew Kushnir (Jack Wilson), John Mann (Lewis Wilson), and Cameron Macduffee (Max Tomson).
Photo by David Cooper

poles' power and potential for further transformation reveal themselves to Tomson through his tracing of their patterns. Without director Dennis Garnhum's magical staging animating the poles' painted carvings, Tomson's crucial reclamation of his Haida identity would come across as flat and insubstantial.

Ruddell's position as informed outsider parallels Wilson's. While it's understandable that he chooses to consciously focus on the white anthropologist's dilemma, his choice limits the argument about tradition and culture to a continuum of polite trespass. Relying on our knowledge of who and what Max Tomson/Bill Reid becomes after and *Beyond Eden* denies the fictional character the complexity and hard-won achievement of his real-life counterpart. In its current form—constrained by self-conscious provenance—*Beyond Eden* begs the question of where a bolder, unfettered take on this heart-of-darkness trope might lead.[3]

The difficulty of revisiting history—of applying a critical lens to distant, often opaque attitudes and maverick individuals—also troubles Marie Clements' *The Edward Curtis Project*.[4] For the better part of several decades from 1904 onwards, Edward Sherriff Curtis set out to capture in images what he considered a "vanishing race." Curtis journeyed to Native communities across North America where he took photographs that have since become iconic portraits of not just First Nations individuals, but of a mythic American West. While Curtis sought to capture "authenticity" in his Native subjects before their complete assimilation or eradication by war or disease, he was also complicit in promoting a romantic fiction of idealized "noble savages" forever frozen in a primitive twilight tradition, surpassed by Western civilization.

The scope of Curtis' *The North American Indian*, its attempt at comprehensive documentation of all tribes, has produced invaluable visual records. To what extent Curtis' images falsify history, are themselves artful interpretation masquerading as authentic record, is at the contentious heart of Marie Clements' inclusively titled, *The Edward Curtis Project*. With photographer Rita Leistner, Clements travelled to many of the communities made famous by Curtis, connecting with descendants of Curtis' iconic images (Clements). Having stared down visionaries like Norval Morisseau in *Copper Thunderbird* and big history (Hiroshima) in *Burning Vision*, Clements easily dispenses with naturalistic niceties for a more free-form approach to historic revisionism. As with Morriseau, her treatment of Curtis is imagistic and fantastic. She embeds fragments of Curtis' story within the action of an Aboriginal journalist's coming to terms with issues of identity, tilting the dramatic plane of *Beyond Eden's* gaze to question Curtis' sweeping perspective from an Aboriginal vantage point.

Co-directed by Clements with Presentation House Theatre's Brenda Leadlay, *The Edward Curtis Project* opened with an arresting image of a hand isolated in complete dark-

The Edward Curtis Project by Marie Clements: Angeline struggles against/within her family. Clockwise from left: Kathleen Duborg (Clara), Stephen E. Miller (father/Curtis), Kevin Loring (Yiska), and Tamara Podemski (Angeline).
Photo by Tim Matheson

ness, fingers flexing in a tight spotlight. As lights come up to reveal Tamara Podemski lying on a bare black stage, we meet Angeline, a contemporary mixed-race Aboriginal woman struggling to make sense of two children's deaths in snow and her guilt and revulsion at reporting the incident. Implicating herself in their deaths, Angeline retreats home only to unravel. There her sister Clara (Katherine Duborg), whose pale skin permits easy identification with the white majority, gives her Curtis' monumental tome, *The North American Indian*.

Angeline, the journalist in extremis, becomes immersed in Curtis' world vicariously. She imagines him alive, ingratiating himself to Indians: offering smokes and drinks, and cooking for her much as he did for the tribes on his exhaustive expeditions. The easy banter of these scenes contrasts with more tense domestic exchanges involving Curtis' neglected wife—another Clara—and the more formal frame of Curtis on his lecture tour, promoting the imagery of the "vanishing race."

Toward the middle of the play, Yiska, Angeline's lover, played by Kevin Loring, confronts Curtis. In one of the show's standout moments, the image of Alexander Upshaw, one of Curtis' Aboriginal interpreters, is superimposed on Yiska who speaks in Upshaw's voice. That image's articulation embodies the dilemma of Curtis' work: how to assert visibility against his sweeping panorama of seductive nostalgia. Yiska openly challenges Curtis' aims and methods, his casual intrusiveness, and automatic proprietary assumptions regarding his pictures. Under attack, Curtis reverts to the postures of his era stripped bare: he accuses Yiska of wanting to scalp him—"Every Indian carries a knife"—as he brandishes a pistol in defence. Near the end, Curtis is shown at the outset of what would become his life work: photographing one of his earliest subjects, Princess Angeline, Chief Seattle's daughter. With Upshaw interpreting, the scene tellingly reveals both parties engaged in wary trade.

Juggling a story of personal recovery against a larger-than-life icon, *The Edward Curtis Project* lacks comforting causality and the lock-step momentum of conventional narrative. Instead the play moves through thematic imagery and emotional logic, interrogating aspects of Curtis' life and work as they relate to Angeline's quest for spiritual equilibrium. Performed without intermission, the production built to a powerful conclusion: snow swirling over Angeline's panic at the discovery of two young bodies in the arctic drift amid layers of choral text and singer/songwriter Leela Gilday's haunting lullaby. The play closes full circle with the image of hands, compelling and strange for being isolated from the body to which, unseen, they nevertheless belong. More oblique than Curtis' epic sweep, Angeline's frozen gaze and complicity in witnessing and recounting a singularly horrific event are stilled rather than resolved.

With different filters and approaches to their monumental subjects, *Beyond Eden* and *The Edward Curtis Project* signal a new phase of engagement with core features of Western culture and its discontents. Neither adopts simplistic strategies or appraisals. Both assert the right of the previously objectified to critique their formerly inviolate curators. The terms of engagement, moreover, are not simply oppositional. *Beyond Eden* and *The Edward Curtis Project* open up new spaces, beyond knee-jerk politicization or aesthetic revisionism. In place, these works suggest how iconography and legend can be taken apart and configured anew, asserting possibilities for talking—even singing—back at the deadening effect of misguided preservationism. At the same time, both shows resist resolution or settlement, least of all of contentious questions of legacy and lasting impact.

Notes

1. Presentation House Theatre premiered *The Edward Curtis Project* theatre production as part of the PuSH International Festival 21–31 January 2010 in North Vancouver. Rita Leistner's photographic exhibit of the same name was presented by Presentation House Theatre 23 January to 23 May 2010 in cooperation with North Vancouver Museum & Archives.

2. Credited with the sound design as composer and arranger, Ruddell's score uses the period music Curtis commissioned to accompany his travelling slide shows, as referenced in the dramatic text. The production's other musical artist, Leela Gilday, is credited as singer/songwriter.

3. Washington's Arena Stage had expressed interest following a transfer to Calgary in March after its Vancouver premiere (Ruddell).

4. Extensive information and visuals of both the production and exhibition can be found at the show's website: www.edwardcurtisproject.ca.

Works Cited

Clements, Marie. Telephone interview. 17 Sept. 2010.

Ruddell, Bruce. Telephone interview. 21 Apr. 2010.

Beverly Yhap keeps an eye on theatre in Vancouver where she lives and writes (http://fishnfowl.blogspot.com/).

Many Stories, Many Voices: Alberta Aboriginal Arts

by Scott Sharplin

Rubaboo [Roo'-bə-boo]: *A Métis stew consisting of anything you can get your hands on.*

Christine Sokaymoh Frederick emceeing the second Annual Rubaboo Arts festival in June 2010.
Photo by Marc Chalifoux

Alberta Aboriginal Arts co-founders/co-directors Ryan Cunningham and Christine Sokaymoh Frederick welcome the audience to the second annual Rubaboo Arts Festival in June 2010.
Photo by Frieda Gladue

When describing the 2nd Annual Rubaboo Arts Festival, Christine Sokaymoh Frederick doesn't dwell on the broad range of Aboriginal theatre, music, and dance artists whose diverse contributions justify the event's name. Instead, her recollections focus on the audience. "It was downtown [Edmonton], and we had people coming in off the street," says Frederick. "To have Aboriginal people see something Aboriginal-themed on their own block was exciting." One particular woman came all four nights, and finally approached Frederick to ask, "What is this all about?" When Frederick began to explain Alberta Aboriginal Arts's role in organizing the festival, the patron interrupted: "What do you *mean,* you're an Aboriginal theatre company?" (qtd. in Frederick).

When they founded Alberta Aboriginal Arts (AAA) in summer 2009, Frederick and co-founder Ryan Cunningham were seeking the answers to similar questions. What can an Aboriginal-themed theatre company contribute to the cultural landscape? What audience(s) does it serve? And—perhaps most importantly—is there even such a thing as Aboriginal theatre? In the same year that AAA was founded, Floyd Favel wrote, in the pages of *Canadian Theatre Review,* that "there exists no Indigenous Canadian theatre" (32)—a declaration that seems to contradict, or undermine, Drew Hayden Taylor's optimism a decade earlier, when he wrote, "Native theatre is strong, popular and practically everywhere in terms of the Canadian theatrical community" (61). As AAA attempts to reconcile this paradox of Aboriginal Canadian theatre—a hearty, complex stew of narratives and disciplines that somehow still remains invisible—it has supplied its own, unique definition: a community-focused, multi-disciplinary arts organization devoted to presenting a wide range of Aboriginal stories.

The apparent scarcity of Native theatre is egregious in Alberta; the province has an Aboriginal population density of 6%, and its two largest cities (Edmonton and Calgary,

Christine Sokaymoh Frederick and Donald Morin in a reading of *Arvus in Excelsus* by Gordon A. Fox for the second annual Rubaboo Arts Festival in June 2010.
Photo by Marc Chalifoux

respectively) have the second and third highest Aboriginal populations of all Canadian cities ("Edmonton"; "Calgary"). Yet Ryan Cunningham recalls "growing up in theatre, going to theatre school, and working in theatre in Edmonton" without ever seeing an Aboriginal play produced. "It wasn't until I moved to Toronto that I was actually aware of Aboriginal theatre" (Cunningham).

And one province's scarcity may well reflect a broader dearth. Obtaining a clear impression of the Aboriginal Canadian theatrical landscape is difficult because, according to Frederick, many companies are "alive on paper, but there's no pulse" (Frederick). No companies with specifically Aboriginal mandates appear to be in operation in Quebec or Atlantic Canada, and between Ontario (e.g. Native Earth, Debajehmujig, Red Sky, Chocolate Woman Collective, and Turtle Gals Performance Ensemble) and Vancouver (e.g. Full Circle) there lies an unlikely cultural desert, punctuated only rarely by oases like Saskatchewan Native Theatre. Cunningham says he owes much of his artistic success to many of these companies, established in the 1980s and 1990s; but he feels that "no one in our generation seems to be stepping up" to maintain a nationwide network of Aboriginal companies (Cunningham).

In fact, while Cunningham was working as an actor "out east" with companies like Native Earth, two Aboriginal theatre initiatives arose in Alberta. In Edmonton, Old Earth Theatre arose when a group of actors, having met in 2005 in Walterdale Playhouse's production of *The Rez Sisters,* resolved to keep working together on original projects (Heather). In Calgary, Crazy Horse Theatre produced professional plays and festivals in Calgary from 2000 to 2007, before its small artistic team succumbed to burnout (Thrush). Such cases are common among small, independent arts initiatives. In an attempt to avoid administrative fatigue, Frederick and Cunningham agreed to adopt a strikingly different model for Alberta Aboriginal Arts.

Both artists, though relatively young, have garnered enough personal experience to know what mistakes to avoid. Frederick (Métis/Cree) has been an actor, writer, and producer in theatre, television and film for over twenty-five years. In addition, she has worked extensively in the Native cultural sector, helping to draft Edmonton's cultural plan *The Art of Living* as well as Alberta's Cultural Policy and the *Provincial Aboriginal Health Blueprint*. Cunningham (Métis) is a board member of the National Indigenous Performing Arts Alliance and an ACTRA and Equity actor with fifteen years' experience. Both artists have worked in administration and publicity, so they know how much work occurs behind the scenes just to make independent theatre feasible.

In a meeting with Canada Council for the Arts Theatre Section advisor Kim Selody, Cunningham learned why so many small companies, Aboriginal or otherwise, expire at an early stage. According to recent research findings, the CCA observed "theatre companies ... folding faster than they were being created, and that was ingrained in how Canada Council

Paula Jean Prudat in Act One of Native Earth's production of *Almighty Voice and His Wife* by Daniel David Moses; Alberta Aboriginal Arts sponsored the October 2010 production in Edmonton.
Photo by Nir Bareket, www.nirbareket.com.

Paula Jean Prudat (foreground) and Derek Garza (background) in Act One of Native Earth's production of *Almighty Voice and His Wife* by Daniel David Moses; Alberta Aboriginal Arts sponsored the October 2010 production in Edmonton.
Photo by Nir Bareket, www.nirbareket.com.

Native Earth's production of *Almighty Voice and His Wife* by Daniel David Moses. Alberta Aboriginal Arts sponsored the Edmonton production in October 2010. (l-r): Paula-Jean Prudat and Derek Garza.
Photo by Nir Bareket, www.nirbareket.com.

was encouraging how people were applying for grants" (Cunningham). The report observed theatre groups "were attempting to become not-for-profit right away, creating the infrastructure, and after two years, they spent so much energy *not* doing art, just doing all the not-for-profit building, that they burnt out" (Cunningham). Selody's suggestion was: "Do not go the not-for-profit route right away. Go for individual grants, project grants; create your mandate as you go" (qtd. in Cunningham).

The co-founders married this advice with their own perceived need to support the existing but unseen community of Native artists: "It seemed very clear, as we were writing our first grant, that [self-promotion] could not be our sole focus. [Cunningham and I] both had plans to do some of our own work at Rubaboo, but it became obvious that so much more could be done if we put our own projects aside for a moment, and focused on making the whole thing for everybody" (Frederick).

The result is a company devoted not to self-promotion, but to becoming "a hub that could support the network of Aboriginal artists in Alberta, as a community" (Cunningham). AAA's flagship project, the Rubaboo Festival, featuring forty playwrights, actors, musicians, and storytellers, illustrates the company's resolve to showcase as many Aboriginal artists as possible; they also collaborated with Dreamspeakers Film Festival, demonstrating their interest in reaching across disciplines to develop new forms of artistic expression.

Along with their commitment to community and collaboration, the willingness to embrace multidisciplinarity makes AAA a quintessentially Aboriginal theatre company: "Aboriginal performing arts [often] interweaves all the disciplines in a much more holistic way than western theatre," says Yvette Nolan, Artistic Director of Native Earth Theatre. "We have always used all the tools at our disposal to tell our stories—song and dance and storytelling—so it seems natural that as contemporary Aboriginal practice develops, we would continue to use all those tools" (Nolan). Native Earth is the first non-Albertan company to work closely with AAA; in October 2010, they collaborated to bring Native Earth's production of Daniel David Moses's *Almighty Voice and His Wife* to Edmonton. Native Earth's productions have toured Canada extensively since the company's creation in 1987; however, until AAA offered to host *Almighty Voice,* the company had only been able to show a single production to Alberta audiences ("not for lack of trying," adds Nolan).[1]

At every level of its operation, Alberta Aboriginal Arts reflects the artistic interweaving described by Nolan. "Aboriginal Art and performance doesn't fall into the western traditional categories of art: theatre, dance, opera, music," says Cunningham. "Our performances, our stories, our art, use all of those at once; you can't separate them" (Cunningham). For AAA, what began as a resolve to include diverse arts events in each season (i.e., one theatre event, one dance event, one music event) quickly became "a synergistic Renaissance" (Frederick). The company still plans to develop theatre using the western model—dramaturging Telly James's new play *Where the Sun Don't Shine* in 2011 and producing Tara Beagan's *Dreary and Izzy* in 2012—but much of their efforts are spent working with non-theatrical Native arts groups, looking for points of congruity.

Even when AAA's projects do focus on conventional theatrical texts, the tone and content of the work contains contradictions and surprises. In 1996, Drew Hayden Taylor described most Native Canadian playwrights' stories as "very, very angry" (67); along with depictions of dysfunction, alcoholism, and abuse, Taylor estimated that "in 75 per cent of the Native plays written and produced, there is a rape" (67). Today, Cunningham and Frederick believe that, while Native writers remain justifiably angry about their cultures' historical treatment and current circumstances, the modes of expressing that anger have changed.

"[Stories of abuse] are definitely an important part of our makeup and history as a people," says Frederick, "I find a lot of non-Aboriginal audiences are surprised—'We're still on about it?'—and yet they acknowledge that it's not taught in schools. So it's a voice that has to get out" (Frederick). But a new generation of Native storytellers are finding "new ways of telling stories that are transformative and hopeful," says Nolan, "we have other things to talk about onstage ... besides having survived ... our role in the larger society, our relationship to a changing environment, [and] our connection to traditional values " (Nolan).

"What do you *mean,* you're an Aboriginal theatre company?" In the case of Canada's youngest company, it means telling ambitious stories in collaborative ways that span artistic disciplines. And it means cheerfully embracing the paradoxes that arise from showcasing Canada's fastest growing and least visible cultures, on both a national scale and right on their very own block.

Note

1 In 2005, Workshop West Theatre (WWT) hosted Native Earth's production of Darrel Dennis's *Tales of an Urban Indian.* WWT also sponsored the first Rubaboo Arts Festival in 2008, and the company's current Artistic Director, Michael Clark, has been instrumental in supporting the foundation of Alberta Aboriginal Arts.

Works Cited

"Calgary." Canada. Statistics Canada. Social and Aboriginal Statistics Division. *2006 Aboriginal Population Profile for Calgary.* www.statcan.gc.ca. 2006. Web. 26 Feb. 2010.

Cunningham, Ryan. Skype interview. 29 Aug. 2010.

"Edmonton." Canada. Statistics Canada. Social and Aboriginal Statistics Division. *2006 Aboriginal Population Profile for Edmonton.* www.statcan.gc.ca. 2006. Web. 26 Feb. 2010.

Favel, Floyd. "Poetry, Remnants and Ruins: Aboriginal Theatre in Canada." *Canadian Theatre Review* 139 (2009): 31–35. Print.

Frederick, Christine Sokaymoh. Skype interview. 29 Aug. 2010.

Heather, Jane. Message to the author. 4 Feb. 2011. E-mail.

Nolan, Yvette. Message to the author. 13 Sept. 2010. E-mail.

Taylor, Drew Hayden. "Alive and Well: Native Theatre in Canada." *Aboriginal Drama and Theatre.* Ed. Rob Appleford. Toronto: Playwrights Canada, 2005. 61–68. Print.

Thrush, Michelle. Message to the author. 30 Aug. 2010. E-mail.

Scott Sharplin is a playwright, director, actor, and theatre educator. He has served as Artistic Director of Sound & Fury Theatre and Walterdale Playhouse, both in Edmonton. He has been involved with many Aboriginal-themed theatre projects, including an adaptation of Thomas King's *One Good Story, That One* and an original play about Louis Riel, entitled *The Burning Blood.* Sharplin presently resides in Glace Bay, Nova Scotia where he teaches Drama at Cape Breton University.

Humanizing Strangers Near and Far: Ethics and Irony in *The Middle Place* and *A Taste of Empire*

by Barry Freeman

The Middle Place *by Project: Humanity. Written by Andrew Kushnir, directed by Alan Dilworth, featuring Akosua Amo Adem, Antonio Cayonne, Jessica Greenberg, Kevin Walker, and the playwright. Staged at Theatre Passe Muraille in Toronto, 21 October to 13 November 2010. Previously staged at Theatre Passe Muraille as part of Summerworks 2009 and toured Toronto-area high schools*

(l-r): Antonio Cayonne, Akosua Amo-Adem, Kevin Walker, and Jessica Greenberg who, with Andrew Kushnir, are the cast of *The Middle Place.*
Photo by Aviva Armour Ostroff

thereafter. Appearing 14 February to 12 March 2011 at CanStage in Toronto; 14 March to 20 March 2011 on the mainstage of Vancouver's Belfry Theatre as part of the Belfry's "Spark Festival", and finally 29 March to 17 April 2011 at the GCTC, Ottawa.

A Taste of Empire by Cahoots Theatre Company. Staged at the Market Kitchen in St. Lawrence Market, Toronto, 29 June to 24 July 2010. Written and performed by Jovanni Sy. Directed by Guillermo Verdecchia and dramaturged by Ric Knowles.

In his book *Cosmopolitanism: Ethics in a World of Strangers*, cultural philosopher Kwame Anthony Appiah asks probing questions about the ethical relationship we may have with "strangers," people we know little about but to whom we may nonetheless be responsible. Appiah writes, "when the stranger is no longer imaginary, but real and present, sharing a human social life [...] you can make sense of each other in the end" (99). While two recent productions I saw in Toronto had little in common in terms of their provenance or tone, they seemed to have in common a desire to make strangers—those close to home and those far away—more real and present.

I encountered the first production on a grey day in 2009 when I filed into a Toronto high school auditorium with the school's students. I had been working on a research project with drama students at the school, and their teacher had arranged for a young company of actors to perform a play called *The Middle Place*. Previous plays this teacher had brought to the school were performed in her classroom, but this play was being performed for the whole school, divided into two audiences that each filled the auditorium. As the students settled into their seats, the atmosphere was boisterous. When the plain-clothed actors stepped onto the massive old stage, I doubted whether they could get this group's attention. They did that and more, transfixing their audience and affirming for me the power and magic of simple, unadorned theatre.

The play was produced by Project: Humanity (P:H), a company with a mandate to engage in youth social issues through art. To date, P:H has initiated or participated in a number of community-based workshops and humanitarian relief efforts. In 2007, the company offered a drama and improv workshop at a Toronto youth shelter called Youth Without Shelter. Quite taken by the personalities and stories of the residents, however, the company, and in particular its new addition Andrew Kushnir, decided to pull some workshop participants aside and interview them. The interviewing took on a life of its own as Kushnir interviewed shelter residents that year and the next. Following through on the company's mandate to bring local social issues to wider public consciousness, Kushnir began to fashion transcriptions of his interviews into a piece of verbatim theatre that would give a human face to youth homelessness. When I saw *The Middle Place* at the high school, the play was partway through its ongoing journey; it premiered at the Summerworks Festival in 2009 to strong reviews, it was about to be picked up in an unusual 2010–11 co-production between Theatre Passe Muraille and CanStage, and it would be seen in Ottawa and Victoria in spring 2011.

Derek Paget coined the term "verbatim theatre" in 1987 to describe a kind of documentary theatre in which the text was derived from interview transcripts or, in the analogue language of the 1980s, "theatre which makes use of taped actuality recording as its primary source material" (317). Since the 1980s, theatre labeled verbatim comprises a variety of forms with varying levels of artistic mediation between source and product. Despite the form's proliferation and enduring popularity, however, verbatim remains the subject of criticism. The objection most commonly heard is that verbatim becomes less artful in the act of lifting its text from "real life," making it indistinguishable, at an extreme, from journalism. In 2010, David Hare wrote what reads like an exasperated apologia for verbatim in *The Guardian*. In it, Hare points out that there is no right or wrong way to create art, and that we ought to be suspicious of anyone guarding its gate. And verbatim theatre is not journalism; where journalism reduces and simplifies, verbatim theatre uncovers complexity and contradiction. Also, says Hare, verbatim departs from journalism in its use of metaphor. My own observation is that however much verbatim theatre is received as somehow more "authentic," it is infused with metaphor and often self-consciously marks itself as the product of careful craft.

The Middle Place is certainly a product of careful craft. The transcripts of Kushnir's interviews at the youth shelter ran 450 pages, whereas the script of the performance runs only fifty. That kind of selectivity is common in verbatim theatre, but Kushnir made two specific choices in crafting the play that were less common. The first is that the actors of *The Middle Place* never saw the videotaped interviews of the youth at any point in the creative process, working purely from transcripts instead. This made their work an act of interpretation as much as one of imitation; while they had to stay faithful to the meticulously transcribed text, having to apply some common understandings of punctuation and typographic convention, they were free to invent vocal and physical qualities for their characters. The second choice would be more visible to the audience: Kushnir's decision to put himself in the play. As the actors onstage cycle through their characters, Kushnir himself moves throughout the audience, asking questions, letting awkward moments languish, or simply just listening as one of his interviewees chooses where to go and what to reveal. This choice throws open the doors on the ethics of the process behind *The Middle Place*, exposing the interviewer's naïveté and missteps but also, conversely, the tact and respect that explains the trust the youth had in him. A particularly poignant monologue in the show (Kushnir refers to each character's most powerful

(l-r): Akosua Amo-Adem, Antonio Cayonne, Jessica Greenberg, and Kevin Walker in *The Middle Place*.
Photo by Aviva Armour Ostroff

monologue as an "aria," a term Paget has also used) comes from the unforgettably fragile and charming character Neveah ("It's heaven, backwards," she says), who slowly lets out a story of family abuse and separation that gets darker with each chapter. Kushnir doesn't prod, but just lets out an acknowledging "right" or "yeah" in between chapters as Neveah turns the pages. Neveah's story unfolds in the context of a relationship, and what might have been staged as a dark revelation is instead a young woman's risky, but hopeful reach for empathy and understanding, a gift we feel lucky to share. Near the end of the play, Kushnir asks the youth: "If there were actors saying your words to an audience, what would you want them to say?" ("Cut—your—shit!" answers Kaaliyah, played by Amo Adem with alpha-female attitude that makes the other characters duck for cover). We delight in the answers not only for their quirkiness and wisdom, but because in that moment we most clearly share the actors' experience of "looking in" on the lives of others. The moment is a beautiful illustration of Brecht's epic theatre as described in his "street scene" essay: actors intervening socially by demonstrating the experience of others.

The Middle Place transcends bleak journalistic portrayals of homelessness by offering unforgettable glimpses into the lives of kind and hopeful youth caught in stasis. With more space, I would say much more about the play. It must be said that Kushnir's finely crafted script is supported by an elegant, dead-simple design. The design rests on a single theatrical metaphor: a large white oval on the stage floor inside of which the actors speak as youth, outside of which they speak as shelter staff. When actors "enter" the shelter by returning to the oval (the middle place), they tap an imaginary buzzer, and a cold, hard sound effect makes palpable the institutional rigidity that shapes their daily lives at the shelter. The stage metaphor also helps delineate the cast of twenty characters with clarity, as do Alan Dilworth's tight direction, Monica Dottor's smartly devised choreography, and the cast's physical precision (four of the play's actors animate sixteen different characters). It should also be said that, pursuant to its social awareness agenda, P:H built an educational project around the show called the "Urban Youth Experience," providing its audience with information on youth shelters and opportunities to discuss the play among other things. The year 2011 will be a big one for P:H, and it will be interesting to watch this talented young company meet creatively the challenge of reconciling their work in professional theatre with their social work in the community.

Where *The Middle Place* made visible the strangers in our midst, Cahoots Theatre's *A Taste of Empire* is about global ethics—the degree to which we feel a sense of responsibility to, or obligation toward, strangers in more distant places. It's also about food.

Part cooking demonstration and part globalization primer, *A Taste of Empire* was staged this past summer at an unusual venue for theatre: the Market Kitchen at the St. Lawrence Market in Toronto, a beautifully renovated professional kitchen usually home to cooking classes and wine tastings. The play, which in this production used the kitchen as a site-specific venue with little embellishment, introduces us to a sous-chef named Jovanni, played by former Cahoots Artistic Director Jovanni Sy. Jovanni (the character), works for the Imperial Seafood Corporation and answers to one Master Chef Maximo Cortés, whose corporate ruthlessness and unsavoury self-promotion we are acquainted with through a video sequence displayed on a screen above the kitchen. Chef Maximo (as Jovanni calls him) was supposed to do the cooking demo for us, the audience, but passed on the duty to his enthusiastic underling Jovanni after being called to another engagement (involving Bono). On the menu is a traditional Filipino dish involving a stuffed fish called *rellenong bangus* (*rellenong* from Spanish for "stuffed," *bangus* a Pacific milkfish). Jovanni (actor and character) actually cooks the meal for the audience as the play unfolds, handling himself in the kitchen with impressive confidence and ease.

As Jovanni steels his knives and sets up the *mise en place*, he begins to tell his audience stories behind *rellenong bangus*. As a consequence of Spanish colonialism in the Philippines, we learn, the *bangus* in the meal gets stuffed with *sofrito*, a mixture of tomatoes, onions, and garlic that is a staple of Spanish cooking. But it is the new imperialism of globalization that takes centre stage in *Taste of Empire*. Systems of food production that have been local for thousands of years now extend the world over, severing our connection with what we eat. The fish being cooked for us came from an aquaculture farm in the Philippines and was flash-frozen before being exported. It's more profitable that way and cheaper for the consumer ("Everyone's a winner!" says Jovanni, parroting boss Chef Maximo's mantra). The real winner, of course, is Chef Maximo and Imperial Seafood, a

Jovanni Sy and Bong-Bong in *A Taste of Empire*.
Photo by Keith Barker

fact we're reminded of when Jovanni periodically interrupts his demo to hawk Chef Maximo's wares: knives, cookbooks, even "Glucomax," a medicinal powder offsetting the effects of diabetes. We don't miss the ironic suggestion here that corporations are selling products to solve problems they created in the first place, an imperial injustice that finds a visceral metaphor in *rellenong bangus* itself: a meal prepared by emptying out the guts of a fish and then using the fish carcass as a sausage casing for a foreign mixture. But as with *The Middle Place*, *A Taste of Empire* digs beneath the social issues to tell the human story. We learn that the fisherman who caught the *bangus* in the meal was once an open-boat hand-line fisherman, but is now a lowly inspector in a fish-processing plant. We learn that a Mexican migrant worker who picked the tomato used for garnish supports his family back home on his minimum wage. (Even the eviscerated fish is personalized with a name: Bong-Bong.) The local and the global, the personal and the political intersect, the layers theatricalized using the projection screen: slides that playfully illustrate the stories cut back to a live video feed close-up of Jovanni's hands as he works on the meal. Visually, our perspective is taken through the web of relationships involved in the act of consumption.

Theatrically, *A Taste of Empire* leans heavily on an important device in relation to global ethics: irony. The play's frame of a corporate cooking demonstration—the presentation on behalf of Imperial Seafood—is a platform from which Jovanni blasts comic irony at a modern system of food production that makes its real-world implications invisible to the supermarket customer. Similarly ironic is the corporate dogma spouted by the significantly absent Chef Maximo, an expert in "Imperial Cuisine" and a stand-in for corporate ignorance and greed. Maximo is a humorous but outlandish villain who cannot be taken any more seriously than Jovanni's obviously servile endorsements of his values or products. There's more than a dash of irony here, and perhaps the hand of the director is visible. Guillermo Verdecchia has said that he uses humour as a point of entry into his work, and uses irony to make it ambiguous: "I like the dynamic of performance," he offers, "where one moment the audience is laughing and the next I am asking them why" (Hansen 176). I wonder, though, whether comic irony might not sometimes have the opposite effect of ambiguity. In a recent article in the *Review of International Studies*, James Brassett looks at the anti-globalization iconography of graffiti artist Banksy, as well as the politically conscious, self-mocking comedy of Ricky Gervais to consider how such artists deal with issues of global ethics by deploying irony. Brassett argues that these artists use irony to increase our sensitivity to the human suffering of others," but he also makes the interesting observation that there is an important "solidarity" in irony, "*the idea that we all get the joke*" (223). That's a good thing for Brassett, because, he writes, ironic positions "suggest some form of community in critique [...] of global ethics" (223).

That strikes me as a provocative idea in relation to *A Taste of Empire,* and by extension to theatrical treatments of global ethics more generally. It's true that we may interpret the irony of *A Taste of Empire* to be indicative of a wider collective cultural backlash against the corporatization of food, a backlash manifested in the organic, locavore and 100-mile diet movements. But while irony might implicitly suggest the maturity of a cultural movement, and while its comic potential is inarguable (if exhaustible), it can also feel as though it doesn't admit a balanced presentation of an issue. For example, as Bong-Bong the fish's back story rolls out, the implicit argument—if we can call it that—for a pre-industrial mode of food production starts to feel a bit romantic. (And I was missing the arguments one could make for the positive environmental consequences of industrial-scale aquaculture.) The play does dig deeper into the issue here by suggesting how the fisherman's quality of life may have actually improved with his job at a processing plant, but this, too, is glazed in irony, and has to be completely discarded when we later learn of the fisherman's cruel treatment at the hands of Imperial Seafood.

I can imagine that the shift to which Verdecchia alludes—from, in my own terms, the comic/ironic to the critical/ethical—is coded into the script in the form of Jovanni's cracking and ultimately shattered faith in the corporate enterprise for which he works. For me, however, Sy's performance had an affected quality that made it hard to believe that he (and by extension, anyone else) really bought Chef Maximo's drivel to begin with. There wasn't a real connection to the audience here, perhaps because the solidarity to which the play's irony appeals is, in fact, itself a hopeful fiction, something that was made most obvious to me when Jovanni made statements to the effect of "I know what you're thinking." Which Jovanni, actor or character, knows what we're thinking? Where the shift did clearly take place, however, was after the applause. When after the show Jovanni served up portions of *bangus* for his audience, you had the unique sensory experience of enjoying the rich flavours of *rellenong bangus* while you were conscious that the meal had a human cost beyond what was paid at the grocery store; a delicious irony perhaps, and one significant to the issues at stake.

Works Cited

Appiah, Anthony. *Cosmopolitanism: Ethics in a World of Strangers.* 1st ed. Issues of Our Time. New York: W.W. Norton, 2006. Print.

Brassett, James. "British Irony, Global Justice: A Pragmatic Reading of Chris Brown, Banksy and Ricky Gervais." *Review of International Studies* 35 (2009): 219–245. Print.

Brecht, Bertolt. *Brecht on Theatre; the Development of an Aesthetic.* London: Methuen, 1964. Print.

Hansen, Pil. "Dramaturgical Strategies: Articulations from Five Toronto-Based Theatre Artists." *Developing Nation: New Play Creation in English-Speaking Canada.* Ed. Bruce Barton. Toronto: Playwrights Canada, 2009. 168–184. Print.

Hare, David. "Mere Fact, Mere Fiction." *The Guardian.* 17 Apr. 2010. Web. 25 Apr. 2011.

Paget, Derek. "'Verbatim Theatre': Oral History and Documentary Techniques." *New Theatre Quarterly* 12.3 (1987): 317–336. Print.

Barry Freeman is an Assistant Professor in Theatre and Performance Studies at the University of Toronto Scarborough. His research interests are Canadian theatre, drama-in-education, performance ethnography, ethics, and interculturalism.

The Politics of Distraction: Spectatorial Freedom and (dis)Enfranchisement in Toneelgroep's *Roman Tragedies*

by Natalie Corbett and Keren Zaiontz

Written by William Shakespeare. Direction by Ivo Van Hove. Dramaturgy by Bart Van Den Eynde, Jan Peter Gerrits, and Alexander Schreuder. With Roeland Fernhout, Renée Fokker, Fred Goessens, Marieke Heebink, Chico Kenzari, Hans Kesting, Hugo Koolschijn, Hadewych Minis, Chris Nietvelt, Frieda Pittoors, Alwin Pulinckx, Halina Reijn, Eelco Smits, and Karina Smulders. Musicians include Bl!NDMAN: Ruben Cooman, Yves Goemaere, Ward De Ketelaere, and Hannes Nieuwlaet. Set and lighting design by Jan Versweyveld. Costume design by Lies Van Assche. Video by Tal Yarden. Music by Eric Sleichim. Produced by Toneelgroep Amsterdam. Co-production by Holland Festival (Amsterdam), La Monnaie (Bruxelles), Kaaitheatre (Bruxelles), Muziektheatre Transparant (Anvers), and BL!NDMAN (Bruxelles). Presented by Festival TransAmériques in Association with Monument-National and Carrefour International de Théâtre de Québec, 28–30 May 2010.

In the five-and-a-half-hour epic *Roman Tragedies,* staged by the prodigious Dutch ensemble Toneelgroep, Shakespeare's tragedies of *Coriolanus, Julius Caesar,* and *Antony and Cleopatra* are performed in a sequence that traces political history from the beginnings of democracy to the globalized world of international politics. The trilogy, billed as "Shakespeare that jumps straight from the headlines [...] hurled into the heart of the contemporary world" offers an updating that seeks to investigate the mechanisms of state power and the nature of "man [sic] as a political animal" (FTA). Key to this twenty-first century interpretation of Shakespeare's texts is the production's encouragement of audience engagement, which implicates spectators as the absent public that bears witness to ongoing political turbulence. Audiences that attended the North American premiere at the 2010 Festival TransAmérique experienced both exceptional physical duration and proximity to the event while circulating between (and within) the auditorium and the stage during timed breaks. Within the context of an international festival known for its contemporary theatre and dance, the dynamics of reception in *Roman Tragedies* are the proud insignia of the "avant-garde" or experimental performance traditions. The production adopts slightly condensed versions of Shakespeare's dramaturgical structures, employs well-established conventions of disruption, and incorporates a realist mode of acting. However, the true experimentality of *Roman Tragedies* lies in linking the direct participation of audiences to a political commentary that dramatizes the dangers of (and desire for) distraction in a hypermediated world.

Jan Versweyveld's set design casts the play's epic actions within a modern, anonymous corporate environment, populated by blandly geometric Swedish sofas, potted plants, Plexiglas and ubiquitous television monitors. Modular configurations within the stage space function interchangeably as committee boardroom and private living room, highlighting the porousness between the public and private lives being staged. Camera operators relentlessly film the actors, whose images are projected onto the screens on stage and in the wings, simultaneously remediated as live news broadcasts. When actors exit the stage they often remain visible on the periphery; hair and makeup stations line the stage right wing, brushing up against one of the stage-side food vendors.

The dynamic of constant visibility created by this aesthetic of surveillance highlights the two most significant alterations to the original Shakespeare texts. Although nothing has been added, all battles have been replaced by extended spectacular sequences of flashing lights and violent bombastic sound, and all scenes in which the citizens speak have been cut. By col-

Julius Caesar: Brutus addresses the masses in a press conference. On stage, audiences seated on sofas watch the television address on screen. (l-r): Renée Fokker, Eelco Smits, Jacob Derwig, and Marieke Heebink.
Photo by Jan Versweyveld

lapsing the unfolding stratagems and defining events of major wars to their final outcomes—and by excising all record of public response to the momentous political events depicted—the edited script presents a narrative relentlessly focused on the psychology of those few individuals within the highest echelons of power. Stripped of the minutiae of developing action, the balanced causal chains of Shakespeare's tragedies are reshaped into contemporary portraits of political manoeuvring, backroom dealings and press conferences, private scandals, and public obfuscation.

The increased biographical bent produced by this narrative condensation lends itself to the acting style of the piece, which is defined at once by the intimacy of filmic realism and by intense, even volatile, emotionalism. The unhinged displays by the ensemble, exemplified by group arguments and giddy encounters between lovers, deliberately risk a performance of excess. Certainly for those spectators on stage—standing or sitting beside the physical scrapes that break out between politicians in *Julius Caesar,* or within arms' reach of the queen and her ladies as they swill champagne and dance boisterously in *Antony and Cleopatra*—these corporeal outbursts allow the audience to inhabit the tragedies in a way that exceeds the traditional prioritization of the word in Shakespearean performance. The intimacy of these encounters do not so much bring spectators into contact with the politics of ancient Rome as with the politics of "personalized" media which feed our desire to be "up close and personal"

with public figures, be they politicians or stars. Politics, separated from the lived consequences for the populace, and framed by the representational logic of the twenty-four-hour news cycle, is displayed largely as a cult of personality.

What *Roman Tragedies* so deftly dramatizes is our insatiable need to come into proximity to, and accumulate intimate details about, the excesses of public figures. The spectacular performance environment shows this very act of accumulation to be mediated by continuous display. Thus, in mining Shakespeare's texts for their many private trysts and public betrayals, director Ivo Van Hove lays bare the aesthetics of contemporary politics. Political power is represented through a disclosure of stagecraft in which theatrical and mediatized effects like makeup, recording technology, and cinematography are shown to produce public figures. As audiences witness how the images of politicians accumulate and circulate through the apparatus of the stage, the function of imitation shifts course. Van Hove expresses this refocused view of mimesis when he insists that the "*Roman Tragedies* are not realist theatre, but a theatre of reality" (FTA). The tragedies do not set out to imitate the spectacle of politics but to show how the contemporary political world is structured *through* imitation.

In a theatre of reality, the constitutive feature is a participatory culture that is permanently "plugged in" to the social world.[1] Scripted into the void left by absent soldiers and citizens, the spectators of *Roman Tragedies* function as a

Coriolanus: Coriolanus refuses to recognize the tribunes. In the context of the scene's staging as a public hearing, Coriolanus' volatile behaviour and violent antics emphasize not only his contempt for the common people, but also his disregard for the negative optics of the televised event. (l-r): Fred Goessens, Fedja van Huêt, Eelco Smits, Alwin Pulinckx, and Jacob Derwig.
Photo by Jan Versweyveld

Julius Caesar: Caesar's slain body rests on the press conference table as a camera operator films the public address. Mark Anthony's superior rhetorical skills are matched in this staging by his savvy in performing for the camera. (l-r): Hugo Koolschijn, and Hans Kesting.
Photo by Jan Versweyveld

Montreal performance, rules structuring audience movement were explained via teleprompter and spoken announcement at the short break after the first scene: mobility was allowed during the breaks (the lengths of which were visible as a countdown displayed on all screens). Placement on stage was highly structured, generally limited to the sofas and a few additional boxes or stools in the offstage space. The implicit (and explicit) contract for the audience to be visible yet silent observers and not participants was quite rigid.

The separation of audience from the depicted action, manifested in their spatial complicity and visible passivity, is further emphasized by a number of traditional alienating strategies employed in the production. As the performance unwinds, the electronic ticker running above the stage provides updates as to the amount of time remaining until the death of each of the key characters. At the conclusion of scenes, spoken and visual announcements inform the audience of what will follow in the next scene, prompting individuals to make an informed choice about what perspective they would like to have on the event. The volume of narrative information presented and the duration of attention demanded by *Roman Tragedies* are almost overwhelming, and yet the devices that appear to support comprehension are suspect. At the top of the production a lengthy history detailing the specific players and conflicts that have culminated in the events prior to the first scene scroll on both the projection screen and digital news crawler at breakneck speed. During battle sequences a rapid summary of events competes with stroboscopic lighting and deafening percussion. The net effect is that of being witness to significant political events that are the products of a causality too complicated to understand either in the unfolding moment, or without specialist knowledge.

The disparity between the event and our understanding (or interpretation) of it is manifested, most compellingly, in the execution of stage deaths. Framing character deaths as facts that can be estimated, announced, and digitally archived, *Roman Tragedies* brings into focus our desire to master the finiteness of life through hard-boiled facts. Finitude is not grappled with, or even mourned, but is managed within the circuits of media as yet another image. Actors, at the moment of their stage deaths, are positioned (thrown, pushed, or voluntarily laid) on a sliding platform that, when thrust into place, triggers an overhead camera to photograph the corpse. The image, projected at the instant of death onto the main screen above the proscenium as well as the onstage screens, evokes an aesthetic of criminal evidence. The unmoving body, still and breathless in photography as no live performer can be, maintains the finality of death, even as the actor rises and walks off stage. The rupture between the liveness of the performance at this moment and the mediated image with its greater diegetic realism, emphasizes the contradictory multiplicity of informational tracks available to the spectator.

mute but networked populace, attempting to comprehend the machinations that shape their world. Ostensibly, the freedom to choose where to sit, to enter the stage space and be in close proximity to the actors, or to opt out of spectatorship, have a sandwich, check e-mail, or tweet updates to the outside world, suggests an enfranchised and flexible engagement with performance. Indeed, autonomous, individual contribution to the event was encouraged by the availability of public computers on stage, and even celebrated through the publication of spectators' Twitter comments on the overhead news crawler. Despite the variability of the configuration, however, participation, as such, is entirely proscribed. In the

End of *Coriolanus*, beginning of *Julius Caesar:* The glass walls and sliding platform (upstage centre) designate the place in *Roman Tragedies* where characters go to die. Above the stage, on screen, an overexposed image of the slain Coriolanus is projected both at the moment of his death and the close of the play. (l-r): Fedja van Huêt, Marieke Heebink, Renée Fokker, Barry Atsma, and Jacob Derwig.
Photo by Jan Versweyveld

Antony and Cleopatra: Antony and Cleopatra surrounded by Cleopatra's retinue. The audience has returned to sit in the auditorium for the final scenes (and play) of the evening. On screen: Chris Nietvelt and Hans Kesting. On stage, (l-r): Eelco Smits, Chris Nietvelt, Marieke Heebink, Jacob Derwig, Hans Kesting, Janni Goslinga, Frieda Pittoors, Alwin Pulinckx, Barry Atsma, Fedja van Huêt, and Hadewych Minis.
Photo by Jan Versweyveld

The distancing effects of *Roman Tragedies*, however, do not thwart engagement so much as serve to raise questions about what kinds of engagement are possible in an era of global accessibility, digital reproduction, and a higher degree of audience choice. Audiences in *Roman Tragedies* contend with scales of distraction that range from spectacular display to microspatial engagement: in the electronic ticker that scrolls across the proscenium arch, providing crucial information in multiple languages at almost unreadable speed; in the large screen above the ticker that projects a live feed of the stage action; in the sandwiches and refreshments served on stage between strictly timed breaks; and in the placement of computers to post updates just inches from the action on social networking sites like Twitter. Audiences witness state power as a dispersed event. The overproduction of the stage image onto multiple screens recharges the content of the tragedies so that state affairs are made to serve the consumptive habit of spectators. This reimagination of the tragedies as a visual display that is endlessly sensationalized—and appropriated into a twenty-four-hour news cycle—does not belong to the "counter-traditions" in which the authority of Shakespeare's texts is tested. Rather, the authority that is challenged in *Roman Tragedies*, with the complicity of roving audiences, is that of mass media.

Note

1   In *Blog Theory*, Jodi Dean's observation about online, participatory culture (by way of Giorgio Agamben's reading of contemporary spectacle), assists us in understanding how publics mirror the politicians and stars that dominate the media landscape by prioritizing individual "usership" online:

> We have been produced as subjects unlikely to coalesce, subjects resistant to solidarity, and subjects suspicious of collectivity. Central to this production is the cultivation and feeding of a sense of unique and special individuality. Every sperm is sacred, so began the story of our unique cellular lives. Or, every potential genetic combination carries with it the remarkable potentiality we locate in our individuated selves. Each voice must be heard (but they don't combine into a chorus). Each vote must be counted (but they add up to less than a movement). Each person must be visible (but then we don't see a group). Personalized "participatory" media is a problem not only because of its personalization of participation. More than that is its injunction that we participate ever more in personalization: make your own avatar, video, profile, blog, mobster, video, and app. Participation becomes indistinguishable from personalization, the continued cultivation of one's person. Leave your mark (82).

Works Cited

Dean, Jodi. *Blog Theory: Feedback and Capture in the Circuits of Drive.* Cambridge: Polity, 2010. Print.

FTA. Festival TransAmérique. Play Program. *Tragédies Romaines.* Ivo Van Hove + William Shakespeare. ToneelGroep Amsterdam. Montreal: FTA, May 2010. Print.

Natalie Corbett is a PhD candidate at the University of Toronto's Graduate Centre for Study of Drama. Her dissertation examines ongoing and evolving preoccupations with "literariness" in theatrical adaptations of Canadian novels for the Canadian stage.

Keren Zaiontz is co-editor of the anthologies *Reluctant Texts from Exuberant Performance: Canadian Devised Theatre* and *Performing Adaptations: Essays and Conversations on the Theory and Practice of Adaptation.* Her current research examines how audiences are enlisted in arts and cultural festivals to promote neighbourhoods and nations through community-based art, installation, audio tours, and other participatory events.

Dancing in the Dark: *Tu vois ce que je veux dire?*

by Natalie Rewa

Tu vois ce que je veux dire?, which was featured during the Festival TransAmériques in Montreal in May 2010, is a time-based *dérive* (peregrination). It partners two complete strangers: one a volunteer signed on by the producers, and the other a ticket-buyer. Before they meet, the ticket-buying partner is blindfolded. Together they will negotiate an urban landscape and some of its interior spaces. The present writer was one of the blindfolded ticket-buyers, hence the point of view.

The first edition of this "urban odyssey" in 2005 was a co-production by Projet in situ in association with three diverse organizations: Théâtre Le Merlan, Lieux Publics (an urban theatre company), and the National Institute for the Blind in Marseille. Three years later it was a contribution to the Biennale de danse in Lyon. The artistic directors of the walk are dancer Martin Chaput (originally from Montreal) and choreographer and anthropologist Martial Chazallon, whose company regularly collaborates with dancers, photographers, and visual and installation artists in France and South Africa. For a decade Chazallon has also been rechoreographing urban environments so as to interrupt the habits of the social and historical body. Such walks engage local sites and local artists as part of a kinesthetic lab, the emphasis being on the physicality of movement rather than descriptive touring. The experience is an active immersion in a kind of acoustic and tactile scenography. The title is playfully ambiguous because what you are told is very minimal and what you "see" in the mind's eye is immensely more than what is told. The seeing partner is under instructions not to describe, identify or confirm the assumptions, suppositions or guesses of the blindfolded one, except to warn about approaching hazards such as curbs and steps.

Initially, the walk is a trust exercise in which the ticket-buying participant's own urban gait and habits of walking are adapted under seeing guidance. Chaput and Chazallon allow for both the heightened acoustic and other sensorial impressions engendered by the blindfold to take hold before the visits to various interior spatial and social environments begin. These will culminate in a final dance in a large gymnasium about two and half hours later. During the walk, generalized aural attention to street sounds is alternated with visits to defined spaces such as a café, a yoga studio, a graphic exhibit, a church, and its internal ritual spaces including a confessional and a music lesson—a different selection for each ticket-holder.

In Montreal the walk started from the second storey Long Haul/Le Corrid'art, a not-for-profit artist's space that

The three-hour walk had a real vibrancy about it for each member of the couple; for the guides, showing the city provided a new perspective.

A volunteer guides the blindfolded walker and each walker is encouraged to take refreshment en route.
Photo by Juan Saez

otherwise serves as a hub for visual artists. Departures for the walk were timed so that there were only two or three ticket-holders in the gallery at any one time, and the briefings were simultaneous with a blindfold fitting.

My guide, Louise, was introduced. Her left elbow was my point of contact. Up to this point *Tu vois ce que je veux dire?* was like any number of trust walks used in workshops; the first five minutes of the walk were taken up with a careful descent to the street, down a circular staircase and to the sidewalk. On the street the guide fell silent and my pace became the measure for the walk. *Tu vois ce que je veux dire?* insists on the participant being immersed in the city and becoming a spectacle while being deprived of sight herself. Initially the walk appears to have absorbed the city—the sidewalks, the textures of fencing or railing, the construction materials of the buildings, and the public fountains and benches—but soon modulates into a complex sense of one's

Commercial and residential areas intrigue the walker as well as the fellow pedestrians and residents.
Photo by Juan Saez

blind jazz musician takes over from Louise. This visit involves a gentle choreography added in small increments. Klang invites me to explore various spaces within the church. At first I climb into a tight, round wooden pulpit and I am instructed to percuss this drum-like structure, then together we test its acoustics; soon we take the volumetric measure of a chapel and the main nave by throwing out sound in quick bursts. This visit finally ends with an exploration of a sculpture in the church. With a kind of transgressive glee, Klang leads me to a sculpture and asks me to describe it. His low giggle suggests an artist-to-artist amusement when I remark on an enormously long and seemingly untrimmed toenail on one of the figures—a physical joke by the sculptor—that perhaps is only available to those who touch the figure.

The final segment of the walk is set some distance from the church. When I arrive, it requires that I remove my

presence in public as the walker is acknowledged both by participating hosts and in random encounters with those who are merely interested in the figure of the blindfolded walker.

Walking on the street primes the walker to give up ingrained urban habits—of vigilance, if not also tension. For the first twenty minutes or so the terrain is all outdoors, on sidewalks, on the crossing of busy streets, and into the respite and cool of a park or square. During this phase sensitivity is profound to the movement of cars on the street and their stink, to the blaring radios and snippets of conversation, all of which coalesce into shifting impressions. Suddenly I am walking on grass, independently, out of touch, out of communication with Louise … quite a thrilling adventure. Conversations, although brief, quickly engage the oddness of the meeting, our perspectives on the occasion, and the (assumed) environment.

Gradually, the walk distills this purposeful movement by crossing a series of thresholds. At each of these junctures the guide and the walker negotiate a new series of moves. Louise's arm, still bent at the elbow is now extended across her back, signaling that I should follow behind directly and hold on to her right shoulder with my other hand. Although the manoeuvre was rehearsed at the outset and has been used at various stages en route, it becomes imperative at this point in order to pass through narrow spaces and portals. In a shop I am left to engage with objects d'art made from recycled materials—all known materials repurposed. At a private house where we listen to two female musicians who play a composition for flute and violin and then reverse the parts, the ensuing minutes involve an intense memory exercise of the music and a discussion with them of the specificity of each instrument. It is not only the music at issue but how I arrange myself to hear it and respond to what I hear from the unseen source. The third visit is to a large church where a

For interior experiences, the blindfolded walker is handed over to a new volunteer. The interior of a church provided a lively acoustical tour by blind volunteers.
Photo by Juan Suez

socks and shoes and cool off before a dancer invites me to take his elbow. This time, no personal introductions; in fact, all this is done in total silence. We begin slowly by walking the length and width of the large indoor space. Gradually our movements are sped up and we add the activation of one arm first, and then the other, and then adjust our breathing in relation to the movement. Just as in the church regarding the soundings, I begin to realize that this movement has another very strong delight in either moving from my physical core through space or choosing to animate my limbs in much smaller movements; I begin to guide my body with my breath and even attempt to resist the direction of this guide. For about twenty minutes I explore the space with what seems to be several dancers, and when I think of being observed I decide that I am now more willing to take a chance on exploring this choreography. When this dance

The final sequence, with a professional dancer, invited a fresh choreography of the social body; seen here is the delight in a convivial stillness.
Photo by Juan Saez

ends, I am reunited with my socks and shoes. Then I am taken to a small room for refreshments and debriefing and finally meeting Louise, my guide, face to face.

The debriefing is a methodical investigation of physical reactions and reading of my performance by Louise. It becomes clear that the performance takes the walker's body through several *scenarii*—the commercial encounter (vigilant body), the purely aural sitting in the domestic "concert hall" (engaged but internalizing body), the ambulant and percussive investigation of the church (ambulant and sounding) to the final heart/breath-motivated dance exploration. The walk allows one to increasingly internalize one's own rhythms and sense of being—and as one listens to them, Chaput and Chazallon have planned a route that encourages greater risks by adjusting the spaces through sound design of architectural reverberation. By the silent dance one knows that one can perform in a large space, and hearing the others in the room, one senses their proximity by breath and sound on the floor. Five kilometres later, the walker enjoys anything but functional locomotion in the dance with space and a social decompression is at least glimpsed.

This walk is part of an active artistic dialogue that Marie Hélène Falcon, the artistic director of the FTA, has made integral to Montreal's festival experience. In its first edition in 1985, the trek north along Saint-Denis delivered spectators to a vacant lot where an installation scenography by Robert Deschênes capitalized on the detritus of modern society by using wrecked cars, painted with an imposing ocean motif, as multiple interior stages imbedded in/as the walls of this temporary urban arena for *Titanic* by Carbone 14. When spectators journeyed south along Saint-Laurent they were confronted by the transformation of a vacant lot by Richard Lacroix (Dene Nation) to support the mythopoetic First Nations vision of Yves Sioui Durand's *Le Porteur des peines de monde*. Years later in 2003, travel through the city was conceived as a series of increasingly complex encounters. An audio tour by La Farine Orpheline directed individuals through east end Montreal in *Coïncidence de potentiel infini* to explore/experience, at least superficially, the economic reverberations subsequent to the withdrawal of significant freight lines through the city (the experience included a stop in a restaurant booth to attend to an installment on the juke box, with an encouragement to order poutine and a soft drink, and ended with an individual personal interview in an on-street video kiosk). That same year, an artistic team from Le Théâtre du Nouveau Monde (headed by Lorraine Pintal and scenographer Danielle Lévesque) collaborated with a chorus of participants from Les Impatients (that offers a place for artistic expression for people with mental health problems) on a theatrical reading of *L'Asile de la pureté* by Claude Gauvreau in a mothballed wing of the Hôpital Louis-H. Lafontaine. Each of these encounters has always implicated the spectators, but in 2010 the interiorization of the scenography engendered by the blindfolds launched an urban dance of the *seen* rather than *seeing* body.

Natalie Rewa is the author of *Scenography in Canada* (University of Toronto Press, 2004), and editor of *Design and Scenography* (Playwrights Canada Press, 2009). She was the co-curator of the Canadian exhibit "Imprints of Process" to the Prague Quadrennial in 2007 and co-editor of its catalogue (2008). She is Professor of Drama at Queen's University with cross-appointments to the Departments of Gender Studies and Cultural Studies. Her current research concerns scenographic dramaturgy in opera with a specific focus on Michael Levine's production design for the *Ring* cycle (Canadian Opera Company 2004–2006).

Upcoming Issues

CTR 148 Fall 2011
Artists in Communities
Edited by Kim Renders, Julie Salverson, and Jenn Stephenson

CTR 149 Winter 2012
Queer Women's Performance
Edited by Moynan King

CTR 150 Spring 2012
Manifestos: Everything you've ever wanted to say about theatre but were afraid to put in print
Edited by V&R Editors Natalie Alvarez and Jenn Stephenson

CTR 151 Summer 2012
Performance Ethnography
Edited by Brian Rusted

Maiko Yamamoto builds Gastown.
Photo by Tim Matheson

For further inquiries, please contact The Editors.
email:info@canadiantheatrereview.com

ctr
canadian theatre review

GREAT THEME ISSUES AVAILABLE ONLINE www.utpjournals.com/ctr

PERFORMANCE AND HEALTH
Edited by Natalie Alvarez and Catherine Graham

This issue of *CTR* features the work of artists, health researchers, and theatre scholars collaborating at the intersections between performance studies and health and traversing the professed boundary between different ways of knowing.

CTR 146 | Spring 2011

THEATRE IN AN AGE OF ECO-CRISIS
Edited by Sheila Rabillard and Nelson Gray

This issue of *CTR* takes a lively, thought-provoking, and sometimes controversial look at the role of theatre with respect to some of the most pressing ecological issues of our time.

CTR 144 | Fall 2010

MEMORY
Edited by Pil Hansen and Bruce Barton

This issue of *CTR* responds to the growing body of Canadian performance projects which examine our understanding of memory and how its complex processes affect artists and audiences in multiple ways.

CTR 145 | Winter 2011

IMPROVISATION
Edited by Ric Knowles

This issue of *CTR* explores the divide between reproductive and productive improvisation – between improv as individual, free-market entrepreneurship and improv as collective, socially responsible intervention.

CTR 143 | Summer 2010

Access these issues online at www.utpjournals.com/ctr

CTR Online features vivid colour photographs and engaging video and audio files that add an innovative new dimension to the text. *CTR Online* is a fully searchable electronic resource that addresses all your research needs. This resource includes a Table of Contents alerting service which automatically sends you a message when a new issue is available online. The *CTR Online* search function allows for easy searching within results and lets you filter your search for selected items. Also, your search results can be organized by article summaries, abstracts, or citations. You can also export links to the articles you are interested in for easy access anytime.

Human Resources in the Canadian Theatre

A Guide to Hiring, Contracts, Positions, Compensation & Benefits

The Professional Association of Canadian Theatres (PACT) presents the newest edition of Human Resources in the Canadian Theatre. This guide to hiring, contracts, positions, and benefits thoroughly updates job descriptions and presents all new compensation data for eight staff positions within the theatre community. To purchase a copy, download an order form at www.pact.ca or email info@pact.ca for more information.

BUILDING EXPERIENCE FOR OVER 100 YEARS

The University of Toronto Press offers a wide range of professional, scholarly, and special-interest journals for every taste.

utpjournals.com

UNIVERSITY OF TORONTO PRESS
Journals

Synergies and University of Toronto Press partnership: a considerable achievement for the dissemination of Canadian research.

Synergies is pleased to announce a partnership with the University of Toronto Press (UTP) for the integration of the scholarly publisher's extensive online collection of peer-reviewed journals. Several months in the making, this substantial endeavor marks the addition of UTP's 23 publications to the Synergies platform, greatly expanding the database's offerings in fields as diverse as theology, dramatic literature, physiotherapy and law.

"Synergies strives first and foremost to offer a unified access to Canadian research results in the Social Sciences and Humanities, most notably to content stemming from scholarly journals," stated Martin Boucher, Executive Director of Synergies. "In light of this mission, the addition of UTP's journals to our platform constitutes an important milestone for Synergies. These 23 titles will greatly enrich our collection, as much in quality as in quantity. We hope this accomplishment paves the way for many such collaborations in the future."

This important aggregation project represents the indexation of 8000 new articles in Synergies' powerful search engine, increasing to over 116 000 the total of articles accessible from the platform.

Founded in 1901, University of Toronto Press (UTP) is Canada's leading scholarly publisher and one of the largest university presses in North America. UTP publishes approximately 200 new books and 30 journals annually in a wide range of disciplines. With the publication of landmark titles, as well as a continuing dedication to groundbreaking new scholarship, UTP has firmly established its reputation for excellence. **http://www.utpjournals.com/**

Synergies is the only Canada-wide distribution platform for scholarly publications and actively contributes to the dissemination of university research by offering privileged access to several types of documents, including journals, books, proceedings, theses, and other research data. Synergies has been developed in close collaboration with the academic milieu to meet the specific needs of the humanities and social sciences academic community, providing researchers with a superior framework recognized by peers. **http://www.synergiescanada.org/**

For further information:

Martin Boucher
Executive Director
Synergies, Université de Montréal
Email: martin.boucher@umontreal.ca
Phone: (514) 343.6111 extension 0693

Anne Marie Corrigan
Vice President, Journals
University of Toronto Press
Email: acorrigan@utpress.utoronto.ca
Phone: (416) 667-7838